"Piper shows how true preaching and true worship go hand in hand in the most natural way. This takes place when the preacher works carefully to exegete the text through the anointing of the Spirit and comes to the pulpit under the same influence. The goal is to bring out the spiritual reality behind each text of the Scriptures to honor the intention of the human writer, but especially to exalt the glory of the divine author who inspired the text. This is what this book is all about. Read it slowly, digest its content carefully, and then bring its principles into practice piously."

Miguel Núñez, Senior Pastor, International Baptist Church of Santo Domingo; President and Founder, Wisdom and Integrity Ministries

"John Piper writes with the expository conviction we expect, encouraging preachers not only to say what is true but also to *show* how the Bible establishes that truth. He writes beyond our expectations, however, when putting his pastoral finger on the chief expository errors within our ranks: the moralistic error ('Just do it!') and the replacement error ('You can't do it, so merely enjoy justification by imputed righteousness'). Finally, he advocates for the preaching we need, urging that in all our expositions 'we would make a beeline *from* the cross to the resurrection to the outpouring of the Holy Spirit to the giving of Scripture to the blood-bought miracle of new birth to the mystery of *Christ in you, the hope of glory*, to the beauties of Christ-permeating, Christ-exalting self-control and sober-mindedness and love.' This is great writing to exult the glorious power of the gospel that pervades all of Scripture."

Bryan Chapell, Pastor, Grace Presbyterian Church, Peoria, Illinois

"John Piper's new book on preaching is a dream come true. I have personally been waiting for this book for nearly twenty years. Piper's first book on preaching was monumental. This book is even better. It was worth the wait."

Jason C. Meyer, Pastor for Preaching and Vision, Bethlehem Baptist Church, Minneapolis

"Piper has written more than fifty books, so there is something a bit outrageous in suggesting that *Expository Exultation* is his best. But such a case can be made. Perhaps that is because I, like John, am a preacher, and was profoundly instructed, rebuked, encouraged, and given even greater hope for my ministry through the insights he provides in this book. I trust John has many more volumes to come, but for my money, this is the culmination of his contribution to pastoral ministry. If you're not a pastor or preacher, read it anyway. If you are in full-time ministry, dig deeply into this immense treasure trove of homiletical insight. I'm confident that if you do, it will radically transform your approach to God's Word and the passion with which you preach it."

Sam Storms, Lead Pastor for Preaching and Vision, Bridgeway Church, Oklahoma City

"John Piper's *Expository Exultation* is fittingly dedicated to Martyn Lloyd-Jones, because it may well do for the present generation what *Preaching and Preachers* did uniquely for previous ones—instruct, humble, challenge, and inspire. Here are heat and light combined—what Lloyd-Jones called 'logic on fire.' All the emphases we have come to expect from Piper are here: God-centered, Christ-focused, Spirit-imbued, with rigorous attention to the text of Scripture and passionate theological conviction. Piper displays a take-you-by-the-throat honesty and a sense of the weight of glory that marks true worship. Here is a book about preaching in which God himself takes center stage. *Expository Exultation* is a stunning utterance, a leave-you-wanting-more kind of book. It prostrates us in the dust, then sets us on our feet, and thus makes us want to be and do better for God. It is simply a must-read for every preacher of the gospel."

> **Sinclair B. Ferguson,** Chancellor's Professor of Systematic Theology,
> Reformed Theological Seminary

"The first time I heard John Piper preach the Bible, I was in my early twenties and had never experienced anything like the passion and power that proceeded from a zeal rooted and tethered to the text. This became for me a blueprint to be emulated. I am grateful that he has written the great lessons of over thirty years of 'expository exultation' for the generations to come. There is gold in these pages, and I am eager for the next group of those who will herald the good news of the gospel to be shaped by it. We are in desperate need of serious preaching in these serious days."

> **Matt Chandler,** Lead Pastor, The Village Church, Dallas, Texas;
> President, Acts 29 Church Planting Network; author, *The Mingling of Souls* and *The Explicit Gospel*

"It is a refreshing change to read a book on preaching that contains almost nothing about technique but rather focuses on the Bible's teaching about the nature and awesome privilege of the task—and, above all, on the majesty of God, whose servants we are and whose glories we are called to proclaim. Many preachers will be spurred on by these pages, as I have been, to keep giving themselves to the solemn and joyful tasks of explaining Scripture and exulting in God."

> **Vaughan Roberts,** Rector, St Ebbe's, Oxford, England; Director,
> The Proclamation Trust; author, *God's Big Picture*

Expository Exultation

Other Books by John Piper

Bloodlines: Race, Cross, and the Christian

Brothers, We Are Not Professionals

The Dangerous Duty of Delight

Desiring God

Don't Waste Your Life

Fifty Reasons Why Jesus Came to Die

Finally Alive

Five Points

Future Grace

God Is the Gospel

God's Passion for His Glory

A Hunger for God

Let the Nations Be Glad!

A Peculiar Glory

The Pleasures of God

Reading the Bible Supernaturally

Seeing and Savoring Jesus Christ

The Supremacy of God in Preaching

Think

This Momentary Marriage

What Jesus Demands from the World

When I Don't Desire God

Expository Exultation

Christian Preaching as Worship

John Piper

WHEATON, ILLINOIS

Library of Congress Cataloging-in-Publication Data

Names: Piper, John, 1946- author.
Title: Expository exultation : Christian preaching as worship / John Piper.
Description: Wheaton : Crossway, 2018. | Includes bibliographical references and index.
Identifiers: LCCN 2017035954 (print) | LCCN 2018005258 (ebook) | ISBN 9781433561146 (pdf) | ISBN 9781433561153 (mobi) | ISBN 9781433561160 (epub) | ISBN 9781433561139 (hc)
Subjects: LCSH: Preaching. | Jesus Christ--Exaltation. | Worship.
Classification: LCC BV4211.3 (ebook) | LCC BV4211.3 .P56 2018 (print) | DDC 251--dc23
LC record available at https://lccn.loc.gov/2017035954

To
Martyn Lloyd-Jones,
who never trifled with the word of God

"We are not, like so many, peddlers of God's word,
but as men of sincerity, as commissioned by God,
in the sight of God we speak in Christ. . . .
We refuse to practice cunning or to tamper with God's word."
—The apostle Paul

Contents

PART 7

Expository Exultation and the Old Testament

The Glory of God, the Cross of Christ, and the Obedience of Faith

Introduction

The Roots and Scope of Expository Exultation

I have dedicated this book to Martyn Lloyd-Jones (1899–1981), minister of Westminster Chapel in London for almost thirty years. No preacher has inspired in me a sense of the greatness of preaching the way Lloyd-Jones did. When he preached, I felt, as with no others, the weight of the glory of heralding the very word of God. When he gave his lectures on preaching at Westminster Theological Seminary in 1969, he gave two reasons why he was willing:

> My reason for being very ready to give these lectures is that to me the work of preaching is the highest and the greatest and the most glorious calling to which anyone can ever be called. If you want something in addition to that, I would say without any hesitation that the most urgent need in the Christian Church today is true preaching; and as it is the great and most urgent need in the Church, it is obviously the great need of the world also.[1]

It was typical of Lloyd-Jones to state things in superlatives. His aim was not to minimize other callings. He knew as well as anyone that in the last day the Lord will reward a person's faithfulness, not his office. He knew that the one who would be great must be the servant of all. And he knew that "neither he who plants nor he who waters is anything, but only God who gives the growth" (1 Cor. 3:7).

But he also knew that to be an ambassador of the King of ages is a

---

1. Martyn Lloyd-Jones, *Preaching and Preachers* (Grand Rapids, MI: Zondervan, 1971), 9.

staggering privilege and burden. He had tasted something of the glory that moved the apostle Paul to say that faithful servants of God's word are "worthy of double honor, especially those who labor in preaching and teaching" (1 Tim. 5:17). He had trembled at the warning, "Not many of you should become teachers, my brothers, for you know that we who teach will be judged with greater strictness" (James 3:1). The supernatural nature of his calling amazed him: "As commissioned by God, in the sight of God we speak in Christ" (2 Cor. 2:17).

He knew that the great aim of preaching is the white-hot worship of God's people. And he knew that this worship is nothing small or constricted or parochial. It finds expression in weekly worship services and daily sacrifices of love, and finally will be freely and fully released in the perfecting of the bride of Christ and her cosmic habitation. And so he knew that this worship is as personal as the heart's deepest desire, as expansive as the universe, as enduring as eternity, and as visible as the radiance of love and the renewal of creation.

He knew that the Bible is true and exists for the glory of God. Therefore, reading it and preaching it share that goal. The unrelenting seriousness of Lloyd-Jones's handling of the glories of God's word has been a great inspiration to me in a world that seems incapable of serious joy. I am deeply thankful that God raised him up in the middle of the twentieth century and gave me a taste of what J. I. Packer meant when he said that Lloyd-Jones's preaching came to him with the force of electric shock and brought him "more of a sense of God than any other man."[2]

The Origin of This Book

This book is an organic outgrowth of two previous books. Together they form a kind of trilogy. The first volume, *A Peculiar Glory* (2016), focuses on how we can know that the Bible is God's word and is completely true. The second volume, *Reading the Bible Supernaturally* (2017), focuses on how to read the Bible—specifically, how to read it in the pursuit of its own ultimate goal that God be worshiped with white-hot affection by all the peoples of the world. This third volume, *Expository Exultation*, now asks, If the Bible is completely true and is

---

2. Quoted in Christopher Catherwood, *Five Evangelical Leaders* (Wheaton, IL: Harold Shaw, 1985), 170.

to be read supernaturally in the pursuit of worship, what does it mean to preach this word, and how should we do it?

Foundations of Worship and Preaching

Most preachers assume that their congregations should gather weekly for corporate worship. Many of us have devoted little time and effort to justifying this practice from the New Testament. We take it for granted. Further, most pastors assume that preaching should be part of that corporate gathering. This too is taken for granted by most, though some fall prey to the predictable put-downs of preaching in every generation. In fact, both of these assumptions—that we should gather for worship and that we should preach—do have explicit biblical foundations. And preachers need to know them. On what basis does the congregation gather for worship, and why is preaching part of it?

Focus on Preaching in Worship

As I set out to write a book on preaching, I assume that perhaps 95 percent of the preaching in the world happens in "worship services" of some kind—whether with a dozen believers in the shade of a tree or with five thousand people in a modern auditorium. Preaching in such worship contexts is what I will be defending and describing and celebrating.

The reason for this focus is not that I don't think preaching belongs on the streets, or in the stadiums, or on the campus quad, or in the jails, or before kings. It emphatically does belong there. I would certainly like to see more of it there. The reason is that I believe with all my heart that preaching in corporate worship is essential for the health and mission of the church. God has appointed preaching in worship, I will argue, as one great means of accomplishing his ultimate goal in the world.

Why Preach in Corporate Worship?

I am aware that my conception of worship and preaching is not shared by all Christians. Nor do all Christians believe that preaching is an essential part of corporate worship. So the first task I set for myself is to show from Scripture that Christian congregations should gather for corporate worship and that preaching should be part of that gathering. That's what I do in parts 1 and 2.

Part 1 is a description and a defense of corporate worship. It may seem strange, in a book on preaching, to devote so much space to corporate worship. But if you believe, as I do, that corporate worship is divinely appointed for a unique and indispensable impact on God's people, and that preaching is uniquely designed by God to assist and express that worship, then the strangeness might vanish. The most important thing to establish about corporate worship is what the *essence* of it is. There will always be a thousand variations of the *forms* of worship around the world in thousands of cultures. But what is the essence? That's the task of chapter 1. What emerges, then, in chapter 2 is that the essence of worship leads Christians to discover how beautifully fitting it is for the people of Christ to gather for corporate worship.

Then, in part 2, I try to show what preaching is and why it belongs in corporate worship. It is precisely *what* preaching and worship *are* that justifies that they should be—and that they should be *together*. So in part 2 I try to show how this extraordinary form of communication—and which I call "expository exultation"—became a biblically sanctioned, normative part of corporate worship. The reasons are both historical and theological (chapters 3 and 4), reaching into the Trinitarian nature of God (chapter 5).

Preaching as Worship and for Worship

One of the primary burdens of this book is to show that preaching not only *assists* worship, but also *is* worship. The title *Expository Exultation* is intended to communicate that this unique form of communication is both a rigorous intellectual clarification of the reality revealed through the words of Scripture and a worshipful embodiment of the value of that reality in the preacher's exultation over the word he is clarifying. Preachers should think of worship services not as exultation in the glories of God accompanied by a sermon. They should think of musical and liturgical exultation (songs, prayers, readings, confession, ordinances, and more) accompanied and assisted by *expository* exultation—preaching as worship. Music is one way of raising and carrying the heart's exultation. Preaching is another. I will argue that preaching *is* worship. And preaching serves worship.

Worship: All of Life, Forever

When I say "preaching serves worship," I don't mean that it serves only "worship services"—not even *eternal* worship services. When I say that the ultimate goal of Scripture and preaching is that God be worshiped with white-hot affection by all the peoples of the world, I am referring to the complete transformation of all God's people and the final renovation and renewal of heaven and earth (Rom. 8:19–23). This transformation of God's people and this renovation of the universe will be such that its greatest effect will be to magnify the supreme value and excellence of God.

What we will see, in more detail and with biblical argument, is that worship means consciously knowing and treasuring and showing the supreme worth and beauty of God. When I say that preaching serves this worship, I am thinking of it in at least three expressions:

1. This worship may be expressed in worship services (Ps. 34:3). We worship together as we *know* God truly in song lyrics, prayers, and other expressions of right doctrine; and as we *treasure* God with awakened affections for his excellence; and as we *show* this in heartfelt singing and praying and hearing—participating in all the forms suitable for the service of worship.

2. This worshipful knowing and treasuring and showing the supreme worth and beauty of God also may happen by magnifying Christ in life and death (Phil. 1:20), as we rejoice in God's sovereign care through the painful sacrifices of loving others (Matt. 5:11–12; Phil. 3:8–10). All of our physical existence becomes "a living sacrifice, holy and acceptable to God, which is [our] spiritual worship" (Rom. 12:1).

3. Such worship will happen completely and perfectly in the resurrection, when we know even as we are known (1 Cor. 13:12), our joyful treasuring of God is perfected (Ps. 16:11), and the fullness of joy's outward display is unimpeded by sin (Heb. 12:23; Phil. 3:12).

This God-glorifying, Christ-exalting, Spirit-sustained worship—expressed in worship services, daily sacrifices of love, and eternal perfection—is the goal of *Expository Exultation*, the act and the book.

So, as I said at the beginning of this introduction, there is nothing small or constricted or parochial about the goal of preaching. It is as personal as the heart's deepest desire, as expansive as the universe, as enduring as eternity, and as visible as the sacrifices of love and the renewal of creation. But the goal is radically God-focused. The Bible exists for the glory of God, now and forever. Reading it and *preaching* it share that goal.

Preaching in the Hands of God, with All Our Might

Worship is not a merely natural act. It is a work of the Holy Spirit. It is supernatural. Therefore, to say that preaching is worship and serves worship raises two questions. One relates to how the preacher is taken up into the supernatural. The other relates to how the preacher uses all his natural powers in the service of the miracle of worship. With regard to the first, we ask: How can preaching, as a human act, also *be* a work of God and *serve* a work of God? How does the preacher preach so that it is not he but God who is acting (1 Cor. 15:10)? How does he become an instrument of God so that his preaching becomes an act of worship and a means of awakening worship? That is the focus of part 3.

The second question is this: What about the preacher's use of his natural powers? Or, what natural means are legitimate in the pursuit of supernatural ends? If the aim of preaching is the Spirit-given worship of the people, can human thinking, explaining, and eloquence be legitimate? If not, what's left of preaching? If so, how does the use of such natural powers become a divine means of spiritual worship? Part 4 addresses these questions.

Text, Reality, and Preaching

Part 5 deals with the question, Do we preach the text or the reality revealed through it? Two of my greatest burdens in writing this book are related to each other paradoxically—as paradoxical as the relation between the divine and human in Jesus Christ. Jesus was human with flesh and bones. But he was so much more. But the more is known through knowing the incarnate man. That's why Paul referred to the "glory of God *in the face of Jesus Christ*" (2 Cor. 4:6). The Bible is like the incarnation in this regard. It is human—words, phrases, clauses, logic, narrative. But it is so much more. It carries and communicates realities that are vastly more than words. You might say, "the glory of God *in the words of Scripture*."

Therefore, it is not enough to say, "What we preach is the text." Nor is it enough to say, "What we preach is the reality behind the text." These two inadequate views correspond to my two burdens.

Two Burdens: Text and Reality

One burden is to plead with preachers to give rigorous attention to the wording of their texts and help people see how the very words of the text reveal the points the preacher is making about reality. The other is to plead with preachers to penetrate deeply into the reality that the words are pointing to. These realities—whether aspects of human nature, God's nature, the way of salvation, the horrors of evil, or the mysteries of providence—are profound. The aim of preaching is that our people see these realities for themselves *in the text*. The certainty of their sight should rest in seeing reality *in the text*, not in the opinion of the preacher. So part 5 deals with "the reality factor" and aims to illuminate the relationship between rigorous attention to the text and radical penetration into reality.

An Author's All-Encompassing Vision of Reality

Part 6 asks more specifically: What is the reality that we preach? It becomes clear that it is inadequate to answer: Preach the reality that the text aims to communicate. This answer is not wrong. But it provides no help in answering the question, What aspects of an author's all-encompassing vision of reality should be included in the exposition of the text? I argue that we must keep in view the author's larger vison of reality (chapter 12). Otherwise, we may draw inferences from the text that are not there. Sometimes this larger vision is communicated in the nearer context. Sometimes not.

Overarching Biblical Concerns in All Our Preaching

If keeping the author's overall vision of reality in view is essential, how shall the preacher decide what aspects of this all-encompassing vision of reality to include in his preaching? My approach to answering this question (part 6) will be to ask three additional questions based on three assumptions. First, I assume that the more ultimate the overarching goal of an author's meaning, the more important it is that it be woven into our preaching of particular texts. So I ask, What is the ultimate goal of the biblical authors?

Second, I assume that what the apostle Paul says is indispensable to *his* preaching should be indispensable to *ours*. So I ask, What does Paul say is indispensable to his preaching?

Third, I assume that there is a way to live the Christian life that leads to final salvation, and there is a way to try to live it that leads to destruction, and that understanding this is relevant for the right handling of every text. So I ask, What way of life is necessary for final salvation?

The answer I give to the first question is: The ultimate goal of the biblical authors is the glorification of God (chapters 13 and 14). The answer to the second question is: Paul said that proclaiming Christ crucified was indispensable to his preaching (chapters 15 and 16). The answer to the third question is: The way of life that is necessary for final salvation begins with being justified by faith alone and proceeds by walking in love through the power of the Holy Spirit by faith. This way of life may be called the "obedience of faith" (Rom. 1:5; 16:26)—the holiness—without which our people will not see the Lord (chapters 17 and 18).

You can see that this is a Trinitarian depiction of the reality we preach—living for the glory of God, magnifying the crucified Christ, walking by the Spirit. I try to make the case that these three realities will not be seen clearly if we think of them as separate from the specific wording of the texts of Scripture. Preaching that drifts (or leaps) away from the particularities of the text in order to preach the reality of the glory of God, or the cross of Christ, or the power of the Spirit, becomes untethered from divine authority and spiritual power. The inspired text of Scripture is where our authority lies. And it is in the very wording of the inspired text where the most vivid, reliable, and explosive revelations of these realities shine forth.

Faithful to the Old Testament's Inspiration

Finally, the question presses to be answered whether we can be faithful to the intentions of the Old Testament authors—who were "carried along by the Holy Spirit" (2 Pet. 1:21)—if we draw out of their texts a steady emphasis on the glory of God, the cross of Christ, and the obedience of faith. To answer that question is the aim of part 7. My answer is yes, we can be faithful to their intentions. In fact, since these Old Testament authors yearned to show more clearly the future implications of their teaching (1 Pet. 1:10–12), they would regard it as contrary to their intentions if twenty-first-century emissaries of the Messiah preached from their writings as though he had not come!

Ultimate Goal

A single ultimate purpose has given rise to the existence, the reading, and the preaching of Christian Scripture. The purpose is that God's infinite worth and beauty be exalted in the everlasting, white-hot worship of the blood-bought bride of Christ from every people, language, tribe, and nation. In the pursuit of that greatest of all purposes, I have written *A Peculiar Glory* to show how we may know that the Bible is the infallible word of God. For that same purpose, I have written *Reading the Bible Supernaturally* to show how we may discover the meaning of that infallible word. Finally, the present volume, *Expository Exultation*, aims to show how preaching becomes and begets the blood-bought, Spirit-wrought worship of the worth and beauty of God.

God has ordained that until his ultimate purpose of white-hot worship is achieved in the regular gatherings of his people, the everyday sacrifices of love, and the everlasting pleasures of the age to come, reading the Bible supernaturally and preaching its reality by the Spirit will not cease from the earth. God's purpose on the earth will advance through Bible-saturated, Christ-exalting, God-centered churches, where the gravity and gladness of eternal worship is awakened and rehearsed each week in the presence and power of expository exultation.

PART 1

A Setting for Preaching

God's People Gathered for Worship

1

The Essence of Corporate Worship

This is a book about preaching in worship. I am hoping to show that preaching *is* worship and *serves* worship. I conceded in the introduction that not all Christians think of the weekly gathering of God's people as worship.[1] If you are among those who think, "Since the New Testament never calls the regular gatherings of the church 'worship' or 'worship services,' therefore it is futile to make a case that we should think of our weekly gatherings that way," may I put some provocative bait on my hook in the hopes of snagging a bit more of your attention?

It may be that we don't mean the same thing by "worship." Maybe if I clarify my view of worship, you might not draw the same lines between services for "teaching" or "edification" or "exhortation," on the one hand, and "worship," on the other.

My provocative bait is to say that the plan to meet weekly, say, for teaching but not worship is like the plan to marry without sex. Or eating without taste. Or discovery without delight. Or miracles without wonder. Or gifts without gratefulness. Or warnings without fear. Or repentance without regret. Or resolves without zeal. Or longings without satisfaction. Or seeing without savoring.

Essence of Worship: Savoring What We See of God

But if you believe, as I do, that *seeing* the spiritual beauty of biblical truth without *savoring* it is sin, then you probably will be slow to

---

1. David Peterson, former lecturer in New Testament at Moore Theological College, Sydney, Australia, has lamented this development. He notes that in reaction against the distortion of the language of worship as referring *only* to a liturgical act, instead of a whole life, "many seem to have abandoned any application of the language to what we do in church. With this development has come an emphasis on meeting for fellowship and mutual encouragement, with little apparent expectation of encountering God together." Accessed June 23, 2017, http://sydneyanglicans.net /blogs/ministrythinking/a_church_without_worship.

minimize worship as a reason for gathering as a church—indeed the ultimate reason. And, yes, I do believe that savoring the glory of God is the essence of true worship.

I wonder if you agree with that. Do you agree that the inner essence of worship is savoring the glory of God in Christ, or being satisfied with all that God is for you in Jesus? Or is that too subjective? Be sure to notice that I am using the word *essence*, not *totality*. I'm not saying that savoring what we see of God is the *totality* of worship—but the essence, without which worship is empty (Matt. 15:8–9).

So it seems to me that the first thing we must do, if we are to make a biblical case for preaching as part of God's plan for the regular worship gatherings of Christ's people, is to make the biblical case that there should be such gatherings. The burden of that argument comes in chapter 2. But it hangs on the claim that the *essence* of worship is the heart's experience of affections that magnify the beauty and worth of God. This is true whether worship is thought of as the obedience to Christ in daily life, or as the tasks of church ministry, or as the gathering for corporate praise.

I have argued elsewhere in some detail[2] that worship in the New Testament, compared to worship in the Old Testament, moved toward a focus on something radically simple and inward, with manifold external expressions in life and liturgy that could be adapted over the centuries in thousands of different cultures. Worship in the New Testament took on the character suited for a *go-tell* religion for all nations (Matt. 28:18–20), as opposed to the detailed rituals prescribed in the Old Testament suited for a *come-see* religion (1 Kings 10:1–13). In other words, what we find in the New Testament is a stunning degree of nonspecificity for worship as an outward form and a radical intensification of worship as an inward experience of the heart.

Biblical Pointer to the Inner Essence of Worship

We can see pointers to this. For one example, in John 4:23 where Jesus said, "The hour is coming, and is now here, when the true worshipers will worship the Father in spirit and truth, for the Father is seeking such

---

2. See John Piper, "The Inner Simplicity and Outer Freedom of Worldwide Worship," in *Let the Nations Be Glad!: The Supremacy of God in Missions*, 3rd ed. (Grand Rapids, MI: Baker Academic, 2010), 239–54.

people to worship him." I take "in spirit" to mean that this true worship is carried along by the Holy Spirit and is happening mainly as an inward, spiritual event, not mainly as an outward, bodily event (cf. John 3:6). And I take "in truth" to mean that this true worship is a response to true views of God and is shaped and guided by true views of God.

For this and other reasons, I argue that Jesus broke decisively any necessary connection between worship and its outward and localized associations. It is mainly something inward and free from locality. "The hour is coming when neither on this mountain nor in Jerusalem will you worship the Father" (John 4:21). This inwardness of the essence of worship is what Jesus had in mind when he said, "This people honors me with their lips, but their heart is far from me; in vain do they worship me" (Matt. 15:8–9). When the heart is far from God, worship is vain, empty, and nonexistent, no matter how proper the forms are. The experience of the heart is the defining, vital, indispensable essence of worship.

So it appears in the New Testament that worship is significantly de-institutionalized, delocalized, deexternalized. The entire thrust is taken off of ceremonies and seasons and places and forms and shifted to what is happening in the heart—not just on Sunday but every day and all the time in all of life.

Godward Essence of Worship

This inner Godwardness in all of life is what Paul intends when he says, "Whether you eat or drink, or whatever you do, do all to the glory of God" (1 Cor. 10:31). And, "Whatever you do, in word or deed, do everything in the name of the Lord Jesus, giving thanks to God the Father through him" (Col. 3:17). This is worship: *to act in a way that shows the heart's valuing of the glory of God and the name of the Lord Jesus.* Or, as we said in the introduction, worship means consciously knowing and treasuring and showing the supreme worth and beauty of God.

But the New Testament uses those greatest of all worship sentences (1 Cor. 10:31 and Col. 3:17) without any reference to worship services. They describe life. Even when Paul calls us to "be filled with the Spirit, addressing one another in psalms and hymns and spiritual songs, singing and making melody to the Lord with your heart, giving thanks always and for everything to God the Father in the name of our Lord Jesus Christ" (Eph. 5:18–20), he makes no reference to a time or a place or a service. In fact, the key words are "always" and "for everything"—"giving thanks *always* and for *everything*" (cf. Col. 3:17). This may, in fact, be what we should do in a *worship service*, but it is not Paul's burden to tell us that. His burden is to call for a radical, inward authenticity of worship and an all-encompassing pervasiveness of worship in all of life. Place and form are not of the *essence*. Spirit and truth are all-important.

Inner Experience Pervading All of Life

My conclusion, then, is that the New Testament shows a stunning indifference to the outward forms and places of worship. At the same time, there is a radical intensification of worship as an inward, spiritual experience that has no bounds and pervades all of life. One of the reasons for this development in the New Testament is that the New Testament is not a detailed manual for worship services. It is, rather, a handbook for living out the Christian faith among thousands of cultures, which are free to put flesh on the spiritual and moral reality of worship found in the New Testament. This is why my most detailed argument for this view of worship in the New Testament is found in my book on missions.[3] The radical shift from the detailed, outward worship forms in the Old Testament to the flexible forms expressing the inner essence of worship in the New Testament is a missiological issue, not just a theological one.

What Is This Inward, Spiritual Experience of Worship?

In place of the longer argument in *Let the Nations Be Glad!*, let me give just one biblical example of how the Bible reveals the inner essence of worship as the *savoring of the glory of God in Christ*, or *being satisfied with all that God is for us in Jesus*. I take it as a given that worship—whether an inner act of the heart, or an outward act of daily obedience, or an act of the congregation collectively—is a magnifying of God. That is, it is an act that consciously shows how magnificent God is. I say "consciously" because the moon and stars show how magnificent God is, but they are not worshiping, since they have no consciousness. But worship is a conscious act (inwardly or outwardly) that reveals

---

3. See note 2.

or expresses how great and glorious God is. Worship is knowing and treasuring and showing the worth of God.

One of the texts that reveals the inner essence of worship most clearly is Philippians 1:20–23:

> It is my eager expectation and hope that I will not be at all ashamed, but that with full courage now as always Christ will be honored in my body, whether by *life* or by *death*. For to me to *live* is Christ, and to *die* is gain. If I am to live in the flesh, that means fruitful labor for me. Yet which I shall choose I cannot tell. I am hard pressed between the two. My desire is to depart and be with Christ, for that is far better.

Notice that Paul's passion in life is that what he does with his body, whether in life or death, will always be worship—that "Christ will be honored" (v. 20). The question then becomes, Does Paul tell us what kind of inner experience exalts Christ in this way? Yes, he does. He shows what it is by the way verse 21 is connected to verse 20.

Notice that "life" and "death" in verse 20 correspond to "live" and "die" in verse 21. And the connection between the two verses is that verse 21 gives the basis for how living and dying can magnify Christ. "It is my eager expectation and hope that . . . Christ will be honored in my body, whether by life or by death. *For* [because] to me to live is Christ, and to die is gain."

Key Connection: Death Gain, Christ Magnificent

Verse 21 describes the inner experience that exalts Christ and is the essence of worship. To see this, let's just take the pair "death" and "die." "My hope is that Christ will be honored in my body . . . by *death*. . . . For to me . . . to *die* is gain." That is, Christ will be magnified in my dying, if my dying is for my gain. There it is. The inner experience that magnifies Christ in dying is to experience death as gain.

But why is that? Why does my experiencing death as gain magnify the greatness of Christ? Verse 23 gives the answer: "My desire is to depart [that is, to die] and be with Christ, for that is far better." This is what death does: it takes us to be "with Christ"—that is, it takes us into a fuller experience of Christ. We depart and we are with Christ, and that, Paul says, is gain. And when you experience death this way, Paul says, you magnify Christ—you make him look magnificent.

Experiencing Christ as gain in your dying magnifies Christ. It is the essence of worship in the hour of death—and in life (as Phil. 3:8 shows).

Gain Means All-Satisfying in Loss

We can now say that the inner essence of worship is cherishing Christ as gain—indeed as more gain than all that life can offer—family, career, retirement, fame, food, friends. The essence of worship is experiencing Christ as more gain than all that life can give. And this is what I mean with the words *savoring Christ, treasuring Christ, being satisfied with Christ.* This is the inner essence of worship. Because, Paul says, experiencing Christ as gain—greater satisfaction—in death is the way Christ is magnified in death.

I love to sum up what I call "Christian hedonism" with the phrase "God is most glorified in us when we are most satisfied in him." If you wonder where I got that phrase, the answer is, right here in Philippians 1:20–21. Christ is magnified in my death, when in my death I am satisfied with him—when I experience death as gain because I gain him. Or another way to say it is that the essence of praising Christ is prizing Christ. Christ will be praised in my death, if in my death he is prized above life. The inner essence of worship is prizing Christ—cherishing him, treasuring him, being satisfied with him.

Next Step: Are Worship Services Essential?

We have not yet established that the regular gathering of God's people for corporate worship is essential or normative. But if we can establish such importance from Scripture, this inner essence of worship would profoundly shape what we do and what preaching is designed to do. In preaching and in every other part of the service, we would "go hard after God," meaning this: we would go hard after *satisfaction* in God, and go hard after God as our *prize*, and go hard after God as our *treasure*, our *soul food*, our *heart delight*, our spirit's *pleasure*. Because we know from Philippians 1:20–21 and 3:8 that experiencing Christ as our supreme gain magnifies him, exalts him, worships him—whether on the street or in the sanctuary.

We turn now to this next step in the argument: Is there a biblical warrant for believing that regular gatherings of local Christian churches for corporate worship are essential for the achievement of God's goal for his people in this world?

2

Corporate Worship

Biblical and Beautifully Fitting

Since the focus of this book is on the nature and method of preaching in the regular gatherings of Christians for corporate worship, it is important to explain why such gatherings are essential in the life of the Christian church. In the previous chapter, I argued that the inner essence of worship is being satisfied with all that God is for us in Christ, or savoring the glory of God in Christ. In referring to the *inner essence* of worship, I mean to imply that there is more to worship than its essence—not less. There are roots to this inner essence, and there are branches. Both are essential to corporate worship.

In the introduction, I defined this totality of worship as knowing, treasuring, and showing the supreme worth and beauty of God—the triune God of Christian Scripture. Knowing the glory of God and his works and ways is the root of the inner essence of worship. Treasuring (or savoring) the manifold glories thus known is the inner essence. And all the ways we outwardly show this inner treasuring are the branches of the inner essence.

Argument from Moral Beauty

The question in this chapter is, Why should regular gatherings for corporate worship be among the many ways that we show the supreme value of God by outwardly expressing in "worship services" what we know and treasure about his glory? My way of answering this question is to argue that such gatherings are beautifully fitting. I take this approach first because of the precedent in Psalm 147:1:

> Praise the LORD!
>   For it is good to sing praises to our God;
> for it is pleasant, and a song of praise is *fitting*.

The word translated "fitting" (*nāwāh*) means "beautiful" or "lovely," as in Song of Solomon 1:5 ("I am very dark, but *lovely*") and 2:14 ("Your face is *lovely*," cf. 4:3; 6:4). But the meaning of the word moved from mere physical beauty to moral beauty. As we might say, "That was a *beautiful* act of love and sacrifice." And when the concept of beauty moves away from the mere physical to include the spiritual or moral dimension of reality, the meaning "fitting" becomes apparent. For what is ultimate, unseen, moral beauty except that something is just as it should be? It fits with ultimate reality.

Hence this same word is used for what is "becoming" or "fitting" or "suitable," as in Proverbs 17:7: "Fine speech is not *becoming* (*nāwāh*) to a fool; still less is false speech to a prince." Fine speech may be beautiful in some people, but in the mouth of a fool it is out of place, unfitting, unsuitable, bizarre. As when Proverb 11:22 says, "Like a gold ring in a pig's snout is a beautiful woman without discretion." Something does not fit. It is not beautiful.

Deepest Warrant One Can Give

So I am going to make my case for regular gatherings for corporate worship on the basis of their beautiful fitness, but not only because there is biblical precedent for this. Moral fitness in the ultimate nature of things is the deepest warrant one can give for anything. If God reveals that something is ultimately *fitting*, he has said the most ultimate thing he can say: it fits with his nature and his ways. Given the way he is and the way he has designed the universe, this fits perfectly. It is beautiful. That is what beauty is—the quality of being in perfect harmony with the way God is.

This is a deeper warrant than the argument that corporate worship is commanded by God. Before corporate worship is commanded, it is beautifully fitting. Worship does not become beautiful because it is commanded. It is commanded because it is ultimately beautiful—

that is, in perfect harmony with who God is and the way he created man to be.

If Fitting in the Old, How Much More in the New?

There are good biblical reasons that account for the two-thousand-year tradition that most Christian churches typically gather at least once a week for corporate worship. And the vast majority of these churches have not stumbled over the use of the word *worship* to describe the primary purpose for why they gather. That too has good biblical warrant.

Let's begin our argument for the beautiful fitness of regular corporate Christian worship with the observation that if such worship was fitting in Old Testament times, how much more it is fitting in New Testament times, when we have such a fuller revelation of the glory of God in Christ. We know from the Old Testament that God ordained that he should be worshiped corporately, not just individually. It is hardly conceivable that corporate worship would be considered less fitting for the new-covenant people of God, who have such greater knowledge of the praiseworthiness of God in Christ. It would be a great anomaly if we discovered that the God revealed in the exodus is manifestly worthy of a gathered assembly uniting in praise, but the God who raised Jesus from the dead did not receive such united and public worship.

The psalmists make clear that God intends his people to gather for corporate worship: "In the midst of the *congregation* I will praise you" (Ps. 22:22). "From you comes my praise in the great *congregation*" (Ps. 22:25). "I will thank you in the great *congregation*; / in the mighty *throng* I will praise you" (Ps. 35:18). "I have told the glad news of deliverance / in the great *congregation*; / behold, I have not restrained my lips, / as you know, O Lord. / . . . I have not concealed your steadfast love and your faithfulness / from the great *congregation*" (Ps. 40:9–10). "Bless God in the great *congregation*" (Ps. 68:26). "Let them extol him in the *congregation* of the people, / and praise him in the assembly of the elders" (Ps. 107:32).

As we have seen, one way to describe God's reason for moving his people to worship him in this way is that it is "good" and "pleasant" and "fitting." "Praise the Lord! / For it is *good* to sing praises to our God; / for it is *pleasant*, and a song of praise is *fitting*" (Ps. 147:1). "Shout for joy in the Lord, O you righteous! / Praise *befits* the upright" (Ps. 33:1).

Calling the praises of God's people "good" and "pleasant" and "fitting" means that their praises in private and "in the great congregation" are not random. They are not arbitrary or capricious. God does nothing that is not "fitting." Praise "fits" with ultimate reality. It fits beautifully, pleasantly. That is why it is "good." There is something about the nature of God and the nature of the human heart (alone and in community) that makes worship fitting—apt, becoming, suitable, appropriate, proper, felicitous, beautiful.

If it was fitting and good and pleasant for the people of Israel to bless and praise and thank God for his deliverances "in the great congregation," it is all the more fitting and good and pleasant for Christians to gather to do the same. And that is what we have done for two thousand years.

The Unique Glory God Gets from Corporate Worship

Another reason for the fitness of the corporate worship of God's people is the greater glory that rises to God from unified corporate worship than from solitary individuals worshiping God alone. To be sure, God is glorified by individual Christians whose selfish hearts have been freed to treasure God above all things. Each conquered soul is a trophy of sovereign grace (Acts 18:27) and is meant by God "to the praise of the glory of His grace" (Eph. 1:6 NASB). Every good tree bearing the fruit of praise is a "planting of the LORD, *that he may be glorified*" (Isa. 61:3).

Nevertheless, there is more divine glory to be savored and shown in the unity of heart and mind and action of a diverse people in corporate worship. There are two reasons for this—two ways that the Lord gets more glory from corporate worship than from individual worship.

Glory of Overcoming More Obstacles

First, such unity is more difficult to achieve than the glory that comes from scattered individuals praising God in their own ways. All genuine, individual praise of the true God is a divine miracle of sovereign grace. But there is another miracle—a greater one—when those individuals are not only brought from death to life, but brought from the *disharmony* of deadness to the *unity* of life. Therefore it is fitting that the Lord receive such unified worship, since it is pleasant and good and beautiful for him to be honored for the greater power he exerts to create such unified corporate worship.

Glory of a New Kind of Beauty

Second, unified corporate worship among diverse human beings brings into being a God-glorifying beauty that does not exist in individual worship alone. We know this because of the analogies we are familiar with in ordinary life—music, sport, military, etc. In music, there is a kind of beauty that rises from four-part harmony among singers that is different from the beauty of powerful sounds in unison. There is a kind of beauty in the unified symphony of instruments that is different from the beauty of the solo virtuoso.

In sport, there is beauty in a stunning individual performance of a star basketball player, but a different beauty in the perfectly executed plays by the team as a whole. There is more beauty when the "corporate" assists under the basket complement the outside shots. In the military, feats of individual heroism are beautiful, but there is another beauty when great movements of troops are orchestrated with flawless precision and bring about a victory for the entire army.

Therefore, when human beings with diverse ethnicities, backgrounds, tastes, expectations, desires, priorities, peeves, admirations, and needs join their hearts and minds and voices and actions in unified worship of the one true God through Jesus Christ, a reality has come into the world that is beautifully *fitting*—it befits the power and the worth of God, whose glory can win such humble, self-forgetting praises from a diverse people.

Corporate, God-Glorifying Images of the People of Christ

Another reality that makes regular corporate worship of Christ's people *fitting* is the nature of the church as revealed in the images used to describe it in the New Testament. I have in mind the terms *body, household, bride, flock, church, temple/house, priesthood, race, nation, possession,* and *people.* Each of these images expresses the corporate nature of the people of God, and each—some more, some less—points to how fitting it is for Christian people to gather to worship Christ.

Body

> The Gentiles are fellow heirs, members of the same *body*, and partakers of the promise in Christ Jesus through the gospel. (Eph. 3:6)

Along with the remnant of true Israel (Eph. 2:12), the Gentile believers are "one body" in Christ by the Spirit. "For in one Spirit we were all baptized into one body—Jews or Greeks, slaves or free—and all were made to drink of one Spirit" (1 Cor. 12:13). There is a double emphasis in the image of "body" for the church. One is that we are "members one of another" (Rom. 12:5; Eph. 4:25). The other is that Jesus Christ is the "head of the body" (Col. 1:18).

The fact that the body has a head implies, for Paul, that Jesus is to be worshiped. Colossians 1:18 continues: "He is the head of the body, the church. He is the beginning, the firstborn from the dead, *that in everything he might be preeminent*." In other words, we are directed to let our corporate identity lead our minds to the absolutely preeminent head, Jesus Christ. Being the body of Christ means being a people whose life as a body is dependent on, and designed to magnify, the preeminence of the head. Therefore, it would be unfitting if this body in its local expressions (1 Cor. 12:12, 21) made no effort to gather, as a body, for the sake of prizing and praising the preeminence of its head, Jesus Christ.

Household

In the term *household* I am including the images of the "children of God" (John 1:12; Rom. 8:16) and "sons and daughters" of God (2 Cor. 6:18) and "brothers" (Matt. 23:8; Heb. 2:11).

> You are no longer strangers and aliens, but you are fellow citizens with the saints and members of the *household* of God. (Eph. 2:19; cf. 1 Tim. 3:15)

This image implies not only the close corporate reality that comes with being one family, but also the relationship of this family to God and Christ. The family has "one Father" (Matt. 23:9). And in the household there is one who is "master of the house" (Matt. 10:25). And the family has one older brother who is preeminent as "firstborn among many brothers" (Rom. 8:29). Each of these relationships points toward extraordinary family worship.

First, there is the assumption that a Father is to be honored uniquely in the family: "Honor your father" (Eph. 6:2). "If then I am a father, where is my honor?" (Mal. 1:6). Then there is the greater honor due to the master of the house: "If they have called the *master of the house* Beelzebul, how much more will they malign *those of his household*" (Matt. 10:25). The logic of this argument depends on the master of the house being worthy of more honor than the members. Given what we know about the real distance between the human members of the household and the divine master of the house, the honor due him points to a worshiping household.

Similarly, Paul points to the worship of Christ among the "brothers" in Romans 8:29 when he says, "Those whom [God] foreknew he also predestined to be conformed to the image of his Son, *in order that he might be the firstborn among many brothers.*" The purpose ("in order that") given for predestining all the family members to be like the unique and only Son of God is "in order that" he might be "firstborn" (*prōtotokon*). The implications of this are made explicit in Colossians 1:18, "He is the beginning, the *firstborn* [*prōtotokos*] from the dead, *that in everything he might be preeminent.*"

In other words, the household imagery for the church points not only to its corporate reality but also to God's intention that he and his Son (Father, Master, Firstborn) be honored as the giver and protector of life, the owner and overseer of all, and as absolutely preeminent. Which is another way of saying that it would be unfitting if the family did not gather to experience and express its honor for the Father, the Master, and the preeminent older brother.

Bride

Jesus is not a polygamist. He has one bride.

> Then came one of the seven angels who had the seven bowls full of the seven last plagues and spoke to me, saying, "Come, I will show you the *Bride*, the wife of the Lamb." (Rev. 21:9)

This implies a remarkable singularity and corporate identity for the people of Christ. This is even more clear when we pause to realize how unfitting it is for individual Christians, especially men, to speak of Christ individually as their husband. Calling the people of Christ his "Bride" is not meant to imply a romance with individual Christians, but rather corporate headship, submission, sacrificial love, and reverence.

Wives, submit to your own husbands, as to the Lord. For the husband is the head of the wife even as Christ is the head of the church, his body, and is himself its Savior. Now as the church submits to Christ, so also wives should submit in everything to their husbands. Husbands, love your wives, as Christ loved the church and gave himself up for her, that he might sanctify her, having cleansed her by the washing of water with the word, so that he might present the church to himself in splendor, without spot or wrinkle or any such thing, that she might be holy and without blemish. In the same way husbands should love their wives as their own bodies. He who loves his wife loves himself. For no one ever hated his own flesh, but nourishes and cherishes it, just as Christ does the church. . . . Let each one of you love his wife as himself, and let the wife see that she respects her husband. (Eph. 5:22–29, 33)

In comparing the relationship between the church and Christ, on the one hand, with a wife and husband, on the other hand, Paul does not reverse the roles. Christ and the church are not interchangeable. That is why the analogy works. Christ leads as head (vv. 22–23). He gives himself in death (v. 25) to save (v. 23) and sanctify (v. 26) and nourish (v. 29) and provide splendor to (v. 27) his bride—all of this so that she will gladly submit to him (v. 22) and reverence him. The word translated "respect" in verse 33 is the word *phōbētai*, which ordinarily means "fear," but should probably be rendered "respect" or "reverence" in this context. So in this imagery of the church as a bride, there are significant pointers to the corporate esteem, respect, and submission the church feels toward Christ.

And it is plain from Paul's language in Ephesians 5 that he wants us to see this relationship as one of *joyful* worship. To be sure, there is reverence and submission. But enveloping all of that is this: Christ loves her, gives himself for her, sanctifies her, cleanses her, removes every spot and blemish and wrinkle (eternal youth!), nourishes her, cherishes her, and presents her to himself. If the church really sees herself this way, would it be fitting that there be no gatherings to give corporate expression to this joy and to our anticipation of the coming marriage supper of the Lamb (Rev. 19:9)?

Flock

I am the good shepherd. I know my own and my own know me, just as the Father knows me and I know the Father; and I lay down my life for the sheep. And I have other sheep that are not of this fold. I must bring them also, and they will listen to my voice. So there will be *one flock*, one shepherd. For this reason the Father loves me, because I lay down my life that I may take it up again. No one takes it from me, but I lay it down of my own accord. I have authority to lay it down, and I have authority to take it up again. This charge I have received from my Father. (John 10:14–18; cf. 1 Pet. 5:1–3)

When all the sheep who are scattered across the world (John 11:52) hear the voice of the Shepherd and are brought to Christ, there will be "one flock" (10:16). That is the corporate emphasis of the imagery. But the emphasis falls heavily on the stunning power and authority of the Shepherd—beyond all ordinary shepherd power. The sheep already belong to him (v. 14), wherever they are in the world, *before* they ever come to him. "I know my own." "I have other sheep." His voice is irresistible when he calls his own (v. 16). "They *will* listen to my voice." That is what he means when he says, "I *must* bring them." The voice will do the bringing.

Then comes the inconceivable words of matchless love and authority: "I lay down my life" for the sheep (vv. 15, 17). "No one takes it from me. . . . And I have authority to take it up again" (v. 18). Now this is no ordinary shepherd, and the response of this flock will surely be no ordinary response of sheep. If it is inconceivably wonderful that a great Shepherd should gather sheep from around the world by dying for them and rising from the dead, then surely it is supremely fitting that this flock will, as with one voice, bleat their praises for such love and authority and power. Surely they will gather in the pastures often, unable to contain their amazement at such a Shepherd.

Assembly, Church

The most common word in the New Testament for the people of Christ is *ekklēsia*, which, over one hundred times, is translated "church." The English word *church* does not give a hint to most people as to the meaning of *ekklēsia*. "Church" is based on an Old English word for "the Lord's" or "belonging to the Lord," hence possibly the "Lord's house" or the "Lord's people." But "house" and "people" are not implied in the word, according to its root. So we do not get much help from the etymology of the English word *church*.

The word *ekklēsia* simply means "assembly"—a group of people gathered for secular or religious purposes. In Acts 19 it is used three times for a secular assembly (vv. 32, 39, 41). Why was this word chosen as the most common reference to the people of Christ in the New Testament?

Probably because the Greek translation of the Hebrew Old Testament (called the Septuagint and abbreviated LXX) loves to translate the Hebrew word for Israel's gathered congregation (*qahal*) as *ekklēsia*. Thus nine of the ten uses of *qahal* in the Psalms are translated in the Septuagint as *ekklēsia*. For example:

> I will thank you in the great *congregation* [*ekklēsia*];
> in the mighty throng I will praise you. (Ps. 35:18; LXX 34:18)

> I have told the glad news of deliverance
> in the great *congregation* [*ekklēsia*];
> behold, I have not restrained my lips,
> as you know, O Lord. (Ps. 40:9; LXX 39:10)

> Praise the Lord!
> Sing to the Lord a new song,
> his praise in the assembly [*ekklēsia*] of the godly! (Ps. 149:1)

This connection between the most common New Testament word for the people of Christ (church) and the Old Testament word for the gathered people of Israel, including her gatherings for worship, means, at least, that corporate worship connotations for the word *church* (*ekklēsia*) are not absent.

Temple, House, Priesthood, Race, Nation, Possession, People

Finally, in our overview of the images of the church in the New Testament the apostle Peter gives us a cluster of six images (house, priesthood, race, nation, possession, and people) explicitly in connection with corporate worship.

> As you come to him, a living stone rejected by men but in the sight of God chosen and precious, you yourselves like living stones are being built up as a *spiritual house*, to be a *holy priesthood*, to offer spiritual sacrifices acceptable to God through Jesus Christ. . . . You are a *chosen race*, a *royal priesthood*, a *holy nation*, a *people for his own possession*, that you may proclaim the excellencies of him

who called you out of darkness into his marvelous light. Once you were not a people, but now you are *God's people*; once you had not received mercy, but now you have received mercy. (1 Pet. 2:4–10)

This is probably the most explicit connection in the New Testament between the existence of the church and the divine purposes of corporate worship. Peter says that Christians are "being built up as a spiritual house, to be a holy priesthood, *to offer spiritual sacrifices acceptable to God through Jesus Christ.*" There is an explicit purpose clause defining the reason for why God is building "a spiritual house [out of individual living stones]"—that is the church. He is doing it *so that* they will "offer spiritual sacrifices acceptable to God through Jesus Christ." I would not go so far as to limit the meaning of such sacrifices to corporate worship, but the imagery of house and priesthood make the corporate worship dimension unmistakable.

Then he states the same purpose for the church again in verse 9, only with different words. "You are a chosen race, a royal priesthood, a holy nation, a people for his own possession, *that you may proclaim the excellencies of him who called you out of darkness into his marvelous light.*" Here he connects our corporate reality as a new race, our royal priesthood, our new holy ethnicity ("nation" *ethnos*), our esteemed status as God's own possession—he connects all of this with our purpose: to proclaim his excellencies.

The point here is not to argue that the word "proclaim" is unique to the language of corporate worship. In fact, I would want to preserve the implication here that Peter *also* has in view the proclamation of God's excellencies with words and deeds to the wider world (see 1 Pet. 2:12). My point is simply to say that this passage is laden with the imagery and the purposes of corporate worship. Therefore, in Peter's mind the very existence and nature of the church points to her calling to be a worshiping people. It would be strange indeed—unfitting—if this "spiritual house," built into a corporate unity out of individual living stones, for the purpose of offering sacrifices of praise, should never gather to do so.

Addressing One Another as We Sing to God
We get another glimpse of the beautiful fitness of regular corporate Christian worship from the apostle Paul. He expresses it with two straightforward exhortations:

> Do not get drunk with wine, for that is debauchery, but be filled with the Spirit, addressing one another in psalms and hymns and spiritual songs, singing and making melody to the Lord with your heart, giving thanks always and for everything to God the Father in the name of our Lord Jesus Christ. (Eph. 5:18–20)

> Let the word of Christ dwell in you richly, teaching and admonishing one another in all wisdom, singing psalms and hymns and spiritual songs, with thankfulness in your hearts to God. And whatever you do, in word or deed, do everything in the name of the Lord Jesus, giving thanks to God the Father through him. (Col. 3:16–17)

Both of these exhortations call for singing "psalms and hymns and spiritual songs" to one another and to God: "addressing *one another* in psalms . . ." and "making melody *to the Lord*" (Eph. 5:19); "admonishing *one another* in all wisdom, singing psalms . . . *to God*" (Col. 3:16). This bi-directional singing—to man and to God—is what makes corporate worship *corporate*, and what makes it *worship*. If we were so atomized that we could not hear each other sing, it would not be *corporate*. And if we were not singing to the Lord (or with reference to the Lord), it would not be *worship*.

Meet for Edification, Not Worship?

This point needs emphasis because just at this point some people veer off into a superficial claim that the New Testament gatherings of Christ's people were not for worship but only for edification. They say that the gatherings were never called "worship services" as we call them today, and so it is misleading to label them that way—misleading because that's not what they were, and misleading also because that's not why we should gather.

I call this a superficial claim for three reasons. One is that it fails to take seriously enough Paul's words in Ephesians 5:18–20 and Colossians 3:16–17. These texts are clearly describing at least part of what happens when Christians gather and why they gather. They gather, among other reasons, to sing. And this singing is Christian worship because they sing "to the Lord [Jesus]." To argue that this singing "to the Lord" is significant only for its effect on the other people around us is like saying that you say thank you for gifts only to teach people gratitude, or that the only reason you kiss your wife is to instruct the children about the meaning of marriage.

Paul is not commending hypocrisy. He is commending—and commanding—heartfelt savoring of the Lord himself—"making melody to the Lord *with your heart.*" To the Lord! From the heart! This is worship. And it is corporate.

What Are We Building People Into?

The second reason I say it is superficial to claim that the New Testament gatherings of Christ's people were not for worship but only for edification is that such a claim fails to penetrate deeply enough into what edification is and how it relates to a vertical focus on God. What if *edify* (*oikodomeō*, "build up") is a description of "being built up as a spiritual house, to be a holy priesthood, *to offer spiritual sacrifices acceptable to God* through Jesus Christ" (1 Pet. 2:5)? What if *edify* means being built into the kind of person who "do[es] all to the glory of God" (1 Cor. 10:31)? What if *edify* means building people who "do everything in the name of the Lord Jesus" (Col. 3:17)? In other words, what if *edify* means helping others to be radically God-centered and Christ-exalting?

It is not at all obvious, when you think about it biblically, that edification (*oikodomē*) is an alternative to worship. In fact, it is *not* an alternative to worship. Rightly understood, it is an *act* of worship. Worship is knowing, enjoying, and showing the glory of God. Edification is one way of *showing* why and how we *know* and *value* God.

The effort to make edification and corporate worship alternatives eviscerates both. Authentic, truth-based, heartfelt, corporate expressions of praise and thanks to God will have an edifying effect on others—it will stir them up to see the truth and feel the value that other believers see and feel. But it will have this effect precisely because God is the focus, not man. Otherwise the praise and thanks are inauthentic and manipulative. It is precisely the intensity and joy of that Godward focus that has the heart-changing (edifying) effect. If you try to say that edification calls for a manward focus, not a worship setting, there will be a subtle (or not so subtle) tendency to bend vertical, God-focused worship into a horizontal affair, and that eviscerates corporate worship.

Similarly edification is eviscerated if it is disconnected from worship. This disconnection implies that the aim of edification is something other than worship. But it's not. Whatever else our edifying efforts may aim to build into others (love, joy, peace, patience, kindness, goodness, faithfulness, etc.), these traits are not Christian unless they are sustained by a zeal for the glory of God in Christ—that is, unless they are expressions of worship. The separation of worship and edification ruins both.

Praising, Thanking, and Edifying in Corinth

The third reason I say it is superficial to claim that the New Testament gatherings of Christ's people were not for worship but only for edification is that it fails to handle carefully Paul's teaching about edification and worship in the gatherings Paul deals with in 1 Corinthians 12–14.

Clearly Paul puts a premium on *upbuilding* (*oikodomē*) as the aim of these corporate gatherings:

> The one who prophesies speaks to people for their *upbuilding* and encouragement and consolation. (1 Cor. 14:3)

> The one who speaks in a tongue builds up himself, but the one who prophesies *builds up* the church. (1 Cor. 14:4)

> The one who prophesies is greater than the one who speaks in tongues, unless someone interprets, so that the church may be *built up*. (1 Cor. 14:5)

> So with yourselves, since you are eager for manifestations of the Spirit, strive to excel in *building up* the church. (1 Cor. 14:12)

> For you may be giving thanks well enough, but the other person is not being *built up*. (1 Cor. 14:17)

> Let all things be done for *building up*. (1 Cor. 14:26)

That's pretty clear. "Let all things be done for building up." But it would be superficial to conclude from this that the aim is upbuilding, or edification, and *not* worship. This is true not only because of what we have seen already about the very nature of edification as an expression of worship, but also because of what Paul says explicitly about the relationship between upbuilding and worship. Consider 1 Corinthians 14:15–17:

> I will *sing praise* [*psallō*] with my spirit, but I will sing with my mind also. Otherwise, if you *give thanks* [*eulogēs*, praise, bless] with your

spirit, how can anyone in the position of an outsider say "Amen" to your thanksgiving [*eucharistia*] when he does not know what you are saying? For you may be giving thanks well enough, but the other person is not being built up [*oikodomeitai*].

Here we get a glimpse into the relationship between vertical worship and horizontal upbuilding, as Paul understands it—indeed as he experiences it. These gatherings at Corinth included various kinds of speech—"the utterance of wisdom . . . knowledge . . . prophecy . . . various kinds of tongues . . . interpretation of tongues" (1 Cor. 12:8–10); "revelation or knowledge or prophecy or teaching" (1 Cor. 14:6). Whatever the form of speech, it included vertical praise and thanks. That is what Paul says in 1 Corinthians 14:15–16. Then he asks: If you or I are praising and thanking God in an unintelligible way, how will anyone say "Amen," and how will they be "built up" (vv. 16–17)?

One thing is crystal clear here. In Paul's mind the causes of up-building include vertical expressions of worship to God. "You may be *giving thanks* well enough, but the other person is not being *built up* [if you are speaking unintelligibly]." Which means that in Paul's mind, authentic, intelligibly expressed passion for God in corporate worship builds people up. Which, as we have seen, is the most natural thing in the world, if the very meaning of edification is moving people toward a life of authentic, God-centered, Christ-exalting worship. People are moved to be real worshipers by being around real worshipers. This is true even of outsiders who come into the Christian gatherings: "The secrets of his heart are disclosed, and so, falling on his face, *he will worship God* and declare that God is really among you" (1 Cor. 14:25).

Corporate Worship Is Beautifully Fitting

From all that we have seen in this chapter, I conclude, therefore, that *it is beautifully fitting for the people of Christ to gather regularly for corporate worship.* By "worship," I mean a radically God-centered, Christ-exalting experience of *knowing, treasuring,* and *expressing* the glory of God through Jesus Christ. There are a thousand good effects that come to a church that follows this practice. But those effects come precisely because the effects themselves are not the ultimate focus. Worship ceases to be worship where pastors try to motivate worship so it will have other good effects. It will. But not if those effects are the focus. The good effects come when the focus of the worship service is the infinite value of the glory of God.

How Often Should We Gather to Worship?

I have not been specific about how often the church should gather for corporate worship or when, or how long, or whether every gathering of the church has the same radical, vertical focus. I will just touch on this as we close this chapter.

The early church seems to have gathered at least once a week on the first day of the week, Sunday, because this was the day Jesus rose from the dead. "On the first day of every week, each of you is to put something aside and store it up, as he may prosper" (1 Cor. 16:2). This reference to a collection for the poor on the first day of the week turns up in the second-century description of weekly worship by Justin Martyr, who lived from about AD 100 to 165. It suggests that Paul is here indeed speaking not of a private act, but a corporate act as part of a worship gathering. Justin writes:

> And on the day called Sunday [τῇ τοῦ Ἡλίου λεγομένη ἡμέρᾳ] all who live in cities or in the country gather together to one place, and the memoirs of the apostles or the writings of the prophets are read, as long as time permits; then, when the reader has ceased, the president verbally instructs, and exhorts to the imitation of these good things. Then we all rise together and pray, and, as we before said, when our prayer is ended, bread and wine and water are brought, and the president in like manner offers prayers and thanksgivings, according to his ability, and the people assent, saying Amen; and there is a distribution to each, and a participation of that over which thanks have been given, and to those who are absent a portion is sent by the deacons. And they who are well to do, and willing, give what each thinks fit; and what is collected is deposited with the president, who succours the orphans and widows, and those who, through sickness or any other cause, are in want, and those who are in bonds, and the strangers sojourning among us, and in a word takes care of all who are in need.[1]

---

1. Justin Martyr, "The First Apology of Justin," chap. 67, in *The Apostolic Fathers with Justin Martyr and Irenaeus*, ed. Alexander Roberts, James Donaldson, and A. Cleveland Coxe, vol. 1, The Ante-Nicene Fathers (Buffalo, NY: Christian Literature Co., 1885), 185–86.

This Tradition Warranted

So I would say that two thousand years of Christian tradition have been warranted and that the baseline for our gatherings should be at least once a week for an all-church corporate gathering to focus intensely on worshiping God through Jesus Christ. In times of great spiritual awakening in the history of the church, the frequency of these gatherings has increased. And besides the all-church gatherings of the people for worship, the New Testament implicitly calls for other smaller gatherings where all the members can be involved in fulfilling the one-another commands of Scripture. I would put Hebrews 10:24–25 in this category:

> Let us consider how to stir up one another to love and good works, not neglecting to meet together, as is the habit of some, but encouraging one another, and all the more as you see the Day drawing near.

And, of course, there is the expectation that not just in formal gatherings, large or small, but in daily interaction, Christians are to exhort each other continually. "Exhort one another *every day*, as long as it is called 'today,' that none of you may be hardened by the deceitfulness of sin" (Heb. 3:13).

Plea for Godward Gravity and Gladness

It seems to me that the New Testament leaves ample room for diversity and flexibility in the frequency, timing, length, and place of church gatherings. This is, no doubt, intentional, because there are thousands of diverse cultures around the world where God wants his church to be indigenous. My plea would be that, whatever else a church gathers to do, it would prioritize gathering at least weekly for corporate worship, and that this service—no matter how small or large—would be intensely focused on the glory of God.

There are 168 hours in the week. Most of those hours are spent focusing on horizontal pursuits. Therefore, most people are unaccustomed to the kind of joyful seriousness that makes a focus on God spiritually possible and deeply thrilling. Gladness mingled with gravity—the weight of glory—is foreign to most modern people, unless they have suffered much. But I think this is our goal—to know, to treasure, and to show the worth and beauty of God and his ways. And to do it together. To do it corporately. Because, given the greatness of God and the wonder of his ways, the nature of his chosen people, and the possibilities of fathomless joy in his presence, it is beautifully fitting that we do so.

From the Beauty of Worship to the Benefits of Preaching

We turn now from the nature and fitness of corporate worship to the question, What is preaching and why should it be an essential part of corporate worship? How did the heralding of good news in the world make its way into the worship of God's people? That is the focus of chapter 3, the first chapter of part 2.

Why Is Expository Exultation Integral to Corporate Worship?

Heralding, History, and Trinity

3

How Paul Brought Heralding
into the House of God

If it is beautifully fitting that Christians gather regularly for corporate worship, what is it about preaching that makes it so important for that gathering? My answer is that preaching itself *is* worship and is appointed by God to awaken and intensify worship. It does this by heralding the reality communicated through the words of Scripture, which was written to create and sustain worship.

To say it another way, the preacher simultaneously *explains* the meaning of Scripture and *exults* over the God-glorifying reality in it. Exultation without explanation is not preaching. Explanation without exultation is not preaching. Therefore, preaching—*expository exultation*— is peculiarly suited for Christian corporate worship, for *worship* means knowing, treasuring, and showing the supreme worth and beauty of God. Preaching helps people do this by doing it. Preaching shows God's supreme worth by making the meaning of Scripture known and by simultaneously treasuring and expressing the glories of God revealed in that biblical meaning.

What Does *Exposition* Mean?

My term for preaching is *expository exultation*. I will have more to say about the meaning of *expository* in the chapters to come. But it may be good to give a brief definition at this point. Here's the heart of it from John Stott, and it is what I mean by *exposition*:

> It is my contention that all true Christian preaching is expository preaching. Of course, if by an "expository" sermon is meant a verse-

by-verse explanation of a lengthy passage of Scripture, then indeed it is only one possible way of preaching, but this would be a misuse of the word. Properly speaking, "exposition" has a much broader meaning. It refers to the content of the sermon (biblical truth) rather than its style (a running commentary). To expound Scripture is to bring out of the text *what is there and expose it to view*. The expositor pries open what appears to be closed, makes plain what is obscure, unravels what is knotted and unfolds what is tightly packed. The opposite of exposition is "imposition," which is to impose on the text what is not there. But the "text" in question could be a verse, or a sentence, or even a single word. It could equally be a paragraph, or a chapter, or a whole book. The size of the text is immaterial, so long as it is biblical. What matters is what we do with it. Whether it is long or short, our responsibility as expositors is to open it up in such a way that it speaks its message clearly, plainly, accurately, relevantly, without addition, subtraction or falsification.[1]

This definition of *exposition* leaves enormous room for different ways of doing what Stott says we should do: take "what is there and expose it to view."

Two Qualifications of Stott's Definition

I want to make two clarifications. One is that not only may the text be of any length, but also it may be of any manageable number. There can be more than one text for a sermon. In other words, exposition can be done thematically and topically. An expository sermon can be about death or love or hope or marriage. What makes it expository is not that there is only one text but that the preaching is actually from biblical texts, and that their true meaning is "brought out and exposed to view."

The other qualification I want to make is that the content of the message, in its essence, is not the biblical text (which, nevertheless, remains indispensable in all its details), but the *reality* that the text is communicating. When Stott says the content of the sermon is "biblical truth," I want to make sure that the word "truth" refers not just to grammatical and historical propositions but to the *reality* that is being referred to—its nature, its value, and its implications for real life now.

---

1. John Stott, *Between Two Worlds: The Art of Preaching in the Twentieth Century* (Grand Rapids, MI: Eerdmans, 1982), 125–26; emphasis added.

If the text is "God is love," the sermon "brings out and exposes to view" the reality of God, the reality of love, and the reality of the relationship between God and love expressed by the word "is." Preaching shows what these realities are, how valuable they are, and why. Preaching urges the implications of these realities. It tries to make plain the value that these realities have for our lives. I will have much more to say about the relationship between text and reality in part 5, but for now, this will suffice to give an idea of what I mean by *exposition*.

Exposition and Exultation Inseparable

The focus of this chapter is not on preaching as exposition but on preaching as exultation—that is, preaching as worship—keeping in mind that exposition and exultation are never separated in true preaching. It is possible to do exposition of texts that you don't even believe, let alone exult over. So I do not regard exposition per se as the defining mark of preaching. The Devil can do biblical exposition—even speaking true propositions about the text's meaning. But the Devil cannot exult over the divine glory of the meaning of Scripture. He hates it. So he cannot *preach*—not the way I am defining it.

Of course, mindless enthusiasts who totally ignore the meaning of texts can exult as they preach, but not in the true meaning of the text and the reality behind it. So exultation per se is not the defining mark of preaching. But together—*exposition*, as making clear what the Scripture really means, and *exultation*, as openly treasuring the divine glories of that meaning—they combine to make preaching what it is.

Vocabulary of Preaching

To give biblical foundation to the claim that preaching is expository *exultation*, we will begin with the New Testament vocabulary of preaching.

The English word *preach* (or some form of it) occurs eighty times in the ESV. Almost every one of these uses come from the Greek words *euangelizomai* ("preach good news"[2]) or *kēryssō* ("preach" or "herald"). Both words refer most often to the public proclamation of a message to the world, not just to a church gathered for worship.

---

2. The ESV translates *euangelizomai* by various phrases, including "preaching" (e.g., Acts 5:42; 1 Cor. 9:18), "preach(ing) the gospel" (e.g., Luke 9:6; Rom. 1:15), "preach(ed) the good news" (e.g., Acts 8:12; Rom. 10:15), and "bring good news" (e.g., Luke 1:19; 2:10).

Heralding in the World—and in Church

Hence Gordon Hugenberger writes:

> "Preach" is somewhat infelicitous as a rendering for these two word groups. "Preach" accurately conveys the typically public and authoritative character of the various speech acts intended by these Greek terms; but it is a misleading translation to the extent that common English parlance uses "preach" to refer to formal sermonizing directed to the faithful, while the NT uses both *kēryssō* and *euangelizomai* to refer primarily (though not exclusively) to evangelistic activity directed to non-Christians.[3]

My response to this observation is mixed. Yes, *preaching* today refers most often to sermons in church (and that is how I am using it), and yes, *kēryssō* and *euangelizomai* in the New Testament refer most often to public speaking to unbelievers. On the other hand, something about the peculiar speech involved in *kēryssō* and *euangelizomai* may make it especially suited to the work of Christian pastors in bringing the word of God to their people.

Notice carefully Hugenberger's words quoted above in parentheses, "though not exclusively." "Both *kēryssō* and *euangelizomai* refer primarily (though not exclusively) to evangelistic activity directed to non-Christians." This concession is important since I am going to argue that Paul did, in fact, model and command the kind of speech implicit in *kēryssō* and *euangelizomai* in the context of the gathered church, not just in the public task of evangelistic preaching.

The fact that in the New Testament, "preaching" translates mainly *kēryssō* and *euangelizomai* suggests that preaching is a peculiar form of speech that derives its character, at least partly, from these public acts of heralding. Preaching was not ordinary conversation. Nor was it identical to teaching. Both *euangelizomai* ("preach good news") and *kēryssō* ("preach" or "herald") have the quality of *announcement*, and since the specific Christian content of the announcement is the good news of Christ's saving work, with all its roots and branches, the announcement quality was not disapproval or indifference, but commendation and acclamation.

---

3. G. P. Hugenberger, "Preach," in *The International Standard Bible Encyclopedia*, rev. ed., ed. Geoffrey W. Bromiley (Grand Rapids, MI: Eerdmans, 1979–1988), 941.

In other words, the fact that in the history of the church the regular address to the people of God in corporate worship has been called "preaching" may not be misleading or infelicitous after all. It may be owing to the fact that crucial dimensions of *kēryssō* and *euangelizomai* are essential to a message about the glories of God addressed to God's people in corporate worship.

Connotations of Euangelizomai

The kind of speaking implied in *euangelizomai*, for example, is that the speaker is animated not by boring or uninteresting or gloomy news, but on the contrary by "good news." We catch the spirit of this kind of communication, for example, in texts like these:

> The angel said to them, "Fear not, for behold, *I bring you good news* [*euangelizomai*] of great joy that will be for all the people. For unto you is born this day in the city of David a Savior, who is Christ the Lord." (Luke 2:10–11)

> The Spirit of the Lord is upon me,
>   because he has anointed me
>   *to proclaim good news* [*euangelisasthai*] to the poor.
> He has sent me to proclaim [*kēryxai*] liberty to the captives
>   and recovering of sight to the blind,
>   to set at liberty those who are oppressed,
> to proclaim [*kēryxai*] the year of the Lord's favor. (Luke 4:18–19)

> How are they to preach unless they are sent? As it is written, "How beautiful are the feet of those who *preach the good news!*" [*euangelizomenōn*] (Rom. 10:15)

Connotations of Kēryssō

The kind of speaking implied in *kēryssō*, in its general use in the first century, was derived not from the focus on good news but from the urgency of being a communication of great import from a significant authority. This is the assumption behind Paul's rhetorical question, "How are they to preach [*kēryxōsin*] unless *they are sent*" (Rom. 10:15)—that is, unless they have some significant authority behind them?

Here again is Hugenberger's summary of the research:

In its broadest and most general (though not the most common) use, *kēryssō* describes the making of a loud, attention-getting noise or of a public oral announcement; hence it can simply be translated "proclaim." A biblical example occurs in Zeph. 3:14, LXX, where Israel is enjoined to "shout aloud" (*kēryssō*) its joyful praise to the Lord (cf. also Ex. 32:5; Hos. 5:8; Joel 2:1; Zec. 9:9; Rev. 5:2). . . .

A *kēryx* [a herald] delivers the message of a king: The Bible offers numerous instances of this more narrow use of the *kēryssō* word group (cf., e.g., LXX Ex. 36:6; 2 K. 10:20; 2 Ch. 36:22; Dnl. 5:29).[4]

No Ordinary Way of Speaking

Therefore, both *euangelizomai* and *kēryssō*, as the primary words behind the English "preach" in the New Testament, describe a kind of speech that involves more than the transfer of information or the explanation of truth that is coming from another source. They both signify a kind of speech that accords with good news, great import, and significant authority.

There is, you might say, in both of them, gladness and gravity. The gladness is in the *euangelizomai*, and the gravity is in the *kēryssō*. Both are serious. Both are weighty. Neither is frivolous, glib, or trivial. If the messenger gave the impression that his news was trivial, he would be speaking out of character. He would be contradicting his calling as one commissioned for this kind of speaking (*euangelizomai* and *kēryssō*).

Use of *Teaching* in Relation to *Euangelizomai* and *Kēryssō*

This is confirmed and clarified when we ponder the relationship between these two kinds of speaking, on the one hand, and *teaching* (*didaskō/didaskalia*) on the other. What we find is that preaching (heralding, announcing, proclaiming) is not identical to teaching. But the closer we focus on the role of preaching in the gathered church, the more interwoven these kinds of speaking appear.

When teaching is mentioned along with *kēryssō* or *euangelizomai*, it is considered to be something, at least in some measure, distinct and in addition to these kinds of speaking. For example:

---

4. Ibid., 942.

teaching + kēryssō

> He went throughout all Galilee, *teaching* in their synagogues and *proclaiming* [*kēryssōn*] the gospel of the kingdom and healing every disease and every affliction among the people. (Matt. 4:23)

> When Jesus had finished instructing his twelve disciples, he went on from there to *teach* and *preach* [*kēryssein*] in their cities. (Matt. 11:1)

> [Paul] lived there two whole years at his own expense, and welcomed all who came to him, *proclaiming* [*kēryssōn*] the kingdom of God and *teaching* about the Lord Jesus Christ with all boldness and without hindrance. (Acts 28:30–31)

> I was appointed a *preacher* [*kēryx*] and an apostle (I am telling the truth, I am not lying), a *teacher* of the Gentiles in faith and truth. (1 Tim. 2:7)

teaching + euangelizomai

> One day, as Jesus was *teaching* the people in the temple and *preaching* [*euangelizomenou*] the gospel, the chief priests and the scribes with the elders came up. (Luke 20:1)

> Every day, in the temple and from house to house, they did not cease *teaching* and *preaching* [*euangelizomenou*] that the Christ is Jesus. (Acts 5:42)

> Paul and Barnabas remained in Antioch, *teaching* and *preaching* [*euangelizomenoi*] the word of the Lord, with many others also. (Acts 15:35)

It would probably be artificial to draw a hard line between preaching and teaching in the instances just mentioned, even though they are mentioned separately. I say this because of the nature of the reality of communication. A herald in the role of a town crier may announce with amazement that the king is offering amnesty to every traitor who will repent and swear fealty to the king. And as he says that, he may realize, by the look on people's faces, that he must explain what *amnesty* and *traitor* and *fealty* mean. In other words, heralding and teaching may necessarily be interwoven, even though, in general, the texts just cited treat them, in some measure, as distinct.

Paul Takes Heralding to Church

This interwoven reality becomes clearer as we turn to ask the question, Does the New Testament portray and command "preaching" in the context of the gathered church? Is preaching—the kind of speech implicit in *kēryssō* and *euangelizomai*—supposed to be part of what the church does when it gathers for corporate worship? If so, how does it relate to teaching?

The apostle Paul takes three words for preaching and proclaiming in public and applies them to the regular gatherings of the church. Besides *euangelizomai* and *kēryssō*, he treats *katangellō* (translated "proclaim" in seventeen of its eighteen occurrences in the New Testament) as a kind of speech directed toward believers, not just the wider world of unbelievers. For the remainder of this chapter, we will focus on the three places where Paul does this.

Katangellō: "I Proclaim"

We begin with *katangellō*—"I proclaim." Paul says in Colossians 1:27–28,

> God chose to make known how great among the Gentiles are the riches of the glory of this mystery, which is Christ in you, the hope of glory. Him we proclaim [*katangellomen*], warning [*nouthountes*] everyone and teaching [*didaskontes*] everyone with all wisdom, that we may present everyone mature in Christ.

Notice that *proclaim* is the main verb, which is then modified by two participles, *warning* and *teaching*. This means that proclaiming is not completely distinct from teaching. Rather, teaching is one aspect of Paul's proclaiming. It also means that proclaiming is what Paul did among believers whom he was seeking to bring to maturity, not just among unbelievers whom he was seeking to convert.

This is implied in the words "we *proclaim*, . . . *teaching* everyone . . . that we may present everyone mature in Christ." In other words, the aim is to bring believers to maturity in Christ, not just convert them. In this text, the main act for accomplishing this maturing process is *proc-*

lamation. Katangellō is the main verb. The other two verbs (*warning* and *teaching*) characterize aspects of how the proclamation is done. The fact that these three verbs (*proclaim*, *warn*, and *teach*) are all present tense in the original Greek underlines the continuing, ongoing work among believers.

This focus on the gathered church is confirmed in Colossians 3:16 by the use of the same two words (*didaskontes* and *nouthountes*) to describe the way to "let the word of Christ dwell in you [Christians] richly"—by "teaching and admonishing [*didaskontes kai nouthountes*] one another." Not only that, but Colossians 1:28 and 3:16 use the phrase "in all wisdom" to describe how this ministry of the word is done. I infer from this that Paul's work of ongoing "proclaiming," which includes teaching and admonishing "with all wisdom," is at least one of the ways he believed that Christians in their worship gatherings should be addressed.

Euangelizomai: "I Preach Good News"

Paul also takes the word that ordinarily signifies the public heralding of good news (*euangelizomai*) and applies it to his ministry to believers within the church. We see this in Romans 1:13–15:

> I do not want you to be unaware, brothers, that I have often intended to come to you (but thus far have been prevented), in order that I may reap some harvest among you as well as among the rest of the Gentiles. I am under obligation both to Greeks and to barbarians, both to the wise and to the foolish. So I am eager to preach the gospel [*euangelisasthai*] to you also who are in Rome.

What Is the Fruit He Hopes to Have?

It is possible that when Paul says, in verse 13, that he hoped to "have some fruit among you as well as among the rest of the Gentiles" (my translation), he meant that he hoped to have some Gentile converts. But of the ten other uses of the word *fruit* in Paul's letters, it never refers to his converts. There is *fruit* that leads to sanctification (Rom. 6:22), and *fruit* of the Spirit (Gal. 5:22), and the *fruit* of righteousness (Phil. 1:11), and the *fruit* of generous giving (Phil. 4:17), but never the fruit of converts.

He had just said in the immediately preceding verses, "I long to see

you, that I may impart to you some spiritual gift *to strengthen you*—
that is, that we may be mutually *encouraged* by each other's faith, both
yours and mine" (Rom. 1:11–12). It would be very natural to see the
"fruit" Paul hopes to have "among you" as the fruit of stronger faith
with all its outcomes for a changed life.

How Will Paul Pursue This Fruit?

How does Paul hope to see this fruit come about? He says in verse 15,
"I am eager to preach the gospel [*euangelisasthai*] to you also who are
in Rome." Notice he is eager to herald the good news *to you* (*humin*,
dative), that is, to believers. This would be one of the ways he hopes to
"have fruit" among them.

This is the way Paul thought about the gospel among believers—
the ongoing application of the gospel by *heralding the gospel* (*euangelizomai*) was a task continually needed to transform and strengthen
believers, not just convert them. For example, Paul writes to the Philippians, "Only let your manner of life be *worthy of the gospel* of
Christ" (Phil. 1:27). In other words, exhortation and instruction in
the way the gospel transforms Christians are needed for believers to
help them live a "life . . . worthy of the gospel." Similarly, when Paul
saw, in Antioch, that Peter's "conduct was not *in step with the truth
of the gospel*," Paul had to press the gospel realities into Peter's mind
again (Gal. 2:14).

So, for Paul, the "fruit" of the Christian life is a "manner of life . . .
worthy of the gospel of Christ." And to bring forth this fruit requires
not just *conversion* by the gospel, but the ongoing *preaching to believers of how the gospel works*. Hence he says to the "brothers" in Rome,
"I am eager to preach the gospel *to you*."

Preaching Good News Belongs in Church

Therefore, it would be a mistake to say that because, in the New Testament, the word *euangelizomai* ordinarily refers to public evangelistic
preaching, it should not be part of how a pastor seeks to "have fruit"
among the saints. On the contrary, Romans 1:15 as well as Colossians
1:28 point in the other direction. There is something about the peculiar
speech involved in *euangelizomai* and *katangellō* that belongs in the
preaching of pastors to their already-converted people.

Kēryssō: *"I Herald"*

Recall that *kēryssō* was ordinarily used to refer to a public heralding on behalf of someone with significant authority on a matter of great importance. It was not a kind of communication that simply transferred information or explained obscurities. It was communication with a comportment that signified the importance of its content and the authority of its author. A herald (*kēryx*) who communicated by his demeanor that he did not revere his king, or regard his message as valuable, was nearing treason. To speak as a herald was to communicate not only the truth but also the value of the message and the majesty of the authority behind it.

Preaching Is Commanded

Now, for the third time, Paul uses such a word (*kēryssō*)—with all these connotations—to describe the way the church should be addressed. In fact, this time he is not describing but commanding. Second Timothy 4:2 is the only place in the New Testament where *preaching* (whether expressed as *kēryssō, euangelizomai,* or *katangellō*) is *commanded* for the gathered community of Christians. Therefore, this passage is unusually important for grasping the (1) setting, (2) content, (3) nature, and (4) importance of preaching.

To clarify these four aspects of preaching, the most immediately relevant context is 2 Timothy 3:16–4:4.

> All Scripture is breathed out by God and profitable for teaching, for reproof, for correction, and for training in righteousness, that the man of God may be complete, equipped for every good work. I charge you in the presence of God and of Christ Jesus, who is to judge the living and the dead, and by his appearing and his kingdom: preach the word; be ready in season and out of season; reprove, rebuke, and exhort, with complete patience and teaching. For the time is coming when people will not endure sound teaching, but having itching ears they will accumulate for themselves teachers to suit their own passions, and will turn away from listening to the truth and wander off into myths.

1. The Setting of Preaching

The command to preach is found at the beginning of 2 Timothy 4:2: "Preach the word" (*kēryxon ton logon*). Already Paul has told Timothy to do his best to "handl[e] the word of truth" (2:15) like a guide who *cuts a straight path* for the traveler (*orthotomounta*, see uses in Prov. 3:6; 11:5). The audience he has in mind is "the elect" (2 Tim. 2:10), that is, the church.

Preaching the truth is one of the ways Timothy will "rightly handle the *word of truth*." Preparing Timothy for the command to preach (in 4:2), Paul reminds him of how reliable the "sacred writings" are, that is, the Old Testament Scriptures that he has been taught from childhood (3:15). These Scriptures "are able to make you wise for salvation through faith in Christ Jesus."

Then Paul gives Timothy the reason these Scriptures are so effective in making him wise and leading to salvation through faith in Christ: they are inspired by God.

> *All Scripture is breathed out by God* and profitable for teaching, for reproof, for correction, and for training in righteousness, that the man of God may be complete, equipped for every good work. (2 Tim. 3:16–17)

Even though the term "man of God," against the backdrop of seventy-six uses in the Old Testament, probably puts the focus on Timothy himself as the beneficiary of the completing and equipping work of Scripture, the clear implication is that if he rightly handles these Scriptures, not only he, but also his people, will be transformed. When the Scriptures have their completing, equipping effect on Timothy, he will be able to *cut a straight path* (2:15) for the fellow travelers in his church.

Therefore, we may infer that when Paul immediately commands Timothy to "preach the word" (4:2), the setting he has in mind is the gathered church. At this point, he is not telling Timothy to "do the work of an evangelist" (4:5). He is telling him to take these Scriptures and preach them to the people of God.

Preaching to a wandering church. The audience of preaching is in need of reproof, rebuke, exhortation, and patient teaching (4:2b). This is a reference not to public encounters with unbelievers, but to ongoing encounters with believers who need patient teaching. Then, in verses 3–4, Paul gives further reason for faithfully preaching the word, namely, that those who are now amenable to sound teaching may not always be:

For the time is coming when people will not endure sound teaching, but having itching ears they will accumulate for themselves teachers to suit their own passions, and will turn away from listening to the truth and wander off into myths.

Paul does not say that his command to preach the word is for the sake of crowds of unbelievers who have wandered into myths. Rather, he says that Timothy is to "preach the word" because the church is in danger of turning away from the truth of God's word and wandering into myths. Preaching is intended to protect them.

I conclude, therefore, that the *setting* for this preaching is the people of God gathered to hear it. Paul has chosen a word for preaching (*kēryssō*) that ordinarily signifies heralding great truth from high authority in the world, and he has used it to signify the kind of speaking that the church needs—"preach the word."

2. The Content of Preaching

Paul commands, "Preach *the word*" (2 Tim. 4:2). The term *word* (*logon*) is not a technical term in Paul's writings that refers only to one thing. Even in the Pastoral Epistles (1 and 2 Timothy and Titus), Paul uses the word twenty times, referring, for example, to trustworthy sayings (1 Tim. 1:15), "words of the faith" (1 Tim. 4:6), "words of our Lord Jesus Christ" (1 Tim. 6:3), "the pattern of . . . sound words" (2 Tim. 1:13), "the word of God" (2 Tim. 2:9), and "the word of truth" (2 Tim. 2:15).

It would be unwarranted to claim that "preach the word" referred to anything less than the word *of Scripture* just mentioned two verses earlier. The chapter break between those verses is misleading. Without the break, it reads like this: "Continue in what you have learned . . . , the sacred writings. . . . All Scripture is breathed out by God. . . . I charge you . . . preach the word" (2 Tim. 3:14–4:2). In other words, preach the *Scripture*. All the Scripture. It is all inspired. It is all profitable. It all makes wise toward salvation in Jesus. It all moves the church toward good works.

The word is written. To underline the obvious but easily overlooked: this means that the word to be preached has come to us in a written form—in a book. In the sentence, "All Scripture is breathed out by God," the phrase, "all Scripture" (*pasa graphē*) refers to all the *writing*—the "sacred writings" (*hiera grammata*)—referred to in the previous verse, that is, the Jewish Scriptures, the Old Testament. Which means that the preparation for preaching will be, in large measure, book work. We must find the content of our preaching in a book.

Of course, the preaching must not be dead. It must not be book*ish*. But it must be book-derived. Book-faithful. Book-saturated. Book-balanced. As we will see in due time, it must be Spirit-given, Spirit-shaped, Spirit-carried, and Spirit-delivered. But the Holy Spirit inspired a particular book—*the* Book—and broods over the Book, and lives to exalt the Christ of the Book (John 16:14). So the content of our preaching is never less than a faithful rendering of this Book.

The word includes the New Testament. There is a clue in the context that the word we preach is not simply the Old Testament, but the New Testament as well. Notice in the next verse (2 Tim. 4:3) the reason Paul gives for preaching the word: "For the time is coming when people will not endure *sound teaching*." Preach the word—because *sound teaching* will not always be loved. What does this "sound teaching" refer to?

Second Timothy 1:13 gives us the answer: "Follow the pattern of the *sound words* that you have heard from me, in the faith and love that are in Christ Jesus." "Sound teaching" in 2 Timothy 4:3 refers to the "pattern of the sound words" transmitted to Timothy by the apostle Paul. "Follow the pattern of the sound words that you have heard *from me*."

Two phrases in 2 Timothy 1:13 carry huge implications for the content of preaching: "pattern of . . . words" and "from me." There is a standard or a pattern of sound teaching. This means that in the early church there was a developing body of fixed doctrine (or teaching) under the care of the apostles that was being faithfully passed on to the churches. That's what "from me" signifies in 2 Timothy 4:3. Paul and the other apostles were the authorized guardians of the "pattern of the sound words" given to the churches.

Good deposit, sound words, standard of teaching, whole counsel. We can see this body of teaching in several other places expressed in different phrases. In 1 Timothy 6:20 and 2 Timothy 1:14, Paul tells Timothy to "guard the good deposit [*tēn kalēn parathēkēn*] entrusted to you." In Romans 6:17, Paul says, "Thanks be to God, that you who were once slaves of sin have become obedient from the heart to the *standard of teaching* [*túpon didachēs*] to which you were committed."

In Acts 20:26–27 he said to the elders of the Ephesian church, "I am innocent of the blood of all, for I did not shrink from declaring to you the *whole counsel of God* [*pasan tēn boulēn tou theou*]."

These four phrases ("good deposit," "pattern of the sound words," "standard of teaching," and "whole counsel of God") point to an emerging, unified body of doctrine that Jesus had promised would be given for the churches: "The Holy Spirit, whom the Father will send in my name, he will teach you all things and bring to your remembrance all that I have said to you. . . . He will guide you into all the truth" (John 14:26; 16:13). This Spirit-given, unified, fixed body of doctrine Paul called the "wisdom of God" in 1 Corinthians 2:7 and said that it was imparted to the churches through the apostles "in words . . . taught by the Spirit" (1 Cor. 2:13).

This is the coherent body of truth that was gathered into the book we call the New Testament.[5] Together with the Old Testament Scriptures that Paul referred to in 2 Timothy 3:16, the New Testament forms the complete word, which Paul, by implication, was referring to when he said, "Preach the word."

3. The Nature of Preaching

The juxtaposition of the word for "heralding" in 2 Timothy 4:2 ("*preach* the word," *kēryxon ton logon*) with the reference to "sound teaching" (*hugiainousēs didaskalias*) in the next verse reveals something crucial about the nature of preaching. "*Preach* the word; be ready in season and out of season . . . with . . . *teaching* [*didachē*]. For the time is coming when people will not endure sound *teaching*." We should not silence the significant and differing implications of either of these words: "preach" (*kēryxon*) and "teaching" (*didaskalias*).

It belongs to the very nature of the case that heralding the word of Scripture must involve significant measures of teaching.[6] The realities heralded must be illuminated. The biblical texts used must be explained.

---

5. For a much fuller treatment of "What Books and Words Make Up the Christian Scriptures," see the section by that title in John Piper, *A Peculiar Glory: How the Christian Scriptures Reveal Their Complete Truthfulness* (Wheaton, IL: Crossway, 2016), 39–87.

6. Of course, other words besides *teaching* are used in the Pastoral Epistles to describe how the pastor speaks to his people. The pastor is to encourage (1 Tim. 5:1), remind (2 Tim. 2:14), declare (Titus 2:15), rebuke (1 Tim. 5:20), let them learn (Titus 3:14), and more. I am not making any claim that these are to be diminished or neglected. I am arguing for the importance of preaching, not the unimportance of other biblical exhortations. These have their place alongside, and as part of, preaching.

And it belongs to the very nature of the case—and the vocabulary Paul uses (*katangellō, kēryssō, euangelizomai*)—that this teaching comes regularly in the form of heralding, that is, preaching.

The message of the preacher, the herald, is not merely a body of facts to be understood. It is a constellation of glories to be treasured. It is, at times, a tempest of horrors to be fled. Any thought that the message of a preacher could be delivered as a detached explanation fails to grasp the significance of Paul's use of the phrase "*Herald* the word!" Or, "*Preach* good news!" Or, "*Proclaim* Christ." Preaching is both accurate teaching and heartfelt heralding. It is *expository exultation*.

The Importance of Preaching

Until now, our examination of 2 Timothy 3:16–4:4 has passed over the most amazing part of this passage. I say "most amazing" because there is nothing quite like it anywhere else in Scripture. I am referring to 2 Timothy 4:1, which forms the introduction to the command "preach the word." I am not aware of any other biblical command that has such an extended, exalted, intensifying introduction (though 1 Timothy 5:21 comes close[7]).

Paul introduces the command, "preach the word," in verse 2 with five preceding intensifiers. Each of them is chosen to strengthen and deepen and heighten the importance of the command to preach. I doubt that anyone has ever overstated the seriousness that Paul is seeking to awaken here.

> I charge you
>> in the presence of God
>>> and of Christ Jesus,
>>>> who is to judge the living and the dead,
>>>>> and by his appearing and his kingdom:
>>>>>> preach the word.

Incomparable Introduction

1. "*I charge you* . . ." The word is *testify* with a prefix that intensifies it and adds weight (*diamarturomai*). Keep in mind that Paul is setting up a command to preach. Yet he uses the word "solemnly testify" for

---

7. "In the presence of God and of Christ Jesus and of the elect angels I charge you to keep these rules without prejudging, doing nothing from partiality" (1 Tim. 5:21).

his own exhortation. What does it mean to say, "I solemnly testify . . . preach the word"? Notice he does not say, "I solemnly *command* . . . preach the word." The word *testify* seems to imply that he is speaking in a court setting with huge things at stake. *Testify* suggests that he has seen something, or heard something, and is not merely speaking his own opinion. He is testifying to something he has seen or heard. And that encounter of seeing or hearing has sobered him in such a serious way that this litany of intensifiers is the result.

2. *"in the presence of God . . ."* "I charge [solemnly testify to] you *in the presence of God . . ."* Now we get a glimpse into the setting in Paul's mind where he is delivering this testimony-command "preach the word." He is in the presence of God. He is conscious of a special and close attention that God is paying to this testimony. The implication is that God is the one who has authorized this command. It is a testimony to the extent that it comes with the firsthand authorization of God. Paul is testifying to the fact that God is behind this command. God is watching over it closely to see that it is delivered. There is no higher authorization and no higher attendant to the proceeding of this testimony. "I testify to you *in the presence of God.*"

3. *"and of Christ Jesus . . ."* "I testify to you in the presence of God and *of Christ Jesus . . ."* Adding Christ Jesus to the attendants at this solemn testimony to preach the word does not increase the authority. There is no authority higher than God. But it does multiply the persons who have a massive stake in what preaching is about. God is the author of the word to be preached, and Jesus Christ is the center of its story. If you are going to sober Timothy as you command him to preach the word, tell him that the command is being delivered in the presence of the *author* and the *subject* of all preaching—indeed all reality.

4. *"who is to judge the living and the dead . . ."* "I testify to you in the presence of God and of Christ Jesus, *who is to judge the living and the dead . . ."* Of the hundreds of things Paul could have said about Jesus, he says this: Jesus is to judge the living and the dead. Why? The point seems to be that when it comes to preaching, the stakes are raised higher than any rewards or threats in this life. In preaching we are dealing with persons and realities that are vastly greater than this world. Their existence and their rewards and punishments

exceed this life. Christ is active in this world, governing the living. And Christ is—and always will be—active beyond this world, dealing justly with those who have died. This glorious person is unavoidable in life and inescapable in death. Everyone meets him as judge sooner or later. These are the great matters of preaching. Paul wants us to feel this weight.

5. *"and by his appearing and his kingdom . . ."* "I charge you in the presence of God and of Christ Jesus, who is to judge the living and the dead, *and by his appearing and his kingdom . . ."* Five of the six uses of the word *appearing (epiphaneian)* in the New Testament occur in the Pastoral Epistles. It refers at least once to the historical appearing of Jesus in the incarnation (2 Tim. 1:10) and at least twice to the future second coming of Christ (1 Tim. 6:14; Titus 2:13). The other two could go either way, including this text (2 Tim. 4:1, 8). Perhaps the ambiguity is intentional. Do you love his appearing (past and future, 1 Tim. 4:8)? And do you feel the weight, for preaching, of the appearing of God himself in history (past and future)?

That is to say, "Preacher, keep this in mind, you herald the word of the coming king of the universe"—the one who came once not to judge but to save (John 3:17), but now will come to judge. In these days, when you are called to preach (between his two appearings!), he may seem distant because he does not appear. But I am telling you to preach knowing this—never forgetting this—he has appeared, and he *will* appear.

And when he does return, he will be king, and his kingdom will be openly established. No longer will he say, "My kingdom is not of this world" (John 18:36). He will reign openly and unopposed. All his opponents will be cast into outer darkness (Matt. 22:13; 25:30). No more will they be a factor. And all the truth you ever preached will be publicly vindicated, and all those who have turned away with itching ears will be put to shame.

Therefore, Timothy, once more, "I solemnly testify to you in the presence of God and of Christ Jesus, who is to judge the living and the dead, and by his appearing and his kingdom, *preach the word.*" That kind of extended, exalted, intensifying introduction to the command to *preach the word* is extraordinary. Therefore preaching—clarifying and heralding, *expository exultation*—is of extraordinary importance.

No Gathering Like Christian Worship

In the previous chapter, I argued from Scripture that it is beautifully fitting for Christians to gather regularly for corporate worship—that is, that they gather to *show* corporately that they *know* the triune God and *treasure* him above all things. In this chapter, I have focused on the nature of preaching with a view to showing why this kind of speech is so important in those regular gatherings for corporate worship. More specifically, the focus has been on the way the apostle Paul brought a public kind of communication—proclaiming, announcing, heralding—into the church and made it serve the ministry of the word for Christian believers.

Why did this happen? My answer is that Paul was drawn to shape preaching in this way by the inner fitness and harmony of such preaching with the nature of God, the nature of Scripture, and the nature of corporate worship. *God* is supremely beautiful and valuable. *Scripture*, as his inspired word, aims to awaken and sustain the true knowledge of God to the end that we might enjoy him and exhibit him to the world. And *corporate worship* gives a visible, united expression to that knowledge, enjoyment, and exhibition.

As these realities transformed the apostle Paul, he saw that the kind of speech appropriate for the gathered church in worship was unique. There was no other gathering like this in the world: a people of God's own possession (1 Pet. 2:9), chosen before the foundation of the world (Eph. 1:4), destined to be like the Son of God (Rom. 8:29), bought with divine blood (Acts 20:28), acquitted and accepted before the court of heaven (Rom. 5:1; 15:16), a new creation on the earth (2 Cor. 5:17), indwelt by the Creator of the universe (1 Cor. 6:19), sanctified by the body of Jesus (Heb. 10:10), called to eternal glory (1 Pet. 5:10), heirs of the world (Rom. 4:13; 1 Cor. 3:21–23), destined to rule with Christ (Rev. 3:21) and judge angels (1 Cor. 6:3). Never had there been a gathering like this. It was incomparable on the earth.

Not only was the gathering unique. So was the Book. All of this glorious truth about the gathered people of Christ was preserved and revealed in a book, and in an apostolic "deposit" that would become the capstone of *the* Book. The God, the Book, and the gathered people under the authority of the God revealed in the Book were incomparable. There was no God, no book, and no people like this. Paul saw this and knew that the gathering of this people would be marked by a kind of communication that was not like any other communication. That included preaching.

No Communication Like Preaching

As Paul proclaimed the unsearchable riches of Christ, and announced the good news of great joy, and heralded the reconciling message of the all-authoritative King, he saw that this kind of proclaiming, announcing, and heralding could not be discarded when this extraordinary people, under this extraordinary God, revealed in this extraordinary Book, gathered for worship. The riches of glory, the goodness of the news, the weight of the truth, and the authority behind it all did not become less because it was being spoken among this gathered people. If anything, it became more.

Therefore, Paul not only *modeled* proclaiming Christ and heralding good news to the people of God, but also *commanded* that the God-breathed Scriptures be heralded in the church: "Preach the word"! (2 Tim. 4:2). But I am stressing that this command (testimony) was not arbitrary, but was constrained by the fitness and harmony that Paul felt between the nature of God, Scripture, and worship, on the one hand, and the kind of speaking called for, on the other.

Paul saw that the proclamation quality, announcement quality, and heralding quality of his public speaking for the risen Christ contained a dimension of celebration, exuberant affirmation, and wonder. It combined a humble recognition that the message did not originate with the herald but with his king. The authority behind it was not his, but his Sovereign's. And the glory and value of the message was directly proportionate to the glory and value of the King. Therefore, the messenger could not be indifferent to the message without being indifferent to the King. That was as unthinkable as not treasuring infinite treasure.

Preaching Too Is Beautifully Fitting

Therefore, nothing was more fitting than that the presentation and explanation and contemplation and application of the King's message among the King's people come with *exultation*. This fitness lay behind Paul's transposition of the music of proclamation to the world into the music of preaching in worship. He saw that preaching as *exposi-*

tory exultation is peculiarly suited for Christian corporate worship. For corporate worship is the visible, unified knowing, treasuring, and showing of the supreme worth and beauty of God. Preaching fits that gathering, because that's what preaching is. Preaching shows God's supreme worth by opening Scripture to make the glories of God known, while treasuring them as supremely valuable. Expository exultation serves corporate worship by worshiping the One whom it shows to be worthy of worship.

Deeper than Paul

This chapter has focused on the implications of Paul's use of the vocabulary of preaching (*katangellō, kēryssō, euangelizomai*). Paul gave authoritative expression to the conviction in the early church that the announcement character and heralding character of these words be brought into the house of God. We have seen that heralding the word of God involves significant measures of teaching. The biblical texts used must be explained. The realities heralded must be illuminated. But the message of the preacher is never a mere body of facts to be clarified. It is a constellation of glories to be treasured. The thought that the message of a preacher could be delivered as a detached explanation fails to grasp the significance of Paul's use of the phrase "*Herald* the word!" Or, "*Preach* good news!" Or, "*Proclaim* Christ." Preaching is both accurate teaching and heartfelt heralding. It is expository exultation.

The roots of preaching as an act of worship, for the sake of worship, go deeper than the uses Paul made of *katangellō, kēryssō*, and *euangelizomai*. They penetrate into the providence of God in history and into the way God has designed for Scripture, faith, and glory to create a people in the image of his Son. These roots even stretch back into the eternal Trinitarian nature of God. To these roots we now turn in the next two chapters.

Four Roots of the Beautiful Fitness of Expository Exultation in Worship

The argument of the previous chapter was not simply that the apostle Paul commanded preaching as part of the church's corporate worship, but that he did so because of an underlying suitableness or harmony between preaching, on the one hand, and the nature of God, his word, and worship, on the other hand. If the deepest argument for corporate worship in chapter 2 was that "praise *befits* the upright" (Ps. 33:1), then the deepest argument for preaching in chapter 3 was that preaching *befits* worship.

The command to preach does not make preaching beautifully fitting. The beautiful fitness creates the command. "Preach the word" (2 Tim. 4:2) is not an arbitrary exhortation. It calls for preaching in the gathering of God's people, because preaching is a *fitting* aspect of corporate worship. It is a fitness that flows from the nature of God and man, the way God governs the world, and the way he transforms his people.

The aim of this chapter is to provide more support for that claim. I will focus on four roots of the fitness of preaching in Christian worship. First are the historical roots of Christian preaching in the Old Testament and synagogue worship. Then comes the fitness that rises from the relationships between (2) preaching and Scripture, (3) preaching and faith, and (4) preaching and human transformation.

1. Historical Roots of Christian Preaching

As with most of God's arrangements in the world, the presence of preaching in the gathered worship of the early Christians did not emerge out of nothing, as if its fitness and harmony were the *sole* cause. Historical roots and precedents prepared the way. Indeed, it is *fitting* that this should be, since God is not only the God who penetrates history in Jesus Christ, but also the God who prepares for that penetration by his providence in history. What follows is a simplified sketch of the historical roots of Christian preaching in worship.

Ezra, Exposition, and Worship

As Nehemiah 8:5–8 demonstrates, already in the Old Testament a kind of Scripture-based exhortation appears in a worship setting of the gathered people of Israel.

> Ezra opened the book in the sight of all the people, for he was above all the people, and as he opened it all the people stood. And Ezra blessed the LORD, the great God, and all the people answered, "Amen, Amen," lifting up their hands. And they bowed their heads and worshiped the LORD with their faces to the ground. Also . . . the Levites, helped the people to understand the Law, while the people remained in their places. *They read from the book*, from the Law of God, clearly, and *they gave the sense*, so that the people understood the reading.

Here we see a divinely authorized "book" (v. 5), the "Law" (v. 7). Then we see that the Levites assisted Ezra: "They read from the book" (v. 8). Then they "gave the sense" of what they had read (v. 8) and helped the people to understand (v. 7). Finally, we see that all of this was in the context of worship: Ezra blessed . . . God; the people said, "Amen, Amen"; they lifted their hands; and they bowed their faces to the ground (v. 6).

Significance of the Synagogue

As an isolated example of Scripture reading, followed by explanation, in the context of worship, this would not be relevant for our purpose. But it is not isolated. It became the pattern of emerging Jewish synagogue worship during the four centuries between the Old and New Testaments. Edwin Charles Dargan, in his *A History of Preaching*, points this out:

> For long years the voice of prophecy was mute, awaiting the coming of the Promised One, the dawn of a new era. During this period the

worship of the Jews had a very important development, and one specially significant in the history of preaching. This was the hortatory exposition of the Sacred Writings in connection with the services of the synagogue. . . . Thus we see that there was a clearly defined basis for Christian preaching in the sacred speech of that people from whom in the divine ordering of events Christianity sprang.[1]

Accordingly, as the New Testament begins, we find Jesus entering the synagogue early in his ministry and following this pattern of Scripture reading and "giving the sense."

He came to Nazareth, where he had been brought up. And as was his custom, he went to the synagogue on the Sabbath day, and he stood up to read. And the scroll of the prophet Isaiah was given to him. He unrolled the scroll and found the place where it was written,

> "The Spirit of the Lord is upon me,
>   because he has anointed me
>   to proclaim good news to the poor.
> He has sent me to proclaim liberty to the captives
>   and recovering of sight to the blind,
>   to set at liberty those who are oppressed,
> to proclaim the year of the Lord's favor."

And he rolled up the scroll and gave it back to the attendant and sat down. And the eyes of all in the synagogue were fixed on him. And he began to say to them, "Today this Scripture has been fulfilled in your hearing." (Luke 4:16–21)

Pattern in Acts

The same pattern is found in the Acts of the Apostles. For example, Acts 15:21 says, "From ancient generations Moses has had in every city those who proclaim him [*kērýssontas autòn*], for he is read every Sabbath in the synagogues." Here we have not only the reading of Moses, but the *heralding* of him in the synagogue. This is a remarkable precedent for what Paul commanded in the church with the same specialized word (*kērýssō*). "Preach [*kērýxon*] the word" (2 Tim. 4:2).

---

1. Edwin Charles Dargan, *A History of Preaching*, vol. 1 (New York: Hodder & Stoughton, 1905), 20–21.

Then we see Paul himself making use of this synagogue pattern to present Jesus as the Messiah. In Pisidian Antioch, according to Acts 13:14–16,

> On the Sabbath day [Paul and Barnabas] went into the synagogue and sat down. After the reading from the Law and the Prophets, the rulers of the synagogue sent a message to them, saying, "Brothers, if you have any word of encouragement for the people, say it." So Paul stood up, and motioning with his hand said: "Men of Israel and you who fear God, listen."

This was the pattern that Paul, no doubt, grew up with in Tarsus and made use of repeatedly in his itinerant preaching as he went from town to town. The Scripture is read, and a word of explanation and application is given; and this is regularly done on the Sabbath as part of the ordinary worship gathering of the Jews (Acts 13:14; 18:4).

I conclude, therefore, with Dargan, that the Christian pattern of Scripture exposition in the context of regular corporate worship has its roots in the pattern of the Jewish synagogue, whose roots are even deeper in the Old Testament. The reading of Scripture and *heralding* of Moses (Acts 15:21) in regular corporate synagogue worship should not surprise us, since the glories of Christianity do not spring de novo from Jesus and the apostles. They have their roots in the Old Testament. We would expect, therefore, that something like *expository exultation* would emerge in the synagogue and its Christian offshoots.

Providence, History, and Preaching

To use the words of Dargan again, "There was a clearly defined basis for Christian preaching in the sacred speech of that people [Israel] from whom in the divine ordering of events Christianity sprang."[2] In other words, the providence of God in the history of Israel and in the Christian church is the ultimate explanation for the emergence of Christian preaching as both historically rooted and beautifully fitted for Christian worship. But that fitness of preaching for corporate worship has roots far deeper than the providentially ordered historical precedents of the synagogue. To those we now turn.

---

2. Ibid.

2. Preaching and Scripture

We saw in the previous chapter that when Paul commanded Timothy to "preach the word" (2 Tim. 4:2), the term "word" referred to nothing less than all of Scripture, including, by implication, both Old and New Testaments.[3] He had just said, "All Scripture is breathed out by God and profitable" (2 Tim. 3:16). His next sentence climaxes with "preach the word" (4:2).

In telling the preacher, in this way, to *herald the Scriptures*, Paul implies that preachers are to become spokesmen for God in bringing to pass the purpose for which God inspired and preserved the Bible. In *Reading the Bible Supernaturally*, I argued that Scripture itself shows that its ultimate goal for the reader and the preacher is that God's infinite worth and beauty would be exalted in the everlasting, white-hot worship of the blood-bought bride of Christ from every people, language, tribe, and nation. And, of course, "worship" here is not limited to worship services, as I argued in the introduction of this book. Worship includes all the ways, in time and eternity—individually, corporately, and cosmically—that the new humanity in Christ knows, enjoys, and shows the beauty and worth of God.

The Aim of Scripture Is the Aim of Preaching

Since Paul tells us to preach the Scripture, therefore, the nature and aim of Scripture dictate the nature and aim of preaching. Both Scripture and preaching aim at worship and are worshipful. Both preaching and Scripture *teach* the truth of God's glory and worth, and both reverberate with more than teaching, namely, with the *treasuring* of God. The heart of the preacher and the hearts of the Author and authors of Scripture overflow with the infinite value of what they reveal. Scripture communicates the *explanation* of God's beauty and worth, and Scripture communicates the *exultation* of its authors over that worth and beauty. Scripture is always true, and never neutral.

Therefore, preaching—aiming at the same ultimate worship as Scripture does—*explains* God's glory and worth and *exults* over God's glory and worth. It always seeks to be true and never allows itself to be neutral about stupendous realities. The preacher speaks

---

3. See chapter 3, pp. 63–65.

as a humble, authentic agent of Scripture. What it aims to produce, he aims to become. He aims to embody the worship the Bible seeks (John 4:23). And then he seeks to open his mouth and make the glories of God in Scripture as clear and as beautiful as he can. By whatever grace he is given through the Holy Spirit, he devotes himself to expository exultation.

Scripture and Preaching Aim at Worship and Act Worship

Therefore, it is clear that this preaching is at home in corporate worship. It fits. It *is* worship, and it *seeks* worship, because it is faithful to Scripture. Scripture is inspired by God in order to awaken, nurture, and bring to final consummation the white-hot worship of the blood-bought bride of Christ from every people, language, tribe, and nation. Preaching is intended by God to herald these Scriptures and advance their purpose. Therefore, preaching aims at worship—that is, it aims to bring into being and sustain a people who know and enjoy and show the glory and worth of God.

Preaching does not contradict its own aim by being indifferent to the glories of Scripture. It aims at worship by being an act of worship. As it clarifies truth, it cherishes the worth of truth. As it explains, it exults. The preacher shudders at the prospect of being indicted with the words of Jesus: This preacher "honors me with [his] lips, but [his] heart is far from me" (Matt. 15:8). His heart is not far from the fire of God's truth. It is near enough to be enflamed. He is "a burning and shining lamp" (John 5:35).[4] Burning with exultation. Shining with exposition.

3. Preaching and Faith

Another way to show that preaching has a fitting home in worship is that its aim is faith, which is designed by God to manifest his glory. Faith is the primary covenant requirement of God precisely because it humbles us and amplifies the trustworthiness and all-sufficiency of God.

Repeatedly Paul lines up preaching—especially the term *heralding* (*kērygma*)—along with *faith* as its goal. For example:

---

4. For an extended meditation on John 5:35 and the implications of "burning" and "shining" for preaching, see Jonathan Edwards, "The True Excellency of a Minister of the Gospel," in *Sermons and Discourses, 1743–1758*, ed. Wilson H. Kimnach and Harry S. Stout, vol. 25, *The Works of Jonathan Edwards* (New Haven, CT: Yale University Press, 2006), 82–102.

> How are they to *believe* in him of whom they have never heard? And how are they to hear without someone *preaching* [*kēryssontos*]? . . . So *faith* comes from hearing, and hearing through the word of Christ. (Rom. 10:14, 17)

> Since, in the wisdom of God, the world did not know God through wisdom, it pleased God through the folly of what we *preach* [*kērygmatos*] to save those who *believe*. (1 Cor. 1:21)

> My speech and my message [*kērygma*] were not in plausible words of wisdom, but in demonstration of the Spirit and of power, so that your *faith* might not rest in the wisdom of men but in the power of God. (1 Cor. 2:4–5)

> Whether then it was I or they, so we preach [*kēryssomen*] and so you *believed*. (1 Cor. 15:11)

> If Christ has not been raised, then our preaching [*kērygma*] is in vain and your *faith* is in vain. (1 Cor. 15:14)

Why Is Faith the Goal of Preaching?

Surely we may say from these texts that the aim of preaching is to beget and sustain faith in God and Jesus Christ. If we ask why faith is so prominent in God's design for his people, the answer is not hard to find. We are to *live* by faith (Gal. 2:20)—that is, do everything in reliance on God for all we need—because the trustworthiness and all-sufficiency of God are magnified in this way. Acting in faith draws attention to the power and mercy and goodness and wisdom of God. Faith glorifies God. This is plain throughout the Scriptures.

Paul underlines this fact, for example, in regard to Abraham's faith in Romans 4:20: "No *unbelief* made him waver concerning the promise of God, but he grew strong in his *faith* as he gave *glory* to God." When we trust God to do what we cannot do (such as having a son when a man is one hundred years old and his wife is barren), we make much of God. When we trust God to be the decisive power behind all our obedience (as with all the saints of Hebrews 11 who obeyed "by faith"), we make much of God's greatness.

This is Peter's point in 1 Peter 4:11: "Whoever serves, [let him serve] *by the strength that God supplies* [that is, by trusting God for his decisive acting in and through our serving]—*in order that in everything God may be glorified* through Jesus Christ." In other words, God is glorified when we serve by faith in his ever-arriving power. This is why faith is essential in our saving relationship with God. It glorifies him. It makes him look like what he really is—trustworthy, strong, gracious, and wise. Faith is the essential root of worship.

What Nonfaith Says about God

This truth is highlighted in Scripture by showing the implications of faith's opposite, unbelief. For example, in Numbers 14:11, God says to Moses, "How long will this people *despise* me? And how long will they *not* believe in me, in spite of all the signs that I have done among them?" In other words, not believing, not trusting God, in spite of all the evidences of his favor and power, is tantamount to despising him. Which is the opposite of glorifying him.

Or again God says to Moses and Aaron in Numbers 20:12, "You did not *believe* in me, to uphold me as *holy* in the eyes of the people of Israel." In other words, not to believe in God's promise is to desecrate his holiness. It is the opposite of glorifying him. Few things that you can say to someone are more dishonoring, or more offensive, than "I don't trust you." That's especially true of God.

When Jesus wanted to explain why the Jewish leaders could not believe on him, he said, "How can you *believe*, when you receive glory from one another and do not seek the glory that comes from the only God?" (John 5:44). In other words, faith is utterly contrary to preferring the glory of man over the glory of God. A love for the glory of God and the experience of authentic, saving faith arise in the heart together. Loving the glory of God and trusting God are inseparable. Faith is the fountain of worship.

Faith Is More Than Trusting God for Gifts

In fact, the heart of saving faith is a spiritual, valuing perception of the beauty of the glory of God in Christ. Faith sees, and at once savors—perceives and at once values—the supreme truth and beauty of Christ in the gospel. Here's the way Paul says this: "The god of this world [Satan] has blinded the minds of the *unbelievers*, to keep them from *seeing* the light of the gospel of the *glory* of Christ, who is the image of

God" (2 Cor. 4:4). But when God "has shone in our hearts to give the light of the knowledge of the glory of God in the face of Jesus Christ" (2 Cor. 4:6), faith happens. There is a valuing perception of the glory of Christ in the gospel. We see and simultaneously savor. We know and we love. We behold and we embrace.

That's the way Jesus described faith in John 6:35: "I am the bread of life; whoever *comes* to me shall not hunger, and whoever *believes* in me shall never thirst." Notice the parallel between *coming* to satisfy hunger, and *believing* to satisfy thirst. Hungering and thirsting refer to the same soul-emptiness. And believing and coming are the same soul-act. *Believing* in Jesus means *coming* to him for the quenching of our soul's hunger and thirst. Faith in Christ means being satisfied with all that God is for us in Jesus.

Preaching for Faith Is Preaching for Worship

Here's the point for preaching: Paul made clear that preaching aims at awakening and sustaining and strengthening faith. The essence of faith is seeing and savoring and being satisfied in all that God is for us in Jesus. When we preachers experience this *in* preaching, and our people experience it *through* preaching, we and they magnify the preciousness and worth of God. Such faith glorifies God. Which means that it is worship—the preacher's worship and the people's. And whatever actions such faith animates and sustains and guides become worship in all of life.

That is what preaching aims to awaken and sustain. The aim of preaching—whatever the topic, whatever the text—is this kind of faith. It aims to quicken in the soul a satisfaction with all that God is for us in Jesus, because this satisfaction magnifies God's all-sufficient glory, and that is worship. Therefore, preaching is at home when the people gather for worship.

4. Preaching and Transformation

When the preacher aims to awaken and sustain vibrant faith for the glory of God, he is aware that faith is the great means by which God changes believers into loving, rather than selfish, people. Here's how Paul makes the connection between trusting Christ and loving people: "In Christ Jesus neither circumcision nor uncircumcision counts for anything, but only faith working through love" (Gal. 5:6). First, there is saving, justifying faith, uniting us to Christ. Then that faith, in the power of the Holy Spirit, frees us from the fear and greed that kill love. Faith "works through love."

This self-denying, sacrificial, loving behavior is the beautiful conduct that both Jesus and Peter say causes other people to see and glorify God (Matt. 5:16; 1 Pet. 2:12). Therefore, not only does faith glorify God by showing him to be trustworthy and wise and powerful; it also glorifies God by "working through love," which causes people to see and admire the glory of God. Therefore, preaching that aims at faith also aims at public displays of God's glory in the new conduct of Christians.

Becoming Glorious by Beholding Glory

But the point of this section is to sketch a different way Paul saw the connection between preaching and the moral transformation of Christian living. This different way of seeing the connection between preaching and transformation also hinges on the glory of God and makes even more clear that the act of preaching is itself a way of worshiping and a key part of Christian corporate worship.

I am thinking here of preaching as the portrayal of Christ with words so vivid that Paul speaks of their effect as *seeing* the very glory of Christ—a seeing so powerful that it transforms the one who sees. The key passage is 2 Corinthians 3:18, and the context is crucial for noticing the connection with preaching.

Paul writes, "We all, with unveiled face, beholding the glory of the Lord, are being transformed into the same image from one degree of glory to another. For this comes from the Lord who is the Spirit" (2 Cor. 3:18). We will look closely at this in just a moment. But, first, note that this is not the only place where Paul's emphasis falls on the transforming effect of *seeing* Christ.

"Before Your Eyes" Christ Was Crucified!

In Galatians 3:1 Paul says, "O foolish Galatians! Who has bewitched you? It was *before your eyes* that Jesus Christ was publicly portrayed as crucified." He calls them foolish because they seem to be drifting away from the gospel. The fact that he is baffled by this—they must be bewitched!—shows how deeply he believes that really *seeing* Christ crucified transforms people. "Before your eyes" in my *preaching*, you saw Christ crucified!

Richard Longenecker is right to say, "The phrase 'Christ crucified' was on Paul's lips an abbreviated form of the gospel (cf. 1 Cor 1:23; 2:2; also 1 Cor 1:13; 2:8; 2 Cor 13:4)."[5] This was the heart of Paul's preaching: "We preach [*kēryssomen*] Christ crucified" (1 Cor. 1:23). "I decided to know nothing among you except Jesus Christ and him crucified" (1 Cor. 2:2). So when Paul says in Galatians 3:1, "Before your eyes . . . Jesus Christ was publicly portrayed as crucified," he means that this happened when he "*preached* Christ crucified." Preaching aims to present Christ in such a way that a spiritual "seeing" happens—a seeing so powerful that the hearers-seers are "transformed into the same image."

Preaching and Beholding Glory

In the context of 2 Corinthians 3:18, the link with preaching is in 2 Corinthians 4:5. Seeing this link is crucial. Recall that the chapter divisions are not original, and often misleading. That is true here. The next sentence after 2 Corinthians 3:18 reads, "Therefore, having this ministry by the mercy of God, we do not lose heart" (2 Cor. 4:1). "This ministry" refers to the ministry he has been talking about from the beginning of 2 Corinthians 3—the "ministry of the Spirit" (v. 8) and the "ministry of righteousness" (v. 9). "This ministry" comes with "more glory" (3:8) than the Mosaic covenant had—"far exceed[ing] it in glory" (v. 9).

Part of that superior glory is "the glory of the Lord" that we behold in 2 Corinthians 3:18, the glory that transforms us when we see it. So 4:1 is not beginning a new topic. It is about the "ministry of the Spirit" that comes with "more glory"—the glory of the Lord, which when beheld transforms (3:18). What Paul stresses in 2 Corinthians 4:1–3 is that when he handles "God's word" concerning this glory, he does not tamper with it. Instead, he is utterly open and candid with it. It is an "open statement of the truth" (v. 2).

It is the Devil, not Paul, who hides things: "Even if our gospel is veiled, it is veiled to those who are perishing. In their case the god of this world [the Devil] has blinded the minds of the unbelievers" (4:3–4).

---

5. Richard N. Longenecker, *Galatians*, vol. 41, Word Biblical Commentary (Dallas: Word, 1998), 101.

Paul's passion is to unveil the glory of Christ in his preaching. Satan's passion is to veil it. Paul's aim is that his hearers might "[behold] the glory of the Lord" (3:18).

The connection with preaching is made explicit in 2 Corinthians 4:4–5:

> The god of this world has blinded the minds of the unbelievers, to keep them from seeing the light of the gospel of the *glory of Christ,* who is the image of God. For what we proclaim [*kēryssomen*] is not ourselves, but Jesus Christ as Lord, with ourselves as your servants for Jesus' sake.

We can see the connections between 2 Corinthians 3:18 and 4:4. Both refer to seeing, or beholding, the glory of Christ, or the Lord. Paul is laboring to unveil it in 3:18, and Satan is veiling it in 4:4. Two things make plain that Paul's effort to unveil Christ's glory is through his preaching. The first is the reference to "gospel" in 4:4. He refers to "seeing the light of the *gospel* of the *glory of Christ.*" In other words, the glory of Christ is seen in the gospel story. When the gospel is preached, the glory of Christ is "publicly portrayed" (Gal. 3:1) in the crucifixion and resurrection.

The other observation that shows the link between Paul's preaching and the unveiling of the glory of Christ is the explicit term for heralding in 2 Corinthians 4:5. The glory that the Devil seeks to veil, we preach, we *herald.* "What we proclaim [herald, *kēryssomen*] is not ourselves, but Jesus Christ as Lord." Here is the all-important word for *heralding* again. The crucified Christ is the risen Lord. Him we herald!

Therefore, I infer from Paul's flow of thought in 2 Corinthians 3:18–4:5 that the crucial statement about transformation in 3:18–19 is a description of what God intends to happen through preaching: "We all, with unveiled face, beholding the glory of the Lord, are being transformed into the same image from one degree of glory to another. For this comes from the Lord who is the Spirit." He includes himself ("We all . . ."), because he too had to see the glory of the Lord in order to be transformed. But Paul's way of extending his own experience of *beholding* to others is to portray Christ crucified (Gal. 3:1) and to preach Jesus Christ as Lord (2 Cor. 4:5).

Preaching, Beholding, Worshiping

The point I am trying to make here is that preaching is supremely suited for corporate worship, because it is uniquely suited by God for unveiling the glory of Christ with a view to transforming people into that glory. Authentic worship always involves some measure of this transformation; otherwise we are hypocrites. Therefore, authentic worship always involves the unveiling of the glory of God in Christ.[6] The heralding of "God's word" with an "open statement of the truth" (2 Cor. 4:2) is how Paul accomplished this unveiling, and how he commanded us to do it: "Preach the word" (2 Tim. 4:2).

Seeing That Wakens Worship

One more crucial observation is needed before we leave this section. "Beholding the glory of the Lord" (2 Cor. 3:18) cannot mean merely seeing what the natural eye can see, or what the Devil's eye can see. Paul said that if the rulers of this age had truly seen the glory of Christ "they would not have crucified the Lord of glory" (1 Cor. 2:8). Paul explained further, "The natural person does not accept the things of the Spirit of God, for they are folly to him, and he is not able to understand them because they are spiritually discerned" (1 Cor. 2:14).

"Spiritually discerned" means that their true beauty and worth are discerned by the help of the Holy Spirit. The "natural person" can see many amazing things about Jesus. Judas certainly did. But the natural person does not "discern" Christ's compelling beauty and worth. The gospel of Christ is folly to them rather than their greatest fortune. He is not the treasure hidden in the field that we sell everything to obtain (Matt. 13:44). He is not the pearl of great price (Matt. 13:46). He is not of "surpassing worth" that by comparison makes all else seem like rubbish (Phil. 3:8). Of such "seeing" Jesus says, "Seeing they do not see" (Matt. 13:13).

But when Paul talks about "beholding the glory of the Lord" so that we are changed by it from glory to glory, he is referring to the spiritual discernment of 1 Corinthians 2:14. He is referring to seeing with the eyes of the heart (Eph. 1:18). He is talking about knowing

---

6. Paul sometimes refers to the glory of God in the face of Christ (2 Cor. 4:6) and sometimes to the glory of Christ who is the image of God (2 Cor. 4:4). This is one glory, not two, and we may sometimes refer to it as the glory of God and at other times as the glory of Christ.

as one ought to know (1 Cor. 8:2). He is talking about the miracle of "comprehend[ing] with all the saints what is the breadth and length and height and depth, and to know the love of Christ that surpasses knowledge" (Eph. 3:18–19). He means, as Peter said, not just attending to Christ but tasting—"if indeed you have *tasted* that the Lord is good" (1 Pet. 2:3). Paul says, "This comes from the Lord who is the Spirit" (2 Cor. 3:18). It is a miracle.

Preaching Must Be Worship

The supernatural nature of seeing the glory of the Lord means that the preaching which aims to impart this miraculous, transforming beholding must have itself beheld the glory. You can't aim at something you cannot even conceive. But the natural man has no conception of this spiritual beholding of the glory of Christ. Therefore, preaching must be spiritual—"from the Lord who is the Spirit." And that means the preacher must have tasted. He must know as he ought to know (1 Cor. 8:2). He must spiritually discern. He must count all else as rubbish. He must renounce all for the pearl and the treasure (Luke 14:33). Which means that, as he preaches this treasure, he is treasuring. As he holds up the pearl, he is prizing. As he invites to the banquet, he is savoring the feast. If he were not, he would be a hypocritical "natural person" and unfit for the ministry.

Therefore, "Preach the word" means show the glory of God as supremely valuable so that people can behold it, treasure it, and be transformed. Which means that the preacher must *aim* at worship and *act* worship. He must exhibit and experience the worth of Christ. He must explain and extol. He must take up the happy burden of expository exultation.

Gift for God's People

What we have seen in this chapter is that Paul's charge to "preach the word" (2 Tim. 4:2) is not arbitrary. It is rooted in the beautiful fitness of expository exultation as part of Christian worship. In the ever-wise providence of God, Christian preaching grew out of the synagogue worship where every Sabbath Moses was heralded (Acts 15:21). In God's beautiful design for how his church is to know and trust and be like the Son of God, God ordained preaching to open Scripture, awaken faith, and reveal glory. In every case, the designed outcome is worship. Preaching is a precious gift to the church—a beautifully fitting gift for his worshiping people.

We turn now to see perhaps the most amazing reason that preaching is beautifully fitting in the ultimate goal of the universe—namely, the goal that God be worshiped for who he is. We turn to the Trinitarian roots of expository exultation.

5

The Trinitarian Roots of
Expository Exultation

We have one more step to take in commending the beautiful fitness of preaching in corporate worship. With this step, we trace the roots of expository exultation back into the unfathomable reaches of God's triune being and his eternal existence. I am suggesting here that the ultimate reason preaching is fitting in worship is that its uniqueness as a form of communication coheres with the nature of God as he *knows* and *enjoys* himself in the Trinity from all eternity.

While it may not be appropriate to say that God *worships* himself, since the word usually connotes a lesser being exulting in a greater, nevertheless the roots of human worship go all the way back into the way the Father, from all eternity, has *known* the Son comprehensively, and the way they have enjoyed each other supremely. Ultimately, we worship the way we do through knowing truth and treasuring beauty and worth because God knows and treasures himself this way. And, I suspect, if we penetrated the words of Jesus all the way to the bottom, this would be implied when he said that the Father is seeking people to worship him in *spirit* and *truth* (John 4:23).

How Jonathan Edwards Conceived the Trinity
I find Jonathan Edwards's conception of the Trinity to be biblically warranted and wonderful. I find its implications for the fitness of preaching in worship compelling. I can only sketch it here, but I recommend that every pastor read his "Essay on the Trinity"—not an unrealistic

recommendation, since it is only thirty pages,[1] and you can find it free online. You may be surprised at the biblical texts he is able to marshal for this admittedly philosophical-sounding conception. Let's begin our sketch where he ends—with a summary of his conclusions:

> This I suppose to be that blessed Trinity that we read of in the holy Scriptures. The *Father* is the Deity subsisting in the prime, unoriginated and most absolute manner, or the Deity in its direct existence. The *Son* is the Deity generated by God's understanding, or having an idea of himself, and subsisting in that idea. The *Holy Ghost* is the Deity subsisting in act, or the divine essence flowing out and breathed forth, in God's infinite love to and delight in himself. And I believe the whole divine essence does truly and distinctly subsist both in the divine idea and divine love, and that therefore each of them are properly distinct persons.[2]

Eternal Begetting of the Son

In other words, the Son exists eternally in God's "having an idea of himself"—a knowledge of himself that carries such a fullness of the divine being that the idea stands forth as a divine Person in his own right, fully God. Since that sounds utterly strange, and inadequate to many people, let's listen to Edwards's effort to help us grasp it:

> If a man could have an absolutely perfect idea of all that passed in his mind, all the series of ideas and exercises in every respect perfect as to order, degree, circumstances, etc. for any particular space of time past—suppose the last hour—he would really, to all intents and purposes, be over again what he was that last hour. And if it were possible for a man by reflection perfectly to contemplate all that is in his own mind in an hour, as it is and at the same time that it is there, in its first and direct existence; if a man had a perfect reflex or contemplative idea of every thought at the same moment or moments that that thought was, and of every exercise at and during the same time that that exercise was, and so through a whole hour: a man would really be two. He would be indeed double; he would be twice at once: the idea he has of himself would be himself again.[3]

---

1. Jonathan Edwards, *Writings on the Trinity, Grace, and Faith*, ed. Sang Hyun Lee and Harry S. Stout, vol. 21, *The Works of Jonathan Edwards* (New Haven, CT: Yale University Press, 2003), 113–31.

2. Ibid., 131; emphases added.

3. Ibid., 116.

Therefore as God with perfect clearness, fullness and strength understands himself, views his own essence (in which there is no distinction of substance and act, but it is wholly substance and wholly act), that idea which God hath of himself is absolutely himself. This representation of the divine nature and essence is the divine nature and essence again. So that by God's thinking of the Deity, [the Deity] must certainly be generated. Hereby there is another person begotten; there is another infinite, eternal, almighty, and most holy and the same God, the very same divine nature.[4]

And this person is the second person in the Trinity, the only begotten and dearly beloved Son of God. He is the eternal, necessary, perfect, substantial and personal idea which God hath of himself. And that it is so, seems to me to be abundantly confirmed by the Word of [God].[5]

Some of the unexpectedness of this view might be reduced if we recall biblical texts like these:

He is the radiance of the glory of God and the exact imprint of his nature. (Heb. 1:3)

He is the image of the invisible God. (Col. 1:15)

Though he was in the form of God, [he] did not count equality with God a thing to be grasped. (Phil. 2:6)

. . . the light of the gospel of the glory of Christ, who is the image of God. (2 Cor. 4:4)

In the beginning was the Word, and the Word was with God, and the Word was God. (John 1:1)

In some sense, the Son of God is the mirroring forth of God the Father. From all eternity, God has had a perfectly clear and full idea of all his own perfections. He has had an "image of the invisible God." This image of God is so complete and perfect that it is, in fact, the standing forth of God the Son as a person in his own right.

Thus, God the Son is not created or made. He is coeternal with the Father. He is thus dependent on the Father as image to original, but

---

4. Ibid.
5. Ibid., 117.

not inferior in any divine attributes, because he is a complete and living image of the Father's perfections. This, of course, is a great mystery—how an idea, or reflection, or image of the Father can actually be a person in his own right. I do not presume to be able to make the infinite exhaustively comprehensible.

Eternal Procession of the Spirit

The third person of the Trinity, the Holy Spirit, has existed eternally because the Father and the Son always have loved and delighted in each other to such a degree, and in such a way, that the Spirit who has processed from them, and between them, has always existed as a person in his own right. Here is Edwards's explanation:

> The Godhead being thus begotten by God's having an idea of himself and standing forth in a distinct subsistence or person in that idea, there proceeds a most pure act, and an infinitely holy and sweet energy arises between the Father and Son: for their love and joy is mutual, in mutually loving and delighting in each other. Prov. 8:30, "I was daily his delight, rejoicing always before [him]." This is the eternal and most perfect and essential act of the divine nature, wherein the Godhead acts to an infinite degree and in the most perfect manner possible. The Deity becomes all act; the divine essence itself flows out and is as it were breathed forth in love and joy. So that the Godhead therein stands forth in yet another manner of subsistence, and there proceeds the third person in the Trinity, the Holy Spirit.[6]

In other words, the love between the Father and the Son is so perfect, so constant, and carries so completely all that the Father and Son are in themselves, that this love stands forth itself as a person in his own right.

C. S. Lewis tries to get this into a conceivable analogy—only an analogy:

> You know that among human beings, when they get together in a family, or a club or a trades union, people talk about the "spirit" of that family, club or trades union. They talk about its spirit because the individual members, when they're together, do really develop particular ways of talking and behaving which they wouldn't have if they were apart. It is as if a sort of communal personality came

---

6. Ibid., 121.

into existence. Of course it isn't a real person: it is only rather like a person. But that's just one of the differences between God and us. What grows out of the joint life of the Father and Son is a real Person, is in fact the Third of the three Persons who are God.[7]

These are great mysteries. But in order to know and love God, I find it helpful to have at least some viable conception in my mind when I affirm that there is only one God and that he exists in three persons. It is our duty and delight to adore our great God. And he is not honored by merely ignorant adoration, for that can only be a charade. Adoration of God as Trinity must be based on some knowledge. Otherwise it is not God himself whom we adore.

Trinity as Foundation of Expository Exultation

How does this conception of the Trinity relate to preaching as *expository exultation*? What we have seen is that, before creation, God related to himself in two ways: God *knew* himself and God *loved* himself, that is, esteemed and delighted in himself. In knowing himself, he begot the Son, the perfect, full and complete personal image of himself. In loving himself, the Holy Spirit proceeded from the Father and the Son.

It is not surprising, therefore, that when God created human beings in his own image, we would have capacities to know and love, and that the highest function of our knowing and loving would be to know and love God. It would not be surprising if the more clearly and deeply we know him, and the more authentically and intensely we love him, the more we would glorify him as the sum of all truth and beauty.

What emerges, then, from the Trinitarian life of God is the profound truth that our capacities to know God and love God are rooted in that very Trinitarian nature. Since we are given these capacities of knowing and loving God in order to glorify God, our aim should be to use both—knowing and loving—as fully as we can to make much of his truth and beauty and worth.

God Glorified by Being Known and Enjoyed

Here is how Edwards explains the way knowing God and loving God glorifies God:

---

7. C. S. Lewis, *Beyond Personality* (New York: Macmillan, 1948), 21–22.

God glorifies Himself toward the creatures also in two ways: 1. By appearing to . . . their understanding. 2. In communicating Himself to their hearts, and in their rejoicing and delighting in and enjoying the manifestations which He makes of Himself. . . . *God is glorified not only by His glory's being seen, but by its being rejoiced in.* When those that see it delight in it, God is more glorified than if they only see it. His glory is then received by the whole soul, both by the understanding and by the heart.[8]

In other words, God gets glory from his creatures in worship by our *knowing* him truly, and by our *enjoying* him duly. Where knowledge of God is defective, his glory will be diminished in our defective knowing. Where delight in God is restrained or hindered or discouraged, his glory will be diminished in our diminished enjoyment. Essential to glorifying God is seeing him clearly and savoring him dearly.

What Worship Leaders Do, Including the Preacher

The implications of this for life and worship are immeasurable. This reality touches us at so many levels and in so many ways, no one will ever trace out all the implications. But for our purpose here, one implication is plain. When Christians gather for worship, the aim of those who lead must be to put before the *mind* of the worshipers the truest, clearest views of God possible, so as to waken in the *heart* of the worshipers the purest and most suitable affections toward God.

I say "suitable affections" to refer to all the emotions we are capable of that correspond appropriately to whatever truth about God is presented to the mind, for example, joy (Phil. 4:4), contentment (Heb. 13:5), delight (Ps. 37:4), fervent brotherly love (1 Pet. 1:22), hope (Ps. 42:5), fear (Luke 12:5), peace (Col. 3:15), zeal and fervency (Rom. 12:11), grief (2 Cor. 7:10), sorrow (James 4:9), desire (1 Pet. 2:2), tenderheartedness (Eph. 4:32), gratitude (Eph. 5:19–20), and lowliness (Phil. 2:3).

Wherever emotions are strong without some truth to warrant them, we call this "emotionalism" and put no value on it. And wherever beautiful and valuable truth about God is clear and there is little response

---

8. Jonathan Edwards, The "Miscellanies," ed. Thomas Schafer, vol. 13, *The Works of Jonathan Edwards* (New Haven, CT: Yale University Press, 1994), 495, Miscellany 448; emphasis added. See also Miscellany 87, pp. 251–252; Miscellany 332, p. 410; Miscellany 679 (not in the New Haven vol.).

of the heart, God is dishonored. Or as Edwards said, "When those that see it delight in it, God is more glorified than if they only see it." And where God is less glorified because the heart is lagging behind the head, worship is jeopardized.

Raising Affections with Truth

Edwards expressed the implications for preaching as powerfully and as carefully as anyone I know. He said:

> I don't think ministers are to be blamed for raising the affections of their hearers too high, if that which they are affected with be only that which is worthy of affection, and their affections are not raised beyond a proportion to their importance, or worthiness of affection. I should think myself in the way of my duty to raise the affections of my hearers as high as possibly I can, provided that they are affected with nothing but truth, and with affections that are not disagreeable to the nature of what they are affected with.[9]

It is his "duty," he says, to raise the affections of his hearers as high as possible. By itself, that would sound like whipping up the emotions of the crowd with lights and fog and music and dozens of artistic techniques. But then Edwards adds, ". . . provided that they are affected with nothing but truth, and with affections that are not disagreeable to the nature of what they are affected with." He gives two qualifications for raising the affections. One is that truth is the agent. And the other is that the affections should be agreeable to the particular content of the truth.

So the truth of hell, depending on the particular angle of the message, should raise the emotion of fear or sorrow or pity or anger, but not happiness, and certainly not playfulness. And the call to eternal glory (1 Pet. 5:10) should raise the emotions of hope and joy and eagerness and love, but not boredom, and certainly not repulsion. God-glorifying emotion must be a response to true and clear views of reality as it relates to God, and the nature of the God-glorifying emotion must be agreeable to the nature of the reality that wakens the emotion.

---

9. Jonathan Edwards, *The Great Awakening*, ed. Harry S. Stout and C. C. Goen, rev. ed., vol. 4, *The Works of Jonathan Edwards* (New Haven, CT: Yale University Press, 2009), 387.

Expository Exultation and the Nature of God

I conclude, therefore, that preaching, as *expository exultation*, is rooted in the Trinitarian being of God. He knows himself and exists as Father and Son. The Father and Son delight in each other and exist as Father, Son, and Holy Spirit. Knowing and delighting are essential to who God is. Human beings have these same capacities: knowing and delighting. God's ultimate purposes in giving them to us is that we might reflect and magnify his beauty and worth by knowing and delighting in him. That is what worship is: truly knowing, duly enjoying, and thus showing the worth and beauty of God.

The gathering of God's people for corporate worship, therefore, by its very nature, calls for a special kind of communication that aims to make the truth of God clear and the worth of God dear. The New Testament calls this special kind of communication "preaching" (see 2 Tim. 4:2). It is more than teaching. And it is more than emotional stimulation—because God's Trinitarian being consists not in *either* knowing *or* delighting, but in *both*. He knows and he delights from all eternity, or he is not God. We experience both, or we are not worshiping—we are not what we were made to be. And preaching embodies both, or it is not preaching. When it embodies both, I call it "expository exultation." It embodies truth by exposition. It embodies joy by exultation. Preaching is uniquely suited to the corporate worship of God's people because it wakens worship and is worship.

Preaching a Miracle

One of the implications of part 2 has been that worship is no mere liturgical action. And preaching, as part of worship, is no mere human performance. Both worship and preaching are beyond what is humanly possible. So we turn now in parts 3 and 4 to the question, How does preaching become a means of the miracle of worship? Part 3 will focus on how the preacher experiences the supernatural power of the Holy Spirit in preaching. Part 4 will focus on how the preacher uses all his natural powers of thinking and speaking without undermining the supernatural outcomes of preaching.

How Does Preaching Become a Means of the Miracle of Worship—Supernaturally?

Expository Exultation in the Power of the Holy Spirit

6

Expository Exultation

A Humanly Impossible Act with a Humanly Impossible Effect

The aim of this chapter and the next is to clarify why worship and preaching are humanly impossible, and what the preacher can do to participate in the miracle of both.

Beauty of Corporate Worship

It is beautifully fitting that Christian people gather for corporate worship every week. When they do, they give united expression to their truth-rooted knowledge of the triune God and their treasure-rooted affections for all God is for them in Jesus. They have seen with the eyes of their hearts (Eph. 1:18) the supreme beauty of God and his ways. And they have come to cherish the supreme worth of this treasure (Matt. 13:44; Phil. 3:8). And when they have completed their corporate exaltation of the glories of God, they continue that worship in a thousand daily tasks where the supreme worth of Christ governs their lives. This is what it means to be Christian.

Why We Need Help in Worship

But it is not as though Christians experience steady-state fullness that is ready every Lord's Day to brim over in joyful praise as they gather for worship. God is glorified in worship not only by those who come full, but also by those who come desperately needy and pinning all their hopes on meeting God. The same heart of worship that says, "Thank you," and, "Praise you," when full, also says, "I need you, I long for you, I thirst for you," when empty. It is the same savoring, the same treasuring.

Corporate worship is not a gathering only for overflow. The full may overflow. That is worship. The languishing come to drink at the fountain of God's life-giving word. That too is worship. It magnifies the necessity and desirableness of God. The soul-hungry come to eat at the banquet that is spread from the rich stores of Scripture. This also is worship.

Woe to the pastor who chastises his people for "coming to get" and not to give. If what the hungry people are coming to get is God, their hunger magnifies the worth of God's soul-satisfying beauty. If they are returning week after week for entertainment, the pastor had better look in the mirror for the cause, not in the people.

In view of this normal neediness of real Christians, God has designed us to depend on other humans to awaken and sustain and strengthen our worship—our knowing and treasuring God. This is clear from many considerations in the New Testament.

God's Design: Hearts Sustained through Humans

First, God has appointed that there be pastors and teachers in the church (Eph. 4:11). He has required that they be "able to teach" (1 Tim. 3:2). This means that God designs for us to be helped by other human ministers of the word, not just by our own private reading and praying.

Second, it is clear that we need other ministers from the example Paul set in strengthening the churches he started:

> They returned to Lystra and to Iconium and to Antioch, *strengthening the souls* of the disciples, encouraging them to continue in the faith, and saying that through many tribulations we must enter the kingdom of God. (Acts 14:21–22)

God did not design Christians to be strong in faith and fervent in worship without other Christian ministers strengthening their souls.

Third, it is clear that our perseverance in joyful, faithful holiness and worship depends on other Christians exhorting us again and again with the truth of God's word:

> Take care, brothers, lest there be in any of you an evil, unbelieving heart, leading you to fall away from the living God. But *exhort one another every day*, as long as it is called "today," that none of you may be hardened by the deceitfulness of sin. (Heb. 3:12–13)

Escaping hardness of heart and persevering in joyful, sin-mortifying faith depend on the exhortation of other believers. We are not designed to survive without the ministry of the word from others.

Fourth, it is clear that we stand in need of others who minister to us, because God designed the body of Christ this way and Paul said we need each other:

> God arranged the members in the body, each one of them, as he chose. If all were a single member, where would the body be? As it is, there are many parts, yet one body. The eye cannot say to the hand, "*I have no need of you*," nor again the head to the feet, "*I have no need of you*." (1 Cor. 12:18–21)

It is clear from Paul's use of the word *need* in 1 Corinthians 12:21 that he does not see the Christian's dependence on other Christians as a defect in our dependence on God. Total dependence on God's grace does not mean no dependence on God's means of grace. If God wills that our dependence on him sometimes be direct and unmediated and sometimes be indirect and mediated then we are no less totally dependent on God in either case. Our physical lives depend on God *and* on food that he gives. Our emotional resources for patience depend on the Spirit *and* on the refreshing sleep that he gives. Our spiritual strength depends on God's word *and* on the ministers whom he sends to us.

Fifth, it is plain from Scripture that we need the ministry of the word from other Christians, because Paul commanded Timothy, "Preach the word" (2 Tim. 4:2). That is not a pointless command. Preaching is commanded because preaching is needed.[1]

Preaching Serves Depleted Worshipers

I have argued that, among all the other ways in which the people of God help each other persevere in faith and lead lives of joyful worship, preaching is uniquely designed for its essential role in corporate

---

1. See chapter 3, pp. 61–63 where I dealt with the context of 2 Tim. 4:2 in detail.

worship. As people gather to give united expression to their *knowledge* of God and their *love* for God, preaching is distinctly designed by God to model this love by its *exultation*, and to serve both the knowledge and the love by its *exposition*.

The need for this assistance from preaching, as we gather for worship, is also clear from our own personal experience and what we see in all the Christians around us. Ordinary Christian living is depleting. We are not designed to live on yesterday's mercies.

> The steadfast love of the Lord never ceases;
>   his mercies never come to an end;
> *they are new every morning*;
>   great is your faithfulness. (Lam. 3:22–23)

Every day has its depleting trouble (Matt. 6:34), and every day has its restoring mercies (Lam. 3:23). When David says, "He restores my soul" (Ps. 23:3), he implies that the soul often needs restoring. Hence, we call out, "Restore to me the joy of your salvation" (Ps. 51:12). "Restore us, O God; let your face shine, that we may be saved!" (Ps. 80:3). "Restore us again, O God of our salvation" (Ps. 85:4).

This experience is universal among Christians. It is partly owing to our being *sinners*. Our old nature wars against the soul and tries to bring it to ruin (Gal. 5:17; Col. 3:5; 1 Pet. 2:11). Part of that warfare is depletion. Another part of our need for refreshing input from other humans is owing to our being *creatures*. We will always be creatures and therefore will always be in need of God's grace. Even perfected and glorified saints will still benefit from the ministry of other saints in the age to come, where there will be no sin. Otherwise, meaningful relationships would be nonexistent. Therefore, whether we think of ourselves as sinners or as creatures, we need help in maintaining a heart of worship.

Preaching is uniquely designed by God to be a central part of this help in corporate worship. *Expository exultation* corresponds to the nature of corporate worship. Its content and its demeanor are suited, by God's design, to restore and enlarge our *knowledge* of God (expository) and to restore and enlarge our *passion* for God (exultation). It does so *not* by standing outside the experience of worship like a coach on the sidelines of the game, or like a director backstage during the play, but by being *part* of the experience of worship itself. Preaching assists worship as worship.

What Our Question Is and Is Not

The aim in this chapter is to show more specifically how expository exultation helps Christians worship authentically—both during the worship service and then in daily life, both of which are meant by God to be demonstrations of his worth and beauty (1 Cor. 10:31; Rom. 12:1–2).

This is a pressing issue because authentic worship—both in liturgy and life—is a miracle, not an effect of merely natural causes. Don't lose sight of what I said in chapter 1 about the essence of authentic worship. "Worship services" as mere performances can be the effect of merely natural causes. But not if the essence of worship is happening in the worshipers. Being satisfied with all that God is for us in Jesus—which is how I defined the essence of worship—is not the effect of merely natural causes.

So the question we are asking is not: What are the natural things that a preacher can do to increase natural knowledge and natural feeling? I have no interest in that question whatsoever. Preaching is not a subspecies of natural rhetoric. It is not a means of using language to persuade the natural mind to act differently. Rhetoric can move the natural mind in stunning ways. Whole movements in society can be awakened by such rhetorical skill. But this effect on the mind may have no taste for the beauty and worth of God. Preaching has no interest in such persuasion. Preaching aims to bring about the spiritual sight of the glories of God in Christ. It aims to awaken and sustain the spiritual "taste" that God is supremely beautiful and satisfying. Rhetorical successes short of this are fatal—especially in the church.

Preaching and Its Aims Are Not Possible by "Natural" Persons

We saw in chapter 4 that "the natural person does not accept the things of the Spirit of God, for they are folly to him, and he is not able to understand them because they are spiritually discerned" (1 Cor. 2:14). "The things of the Spirit of God" refer to the content of true preaching. They are the glories of Christ crucified and risen and reigning, and all that God is for us in him. Paul had just been referring to what he imparted through preaching.

> The word of the cross is folly to those who are perishing, but to us who are being saved it is the power of God. (1 Cor. 1:18)

> Since, in the wisdom of God, the world did not know God through wisdom, it pleased God through the folly of what we preach to save those who believe. (1 Cor. 1:21)

> I decided to know nothing among you except Jesus Christ and him crucified. (1 Cor. 2:2)

> We impart this in words not taught by human wisdom but taught by the Spirit, interpreting spiritual truths to those who are spiritual. (1 Cor. 2:13)

This is what the "natural person" cannot grasp. This is what is "spiritually discerned." This is what the rulers of this age did not perceive when they killed the Son of God: "None of the rulers of this age understood this, for if they had, they would not have crucified the Lord of glory" (1 Cor. 2:8).

So the chief and ultimate aim of preaching—to bring people to see and savor and show the glory of Christ, and all that God is for us in him—is an aim that cannot be accomplished by a preacher who is a "natural person." It cannot happen in a people who are "natural persons." Rhetoric can achieve amazing things by way of excitement and persuasion. But that is not the aim of preaching. What makes preaching unique is that it is a miracle aiming to be the agent of miracles. And the main miracle it aims to experience and bring about is the spiritual sight and spiritual savoring of the glory of God revealed in Scripture.

Aiming for "Spiritual," Not "Mystical"

The word *spiritual* in 1 Corinthians 2:14 ("spiritually discerned," *pneumatikōs anakrinetai*) does not mean "religious" or "mystical" or "otherworldly." It means originating by the Holy Spirit and having the quality of the Holy Spirit. We can see this in Romans 8:7–9 where the "natural person" of 1 Corinthians 2:14 is described as having a "mind that is set on the flesh," with the same result, namely, hardness against God's glorious supremacy, and an inability to welcome and please God:

> The mind that is set on the flesh is hostile to God, for it does not submit to God's law; indeed, it cannot. Those who are in the flesh cannot please God. You, however, are not in the flesh but in the Spirit, if in fact the Spirit of God dwells in you. Anyone who does not have the Spirit of Christ does not belong to him.

But notice that the opposite of the "mind that is set on the flesh" is not a vague spirituality, but the presence of the person of the Holy Spirit: "You, however, are not in the flesh but in the Spirit, if in fact *the Spirit of God dwells in you.*" The opposite of a natural person is not a religious, mystical person, but a person who is indwelt by the Holy Spirit, who is bringing about the miracle of spiritual discernment.

Preaching and Its Aims Are Possible Only by the Spirit

Therefore, the chief and ultimate aims of preaching are impossible apart from the miraculous working of the Holy Spirit. Without his supernatural work, neither the preacher nor the people can see or savor the beauty and worth of God. But when the Spirit works this wonder, he raises the spiritually dead (Eph. 2:5). He goes beyond what "flesh and blood" can do and reveals the truth of Christ (Matt. 16:17). He removes our blindness to the glory of Christ (2 Cor. 4:4). He shines "in our hearts to give the light of the knowledge of the glory of God in the face of Jesus Christ" (2 Cor. 4:6). He enlightens the eyes of the heart (Eph. 1:18). He unveils our face, and reveals the beauty and worth of Jesus, and transforms the beholder: "This comes from the Lord who is the Spirit" (2 Cor. 3:18).

In other words, without the sovereign, life-giving, blindness-removing, heart-illumining, glory-revealing work of God's Spirit, preaching, as expository exultation, cannot achieve its aims—indeed it cannot exist. Preaching is worship seeking worship. And neither of these acts of worship is less than the miraculous seeing and savoring of the beauty of Christ, which the natural man regards as foolishness. He cannot see Christ for who he really is—supremely beautiful and valuable.

How Can the Preacher Become the Means of the Miracle?

Therefore, the question that we are asking is, How can a preacher become the means by which the Holy Spirit works the miracle of worship in the hearts of the people? How can he become the means by which the Holy Spirit grants the seeing and savoring and showing of the beauty and value of Christ? In answer, I will start at the bottom. By "bottom," I mean something so foundational that anything done without it is built on sand. Without this bottom reality for support, all else is counterproductive. It is not Spirit-releasing or worship-producing. This bottom reality must be in place before other things happen. Otherwise, they are not spiritual and will not bring about spiritual reality. Without this there is no supply of the Spirit.

The Bottom Is Hearing with Faith

At the bottom of how a preacher becomes the means by which the Holy Spirit brings about the miracle of worship in the hearts of the people is *faith*—faith in the blood-bought promises of God to help the preacher in whatever way he needs it. I base this primarily on Galatians 3:5: "Does he who *supplies the Spirit* to you and works miracles among you do so by works of the law, or *by hearing with faith*?" The question Paul is answering here is how to have a "supply of the Holy Spirit." The answer Paul expects to his rhetorical question is, "God supplies the Spirit by our *hearing with faith*." Therefore, if we hope for a supply of the Spirit that will work miracles through our preaching, then Paul counsels, "Hear with faith."

By "hearing" I take him to mean, "Hear the word of God," and in particular the promises of God to give us what we need at every moment in ministry. In the immediate context, the hearing was first and foremost the gospel of Christ. But the blood-bought benefits of the gospel of Christ's sacrifice include *all* the promises of God. "All the promises of God find their Yes in him" (2 Cor. 1:20). "In him"—that is where every Christian is by faith. And that is where all the promises of God are yes.

Another staggering way of saying it is in Romans 8:32: "He who did not spare his own Son but gave him up for us all, how will he not also with him graciously give us *all things*?" Or as Paul said it in Philippians 4:19, "God will supply *every* need of yours according to his riches in glory in Christ Jesus." "All things"—"every need" that we require to do God's will and glorify his name—were bought and secured for us by the blood of Jesus.

Now back to Galatians 3:5. The God who supplies the Spirit to us and works miracles in us and through us (and through our preaching) does so "by hearing with faith." That is, the supply of the Spirit flows through faith in the blood-bought promises of God. Do we want to preach in the power of the Holy Spirit? Then we should pinpoint some relevant promises of God and trust them hour by hour in our preparation, and as we step into the pulpit.

———

We could leave the matter there. I could say that we have clarified why worship and preaching are humanly impossible. And I could say that we have answered the question of what the preacher can do to participate in the miracle of both—namely, receive the supply of the Spirit by trusting the promises of God. The miracle-working Spirit is supplied through "hearing with faith." But there were years when I tasted how frustrating it is to hear a prescription like that—preach with faith—and yet not know how to do it in actual practice. So I don't want to leave you here with similar frustrations. In the next chapter, I will take you with me into the experience of thirty years of practicing this prescription and try to be as practically helpful as I can.

7

Expository Exultation by Faith

How I Pursued the Miracle in My Preaching

In part 3 we are trying to clarify why worship and preaching are humanly impossible, and what the preacher can do to participate in the miracle of both. In chapter 6, we saw that worship is not a human performance that one can do at will. It is the fruit of supernatural new life in Christ, and in its essence is being satisfied with all that God is for us in Jesus. This kind of spiritual taste for the glories of God is not native to fallen human beings. It is a gift. A miracle of new life and new spiritual tastes.

We saw also that preaching is not a species of natural rhetoric that sways the congregation to think new thoughts and embark on great exploits. Orators have done that for centuries without any empowering from the Holy Spirit. That is not what expository exultation is. The aim of expository exultation is to become an instrument in the hands of God so that by seeing and savoring and showing the glories of Scripture, the church might be supernaturally awakened to see and savor and show the same—that is, that they might worship.

We saw from Galatians 3:5 that the key to experiencing the supply of the Spirit who works miracles is "hearing with faith." By this means we may be led by the Spirit and walk by the Spirit and bear the fruit of the Spirit. That is, by this "hearing with faith," we may experience the miracle of acting in such a way that it is not merely us who are acting but the grace of God through us (1 Cor. 15:10). By this means we can experience the miracle of preaching.

How Did I Approach the Actual Event of Preaching?

In this chapter, I want to try to flesh out the miracle of preaching from my own experience of thirty-three years of pastoral preaching in one church. I'm focusing here on the actual act of preaching, not on the preparation of the message. Most of what I have to say about preparation—the actual wrestling with the biblical text to discern its meaning—I said in *Reading the Bible Supernaturally*.[1]

But there is a significant overlap in how I seek to do both preparation and delivery by the Spirit. In both I follow the steps of A.P.T.A.T. This is an acronym that guides me in my quest to preach by the Spirit or do anything else by the Spirit—"live by the Spirit" (Gal 5:25), or "walk by the Spirit" (Gal. 5:16), or be "led by the Spirit" (Gal. 5:18; see also Rom. 8:14), or "put to death the [sinful] deeds of the body" by the Spirit (Rom. 8:13), or "worship by the Spirit" (Phil 3:3).

A.P.T.A.T. stands for *Admit. Pray. Trust. Act. Thank.* Those are the steps I think we are to take as we seek the "supply of the Spirit" for the act of preaching. It is a great mystery how this happens. A human being is told to do something *by another*. We are to preach *by the Spirit*. We are to do it. And yet *another* is to do it through us. This is profoundly supernatural and wonderful. It is the great goal of life—to live, and yet so live that another is living in us and through us so that the other gets the glory.

I Preached, but It Was Not I

This "I, yet not I," is woven deep into the way Paul sees the Christian life and ministry:

> I have been crucified with Christ. *It is no longer I who live, but Christ who lives in me.* And the life I now live in the flesh I live by faith in the Son of God, who loved me and gave himself for me. (Gal. 2:20)

> By the grace of God I am what I am, and his grace toward me was not in vain. On the contrary, I worked harder than any of them, though *it was not I, but the grace of God that is with me.* (1 Cor. 15:10)

---

1. John Piper, *Reading the Bible Supernaturally: Seeing and Savoring the Glory of God in Scripture* (Wheaton, IL: Crossway, 2017), 179–390.

> I planted, Apollos watered, but God gave the growth. So neither he who plants nor he who waters is anything, but *only God who gives the growth*. (1 Cor. 3:6–7)

> Work out your own salvation with fear and trembling, for it is *God who works in you, both to will and to work for his good pleasure.* (Phil. 2:12–13)

This is the precious mystery of the Christian life, and the mystery of ministry—which means it is the mystery of preaching. "It is no longer I who preach, but Christ who preaches in me." "It was not I who preached, but the grace of God that was with me." "I preached, but he who preached isn't anything but only God who gives the growth." "Preach, for God is the one willing and acting the preaching in you."

So the greatest question for me in how to preach has been: How can it be that I am fully acting, and yet it is not I? How can I pour myself out in a message with all my powers in full action and yet experience the Holy Spirit in such a way that it was not I but the grace of God with me? *How do I become the means by which the Holy Spirit works the miracle of worship in the hearts of the people?*

My Experience with A.P.T.A.T. in Preaching

My answer is A.P.T.A.T. Picture me sitting on the front pew in our sanctuary. It is one or two minutes before I am to preach. The text is being read by one of the elders or apprentices. This is not the first time I apply A.P.T.A.T. in preparing to preach this sermon. But it is the most urgent. I walk through A.P.T.A.T. in my mind, seeking God's help to be as sincere and earnest as I can.

A—Admit. I say quietly, "I *admit*, Father, that I am utterly dependent on you now as I step into this pulpit. Without your providence, I would not have life or breath or anything (Acts 17:25). Without your supernatural help as I preach, no one in this room will be converted to Christ. No one will be raised from spiritual death. No one will have the heart of stone taken out and a heart of flesh put in. No one will discern the true meaning of this text. No one will see spiritual beauty. No one will savor your infinite worth. No one will be transformed into your likeness." I *admit* this utterly and willingly.

P—Pray. Then I *pray* for the help I need. I might just say, "Help me!" But usually I am feeling some particular burden or challenge or weakness or need. So I ask for specific help. "Father, grant me self-forgetfulness and humility. Grant me clarity of mind and expression. Grant freedom from my manuscript, and don't let me get lost or confused. Grant protection from the Evil One and all the ways he steals the word. Grant joy in the truth I speak, and give me the affections that correspond to the gravity or gladness of what the text says. Grant me to feel love for your people, and compassion for the lost and the weak. Make me real."

T—Trust. This step is decisive. *Trust.* This is the link with Galatians 3:5 that we examined in chapter 6. "Does he who supplies the Spirit to you and works miracles among you do so by works of the law, or by hearing with faith?" God supplies the Spirit and works miracles through our preaching by our "hearing with faith." The Spirit comes through our hearing one of God's blood-bought promises of help, and believing it.

At this point, I think many of us miss out on the fullness of God's blessing by defaulting to vague generalities. Instead of focusing on very concrete, particular biblical promises, we don't focus on any promise at all. We think generally about God's goodness or power. There is nothing wrong with this, but I think God is offering us something better. At least this has proven true for me. Three practices became wonderfully habitual over the years.

Practicing the "T"—Trust: First Habit

The first is to call to mind 1 Peter 4:11 in the prayer room with others who are praying, about half an hour before the service. I am sure that this text was the most often cited in the prayer gathering before our worship services.

> Whoever speaks, [let him speak] as one who speaks oracles of God; whoever serves, as one who *serves by the strength that God supplies*—in order that in everything God may be glorified through Jesus Christ. To him belong glory and dominion forever and ever. Amen.

I love this exhortation and promise. It sets the stage for what is going to happen in a more urgent and final way in the minutes before I preach.

It makes plain that it is *I* who must speak and serve. It also makes plain that my speaking and serving are to be done "by the strength that *God* supplies." And it makes plain why that is important: "in order that in everything God may be glorified." The giver of the strength gets the glory for the message. That text has been the launching pad for hundreds of messages over the years.

Practicing the "T"—Trust: Second Habit

The second practice is to keep a precious store of promises in my memory, ready to be trusted precisely at this point in A.P.T.A.T.—the first T, *trust*. These promises are of such a breadth that they are always relevant no matter the preaching setting or topic. Three of these are:

> Fear not, for I am with you;
>   be not dismayed, for *I am your God*;
> *I will strengthen you, I will help you,*
>   *I will uphold you* with my righteous right hand. (Isa. 41:10)

> No eye has seen a God besides you,
>   who *acts for those who wait for him*. (Isa. 64:4)

> *My God will supply every need of yours* according to his riches in glory in Christ Jesus. (Phil. 4:19)

These promises stand ready in my memory for any preaching challenge—ready to be trusted. And in that trust, they stand ready to become a channel for the supply of the Spirit. But before I mention how I embrace these promises for preaching, consider the third practice.

Practicing the "T"—Trust: Third Habit

The third practice is to ransack the Scripture for a special, God-given promise early Sunday morning during my private time of prayer and meditation. In other words, as I walk through my usual Bible reading for the day—or broaden my reading—I am on the lookout for a specific, tailor-made promise that God may apply to me in a special and personal way as suitable for this very morning.

For example, suppose my wife and I have had a serious conflict in the past few days. I feel guilty and discouraged. I have taken steps to make it right. But I feel defeated in my sinful attitude. This looms as a huge obstacle to preaching with freedom and joy. How will I be able to preach? How will I be able to count on the Lord's help when I feel like such a failure?

As I cry out to him for help, he leads me to Psalm 25, and I read,

> Good and upright is the LORD;
>   therefore he instructs sinners in the way.
> *He leads the humble in what is right,*
>   and teaches the humble his way. (vv. 8–9)

The Lord takes this (he has done this often!) and preaches it to me. He reminds me that he will guide me as I preach, sinner though I am, because "he instructs sinners in the way." There it stands. Right there in Scripture. Here is a concrete, particular promise tailor-made for my situation. This specificity of God's word to me has proved more powerful than the generalities about grace that I have in my head (glorious as they are!). Perhaps this is a weakness of mine. Perhaps it shouldn't be this way. But it seems to me that the reason God has given so many dozens of concrete, particular promises in the Bible about so many situations is precisely so that they will take hold of us and give us a very specific word to trust.

Indeed there are many tailor-made promises for the preacher. If I am anxious about not preaching clearly or powerfully, he may give me this:

> Do not be anxious how you are to speak or what you are to say, for *what you are to say will be given to you in that hour.* (Matt. 10:19)

If I am discouraged by the thought that it seems very little comes from my preaching, he may give me this:

> As the rain and the snow come down from heaven
>   and do not return there but water the earth,
> making it bring forth and sprout,
>   giving seed to the sower and bread to the eater,
> so shall my word be that goes out from my mouth;
>   *it shall not return to me empty,*
> but it shall accomplish that which I purpose,
>   and shall succeed in the thing for which I sent it.
>   (Isa. 55:10–11)

If I am attacked by thoughts that what I have to say is of little account and will probably be discounted by the people, God may give me this:

> The precepts of the LORD are right,
>   rejoicing the heart;
> the commandment of the LORD is pure,
>   enlightening the eyes. . . .
> *More to be desired are they than gold,*
>   *even much fine gold;*
> *sweeter also than honey*
>   *and drippings of the honeycomb.* (Ps. 19:8, 10)

If I am in a hostile setting and fear for my life in preaching God may give me this:

> Do not be afraid, but go on speaking and do not be silent, for I am with you, and no one will attack you to harm you, for I have many in this city who are my people. (Acts 18:9–10)

If I am sick and my nose is running, and I have a tickle in my throat that puts me on the brink of coughing, he may give me this:

> My grace is sufficient for you, for my power is made perfect in weakness. (2 Cor. 12:9)

If I made the mistake of reading my email just before coming to the church and saw there a stinging criticism because of a conviction that I hold, the Lord may give me this:

> Blessed are you when people hate you and when they exclude you and revile you and spurn your name as evil, on account of the Son of Man! Rejoice in that day, and leap for joy, for behold, your reward is great in heaven. (Luke 6:22–23)

The Moment Just before Preaching

So there I sit on the front pew, having admitted (*A*) that I will be utterly ineffective without the Spirit's help, and having prayed (*P*) for the kind of help I especially need, and having laid hold on a promise to trust (*T*). Now comes the real test. Will I, in this hour of actual preaching, trust the promises of God? Paul did not promise the supply of the Spirit to *A—admitting need*, or *P—praying for help*. He promised it to *T—trusting* the blood-bought promise. (The reason I stress "blood-bought" from Romans 8:32 is that it makes *Christ's* work, not mine, the basis of my confidence.)

I take the promise I have settled on, and right there on the front pew, seconds before I preach, I recite the promise to my own soul. I say to the Lord, "I trust you." Sometimes I say, "I believe; help my unbelief!" (Mark 9:24). I turn my mind away from myself—introspection at this point is a hopeless practice, since you can always doubt the adequacy of what you see in your own soul. I turn to the promise, and I say it to myself again, often as I am walking to the pulpit.

I say the promise to myself as if God is saying it to me. I seek to hear his voice saying it to me. I have a special affection for the very word of God spoken to me personally by God himself in these moments. I resonate with Charles Spurgeon when he exults in the personal "shalls and wills" of God. In his sermon "The Rainbow" from Genesis 9:16, Spurgeon said,

> O dear friends, one's heart rejoices to think of those potent *shalls* and *wills*—those immoveable pillars which death and hell cannot shake—the *shalls* and *wills* of a God.[2]

So I say in the words of God from Scripture, "I will help you." "I will strengthen you." "I will uphold you." "I will give you what you need to say." "I will protect you from the Evil One." "I will make your words effective." "I love you." "I have called you." "You are mine." "I have helped you a hundred times, have I not?" "Now go! Be strong. Be of good courage. I am with you. I am with your mouth." I actually say these words, to myself, or ones like them, as I walk to the pulpit. I know of no other way to experience the exhilaration of saying with the apostle Paul, "The Lord stood by me and strengthened me, so that through me the message might be fully proclaimed" (2 Tim. 4:17).

The Act of Preaching Is Now Here

A—Act. This is the great paradox: *Act.* Paul says, "Work out your own salvation . . . , for it is God who works in you, both to will and to work"

---

2. C. H. Spurgeon, "The Rainbow," in *The Metropolitan Tabernacle Pulpit Sermons*, vol. 9 (London: Passmore & Alabaster, 1863), 364.

(Phil. 2:12–13). You work because God is bringing about the working. He *creates* the miracle of Spirit-sustained speech. You *act* the miracle.[3] Jonathan Edwards captures the paradox this way:

> We are not merely passive in it, nor yet does God do some and we do the rest, but God does all and we do all. God *produces* all and we *act* all. For that is what he produces, our own acts. God is the only proper *author* and fountain; we only are the proper *actors*. We are in different respects wholly passive and wholly active.[4]

Even though I am trusting the promise that God is going to be the decisive power in this preaching, I use my mind to discern the moment, and I use my will to decide now to go to the pulpit, and I use my muscles in my legs to get me there, and I use my mind and will and throat to say, "Let's pray." I am acting. And by faith in God's promises, I believe I am serving "by the strength that God supplies" (1 Pet. 4:11).

Rarely while preaching does my mind return to the promise I took hold of as I entered the pulpit. I am so utterly focused on the text and exposition at hand that I seldom have the mental freedom to look away to another text as I am preaching. But it does happen. Sometimes it is in a moment of confusion when I have lost my bearings and I am trying to find my place. The promise will flash in my mind, just for a split second, and speak its encouragement to me. But ordinarily I give my attention totally to the task at hand, resting in the *reality* of the promise, if not the *consciousness* of it. That too is a mystery—resting in a reality that is not in your immediate consciousness.

Even though I rarely return consciously to the initial promise while I am preaching, it is fairly common that my mind will have the freedom to whisper prayers to God while I am preaching. These are usually very short, one- or two-second calls for help, perhaps in general, or specifically because I can't remember something, or I see a person in the audience who looks as if he or she needs God's touch. I think these prayers are simply the overflow of the faith in which I stand at that moment.

---

3. We devoted an entire conference and a short book to this paradox: John Piper and David Mathis, eds., *Acting the Miracle: God's Work and Ours in the Mystery of Sanctification* (Wheaton, IL: Crossway, 2013).

4. Jonathan Edwards, *Writings on the Trinity, Grace, and Faith*, ed. Sang Hyun Lee and Harry S. Stout, vol. 21, *The Works of Jonathan Edwards* (New Haven, CT: Yale University Press, 2003), 251; emphasis added.

By Faith We Know God Is Working

Galatians 3:5 assures me that through my faith, the Holy Spirit is at work. This is so important that it is worth quoting again: "Does he who *supplies the Spirit* to you and *works miracles* among you do so by works of the law, or by *hearing with faith*?" This is the miracle of preaching. This is the point where the supernatural reality happens. You may feel something unusual in the "sacred anointing," or you may not. Goose bumps are not promised, but only that the Spirit will be supplied and do his wonders. Sometimes you can see evidences of his working in the people immediately. Usually it is better not to presume that what you see is spiritual. There are many unspiritual responses to anointed preaching that look significant, but are not. And there are miracles you cannot see. It is better to trust that God is at work, and then make yourself available to speak afterward with anyone who would like to talk or pray.

When the Message Is Over

T—Thank. Finally, the message is finished and I step out of the pulpit. We sing. I give the benediction. And I stand available to talk and pray with the people. During the closing song, my heart says, *"Thank* you." That is the final T. And as I talk to people, I sometimes whisper, "Thank you." And when I am walking home, I will often say out loud on the 11th Avenue bridge, "Thank you. Thank you."

I don't know all the good things God did or will do through the message. But I do know that I am alive. I didn't completely botch the message. I felt his favor and his freedom—sometimes more, sometimes less. I saw fresh things in the text, even as I preached. I felt the sweetness of the truth of the text more intensely as I opened it than when I was studying it. I heard several sincere expressions of folks who were helped. I feel, even now as I write this, the incalculable privilege of being an ambassador of the King of the universe. And so I say again, "Thank you."

Preaching by the Spirit for the Sake of Worship in the Spirit

So it is that I have sought to preach by the Holy Spirit so that my people would be helped to worship—now and forever—by the Spirit. I am not interested in entertaining my people or merely persuading them of doctrinal truths. The Devil is more accomplished in entertainment and doctrine than I am. And it does him no good. Nor does he do any good by it. I do not want to devote my life to doing what the Devil does, and does even better than I.

What the Devil cannot do is see the glory of Christ as supremely beautiful and supremely valuable. He cannot savor this beauty above all things, and he cannot live to make it known. But that is why the universe exists, why the church exists, why corporate worship exists, and why preaching exists. Apart from the supernatural work of the Spirit, this purpose for worship and preaching will fail. Therefore, God has designed that in corporate worship the human activity of preaching be done in the power of the Holy Spirit. As such, preaching becomes worship and awakens worship. By the Spirit, preaching sees and says the glorious truth of Scripture. And by the Spirit, preaching savors and celebrates the glory of those truths. Those who hear are helped by this seeing and savoring to do the same. Thus preaching, as expository exultation, advances worship by worshiping—in the Spirit.

Live the Miracle

In part 3 our focus has been on the supernatural dimension of preaching and what happens in the congregation. The pastor's preaching and the people's worship are a miracle. I have tried to walk with you through the biblical teaching on how preaching happens "in the Spirit." And I have used my own experience of A.P.T.A.T. to illustrate how I think this biblical teaching is put into practice.

Now we shift our focus from the supernatural to the natural. The preacher uses human language. He uses logic. He clarifies history and theology and the paths of obedience. His goals are always supernatural. He aims to help people *see* with the eyes of the heart, and *savor* with spiritual taste, and *show* with Spirit-formed action, the worth and beauty of God. All of that is impossible apart from the supernatural work of the Spirit. Is the preacher then to put all his natural powers to work in the service of this miracle? That is what part 4 is about.

How Does Preaching Become
a Means of the Miracle of
Worship—Naturally?

Expository Exultation and the Use of All Our Natural Powers

8

Expository Exultation

*Loving People with Clear
Thinking and Valid Logic*

Authentic worship and the preaching God uses to sustain it are supernatural experiences. Worship is seeing, savoring, and showing the supreme beauty and worth of the triune God. Preaching is one act of that worship. But human beings cannot see or savor or show this God as their supreme treasure apart from the supernatural work of the Holy Spirit. He is the One who reveals his glory (2 Cor. 4:6), enlightens the eyes of the heart (Eph. 1:18), opens the darkened mind (Luke 24:45), and gives a glimpse of the glory of Christ that the "natural person" cannot perceive (Matt. 16:17).

That is what we saw in part 3. In answer to the question of how the human act of preaching can waken worship, if worship is a work of God, we answered that the preacher *admits* his helplessness, *prays* for divine power, *trusts* the promises of God for supernatural intervention, *does* the human act of preaching, and then *thanks* God. This, we said, is a great paradox—that the aims of preaching and the experience of worship are supernatural, and yet preaching is the act of a mere mortal. Preaching is not only the work of the Holy Spirit; it is also the real effort of human reason and will.

Making the Fullest Use of Our Natural Powers
The focus of part 4—this chapter and the next—is not on God's supernatural power, but on the use of all our natural powers. How do

the supernatural and the natural intersect in the act of preaching? The emphasis will be on the fact that God *intends for preachers to make the fullest use of their natural powers in preaching*, even though the aim is to waken and sustain worship that is possible only in the supernatural power of the Holy Spirit.

When I speak of *natural powers*, I am referring to everything the preacher and people are capable of, simply by virtue of being human and having received a basic education along with ordinary life experience.[1] For example, the preacher and the people have the natural power to listen and speak. They can identify the existence of words and phrases and clauses (even if they do not know the terms *phrase* or *clause*). They can construe a speaker's or author's intention from what he said or wrote. Otherwise, ordinary people would not be communicating. They can see relationships between the different parts of what they hear. They can see connections between what they learn and other things they already know. They can remember things they've discovered. They can get enough sleep and food and exercise (or coffee) so that their powers are assisted by mental alertness and physical vigor. And they can seek help from other people (in books or in person). And so on. This is what I mean by our *natural powers*.

Supernatural Grace Does Not Replace Means of Grace

God's ordinary way of revealing his glory to the hearts of his people is not by circumventing their natural powers but by making those powers the means of supernatural discovery. When Jesus said, "No one knows the Father except the Son and anyone to whom the Son chooses to reveal him" (Matt. 11:27), he did not mean that people should not use their natural ability to look at him and listen to him. The miracle of seeing Jesus as the all-satisfying Son of God was a miracle mediated through the natural act of listening to Jesus and looking at Jesus. The supernatural sight happened through the use of natural powers. Supernatural grace does not replace means of grace.

---

1. I am aware that millions of people in the world do not have access to education. Many are preliterate. Adjustments would have to be made when doing expository exultation in those settings. But even in such settings, it is possible to do exposition of the Scriptures. But here in this chapter, I am assuming basic literacy and mental faculties. A pastor will seek to be aware of the mentally disabled in his congregation and what kinds of adjustments he might make for their good. I think we should be very slow to assume that small children and intellectually challenged adults cannot benefit from expository exultation.

It is the same with regard to preaching. In Luke 24:45, when Jesus "opened their minds to understand the Scriptures," he did not mean that this miracle happened apart from their natural knowledge of the Scriptures. The supernatural understanding happened *through* the use of the natural powers of reading and hearing. As Paul said in Ephesians 3:4, "When you *read this*, you can perceive my insight into the mystery of Christ" (Eph. 3:4). That was a supernatural perception. It came by divine enlightening of the eyes of the heart (Eph. 1:18). But it came through natural reading.

The human effort of mind and will and body that goes into preaching is not contrary to the purposes of God to bring about supernatural effects. And, therefore, my plea in this chapter is for preachers to expend every effort in thinking[2] and explaining and arguing and illustrating with all their rational powers to make the intention of the biblical authors clear and compelling. We will do this knowing that only the supernatural grace of God will bring about the desired seeing, savoring, and showing of the glory of God.

Human Thinking and Divine Illumination Are Not Alternatives

Good preaching and good hearing involve good thinking. The apostle Paul makes clear that the *effort* of human thinking and the *gift* of divine illumination are not alternatives. They belong together. He explains to Timothy, in one sentence, how these two work together: "Think over what I say, for the Lord will give you understanding in everything" (2 Tim. 2:7). *We* make the effort to think. *God* freely gives understanding. Both-and. Not either-or.[3]

Some preachers swerve off the road to one side of this verse or the other. Some stress the first part: "Think over what I say." They emphasize the indispensable role of reason and thinking, and then minimize the supernatural work of God in making the mind able to see and embrace the glory of truth. Others stress the second half of the verse: "The Lord will give you understanding in everything." They emphasize the futility of reason. Then their preaching veers into emotional manipulation or mysticism.

---

2. I have tried to probe the nature and biblical foundations and aims of human thinking in the service of Christ in John Piper, *Think: The Life of the Mind and the Love of God* (Wheaton, IL: Crossway, 2010).

3. This discussion of human effort and divine gift is discussed more fully in John Piper, *Reading the Bible Supernaturally: Seeing and Savoring the Glory of God in Scripture* (Wheaton, IL: Crossway, 2017). I am using some of the thoughts found there (see pp. 240ff.).

Divine Gift Grounds Human Effort

But Paul will not be divided between studious meditation and supernatural illumination. For Paul it was not either-or, but both-and. "Think over what I say, *for* the Lord will give you understanding in everything." Notice there the word "for." It means that God's design for the preacher—as he prepares and as he preaches—is that the divine *gift* of understanding be the basis of our *effort* to gain it by thinking. His supernatural giving does not replace our natural thinking; it encourages and supports it. "Pursue understanding by thinking, *because* the Lord gives understanding." This is true for the preacher as he speaks, and for the people as they seek to understand what he says.

Paul does not say, "God gives you understanding, so don't waste your time thinking over the Scriptures." He does not encourage us to substitute prayer and faith for thinking, but rather to saturate our thinking with prayer and faith. Benjamin Warfield, the great theologian at the beginning of the twentieth century, said, "Sometimes we hear it said that ten minutes on your knees will give you a truer, deeper, more operative knowledge of God than ten hours over your books. 'What!' is the appropriate response, '. . . than ten hours over your books, on your knees?'"[4]

On the other hand, neither does Paul say, "Think hard over what I say because it all depends on your rational powers, and God does not illumine the mind." No. He emphatically makes God's gift of illumination the *ground* of our deliberation. He makes God's gift of light the reason for our effort to escape the darkness of not understanding. "Think over what I say, *for* the Lord will give you understanding."

Think for the Sake of a Mature, Thinking People

So preachers should cultivate in themselves and in their people the habit of rigorous thinking about Scripture. A pastor's preaching should be marked by lucid thinking, and over time he should draw his people into the habit of thinking carefully about the meaning of Scripture. When Paul told Timothy, as a pastor, to think about the apostolic teaching (2 Tim. 2:7), he did not mean that the people don't have to—as if the job of the pastor was to do all the thinking for the people. Paul said to

---

4. Benjamin Warfield, "The Religious Life of Theological Students," in *The Princeton Theology*, ed. Mark Noll (Grand Rapids, MI: Baker, 1983), 263.

the whole church, "Do not be children in your thinking. Be infants in evil, but in your thinking be mature" (1 Cor. 14:20).

A people with powers of mature thinking about biblical truth is one of the goals of pastoral ministry. Paul said in Ephesians 4:12–14 that pastors should aim

> to equip the saints for the work of ministry, for building up the body of Christ, until we all attain to the unity of the faith and of *the knowledge of the Son of God, to mature manhood,* to the measure of the stature of the fullness of Christ, so that we may no longer be children, *tossed to and fro by the waves and carried about by every wind of doctrine,* by human cunning, by craftiness in deceitful schemes.

In other words, one of the marks of immature thinking is instability. The people are "tossed to and fro" by winds of doctrine. Why? Because they have not been equipped to be mature in thinking. So the preacher, in his preparation and preaching, and the people, in their meditation and listening, should be thinking carefully. Their minds should be engaged with the care that catches mistakes in reasoning and that exults in clear, compelling, logically consistent presentations of the truth.

Right Thinking Really Matters

In pleading for clear, compelling, rigorous thinking in preaching, I am aware that I am swimming against the cultural current that minimizes thinking and reasoning in favor of spectacle and visual impact and sound bites and musical atmosphere and emotive persuasion. All over the world "logic on fire"—which is how Martyn Lloyd-Jones defined preaching—is being replaced with fire—or sparks—without logic. Many preachers expend little mental effort to do the difficult work of digging into the language of a passage of Scripture to discover how it actually works to make its point.

Then there is a similar neglect of the mental effort to create a message that shows the people, with compelling logic and authentic passion, what the text means and how it applies to their lives. This minimizing of rational effort is part of the cultural air we breathe. We have been breathing it for many decades. And we are not the better for it.

Light from a Contemporary Novel

Daniel Taylor, former professor of English at Bethel University, wrote a novel that exposes the tragedy of this truth-escaping miasma that we have been breathing. *Death Comes for the Deconstructionist* is a clash between Richard Pratt, the avant-garde, postmodern English professor, and Daniel Abrahamson, the old-fashioned Jewish intellectual, and Verity Jackson, an African American scholar and lover of stories.[5]

For Pratt, reasoning and truth are outdated, soul-quenching power moves of the establishment. Words are toys—playthings in the language games of the liberated university. For Abrahamson (with a keen memory of Nazi distortions of truth) and Jackson (who knows that truth is sometimes the only friend that the poor have), words and the way they are put to use are a matter of life and death.

John Mote—the failed graduate student turned detective, and "hero" of the story—had his own reasons for lamenting the influence of Richard Pratt. Pratt had "liberated" him from "Holy Writ and Holy Reason." And with them had disappeared the "stable, knowable world." And in the absence of stability, Mote's mind was spiraling toward self-destruction. "I am drawn to the edge of the mind where thought descends into randomness and randomness into emptiness and emptiness into oblivion."[6] In other words, when the apostle Paul says, "Think over what I say," more is at stake than at first may appear.

Loving People Means Using Clear, Compelling Logic

Right thinking, clear logic, the valid use of reason, and the respectful, honest handling of words are utterly crucial in loving people. They are an indispensable window into truth, a bulwark against totalitarian abuses of power, a friend of the poor, and a rock of stability in the quicksand of randomness, emptiness, and oblivion. Preaching that fails in the mental effort to dig into the thinking of the biblical authors, and then turn their meaning into a clear, logically consistent, existentially urgent message, dishonors those authors, depreciates the inspiration of Scripture, and falls short of equipping the saints to discern the deceptions of false doctrine. Drawing people into right thinking in preaching really matters.

---

5. Daniel Taylor, *Death Comes for the Deconstructionist* (Eugene, OR: Wipf & Stock, 2015). My full review of the book can be found at http://www.desiringgod.org/articles/who-killed -postmodernism.

6. Ibid.

The Bible, which is the basis of all preaching, is a book. And books must be read to be understood. And good reading means good thinking.[7] There is no getting around it. Reading for maximum understanding is hard mental work. Therefore, the preacher's task involves enormous efforts of thinking week after week, year after year. And either we do it well or we do it poorly. I am pleading for preachers to embrace this task, and do it well.

Paul's Passion for Clear and Open Declarations of Truth

Paul was passionately committed to a kind of communication that was transparent, clear, understandable, and free from artifice, deception, and spin. Listen to the kind of communicator Paul was:

> Our appeal does *not spring from error or impurity or any attempt to deceive*, but just as we have been approved by God to be entrusted with the gospel, so we speak, *not to please man, but to please God* who tests our hearts. For *we never came with words of flattery*, as you know, *nor with a pretext for greed*—God is witness. *Nor did we seek glory from people*, whether from you or from others, though we could have made demands as apostles of Christ. (1 Thess. 2:3–6)

> We are *not, like so many, peddlers of God's word*, but as men of *sincerity*, as commissioned by God, *in the sight of God we speak in Christ*. (2 Cor. 2:17)

> *We have renounced disgraceful, underhanded ways. We refuse to practice cunning* or to *tamper with God's word*, but by the *open statement of the truth* we would commend ourselves to everyone's conscience *in the sight of God*. (2 Cor. 4:2)

This is an amazing passion for truth and clarity and openness and understandability. He is utterly committed to being free from pretext and flattery and greed and man pleasing and cunning and distortion. And all this is under oath, in the sight of God, and before all men. Christian speech is not private-code language. It is open, public, comprehensible, shareable. The Christian preacher has nothing to hide. The Devil is in the business of hiding. The preacher reveals. The Devil obscures. The preacher clarifies. The Devil dulls the mind and heart. The preacher

---

7. I wrote a chapter on this called "Reading as Thinking," in Piper, *Think*, 41–56.

shines and burns. He is ashamed of nothing in his message. And this has everything to do with logic and right reason.

Logic Is Universal, Not Parochial

The preacher submits his thinking openly to the tests of logic. He preaches with the conviction that his sentences must be consistent. They may not be contradictory. He humbles himself under the demands of logical consistency because he believes that logic is not parochial but universal. It is rooted in the way God is and the way he made the world. It is not a creation of Western philosophy. It is not a cultural quirk of societies that think in linear ways. The Bible itself—especially Jesus—shows that so-called Aristotelian logic is not unique to Greek or Western thought.

Pharisees' Selective Use of Reason

Take Matthew 16:1–4, for example. This text is one of the reasons I wasn't impressed with those distinctions.

> The Pharisees and Sadducees came, and to test him they asked him to show them a sign from heaven. He answered them, "When it is evening, you say, 'It will be fair weather, for the sky is red.' And in the morning, 'It will be stormy today, for the sky is red and threatening.' You know how to interpret the appearance of the sky, but you cannot interpret the signs of the times. An evil and adulterous generation seeks for a sign, but no sign will be given to it except the sign of Jonah." So he left them and departed.

What is Jesus saying to these Pharisees and Sadducees? In verse 2 he says, "When it is evening, you say, 'It will be fair weather, for the sky is red.'" What does that mean? It means that these Hebraic (non-Western) Pharisees and Sadducees are thinking in so-called Aristotelian syllogisms.

> Premise 1: Red skies in the evening portend fair weather.
> Premise 2: This evening the skies are red.
> Conclusion: Therefore, the weather will be fair.

That is solid, so-called Aristotelian logic. Jesus responded to this use of accurate observation and sound reasoning: "You know how to interpret the appearance of the sky" (v. 3b). In other words, you know how to use your eyes and your minds to draw right conclusions when it comes to the natural world. He *approves* of their use of empirical observation and rational deliberation. In fact, it's precisely this approval that makes the following disapproval valid and powerful.

He says in verse 3c, "But you cannot interpret the signs of the times." And when he says, "You *cannot*," he does not mean you don't have the sensory and rational capacities to do what needs to be done. He had just shown them that they *do* in fact have the sensory and rational capacities to do what needs to be done. They are very adept at accurate observation and logical deliberation when it comes to getting along in this world. Saving their own skin.

In this way Jesus uses the common ground of consistent logic to expose the hypocrisy of the Pharisees and Sadducees. But he condemns the selective use of this logic that puts it to good work for maritime safety, but leaves it unused to discern spiritual truth.

Getting the Precious Use of "Therefore" Right

Therefore, I do not buy into the view that the demand for sound logic is a parochial, Western, culturally relative claim. Jesus assumed it and commended it. And he does so throughout the Gospels. Sound logic, of the sort Jesus commended and expected, is pervasively crucial for grasping the meaning of Scripture and making it clear and compelling in preaching.

When I speak of "sound logic"—or you could use the phrase "sound reason"—I mean, for example, the way of thinking that enables us to see how the word *therefore* works in biblical argument—or any argument. Sound reasoning keeps us from using it wrongly. For example, when sound logic or sound reason is working well, you don't say things like, "All dogs have four legs. This horse has four legs. *Therefore*, this horse is a dog." If you heard this you would say, "No, that conclusion is not true." And the reason it's not true is that the conclusion does not follow, with sound logic, from the premises. "All dogs have four legs" doesn't mean *only* dogs have four legs. Therefore, a horse may have four legs and is not a dog. The premises don't lead you to believe that a horse is a dog. In the Bible, eternal things may hang on getting *therefore* right.

What a wonderful revolution would come into much preaching if preachers were as passionately committed as Jesus and Paul were never to use any invalid syllogism, and never to use any untrue premises! What a wonderful thing it would be if preachers were so committed to careful preparation, and truthful premises, and valid logic, that they would never say, for example, things like, "The Bible says we are justified by faith apart from works. *Therefore*, we know that obedience to Christ's commandments are not required for final salvation." What's the problem with that? Quite apart from whether the conclusion (introduced by "Therefore") is true, it is definitely *not* valid. The *therefore* is invalid. It is misused. The conclusion does *not* follow logically from the premise.

The reason it doesn't is that "justified" in the premise is not identical with "final salvation" in the conclusion. So we cannot validly infer from justification being "apart from works" that final salvation requires no "obedience to Jesus's commands." That is sloppy thinking and unsound reasoning. It damages the people of God. It is unloving. Preaching should shun all such slipshod uses of the glorious gift of the human mind.

Ordinary Folks Love to Be Treated as Able to Reason

You may think that I am overdoing the demand for logical consistency in sermons, because most ordinary people don't know anything about all this logic talk and don't care to know. That is true. They don't. But that's not relevant for two reasons. One is that the preacher is accountable first to Jesus, not first to the people. "As commissioned by God, in the sight of God *we speak in Christ*" (2 Cor. 2:17). And we have seen that Jesus does not approve of using logic well only when sorting out the weather predictions, but not when it comes to matters of infinite importance.

The other reason it is irrelevant that most people don't know logic language (and don't want to know it, and, I would add, don't need to know it) is that, whether they know it or not, they are wired by God in their humanity to think logically when they are at their best. And over time they come to love (perhaps without even knowing why) the strength and solidity and reliability and power of sermons that are logically consistent and compelling.

They also have an uneasy sense that something is amiss when there is a pattern of preaching in which the points do not logically follow from true premises. The people don't need to know the language of premises and logic and validity and consistency and noncontradiction. These realities are written by God on their minds as human beings. They know intuitively that something cannot *be* and *not be* in the same way at the same time. And they know that a horse is not a dog. They can smell invalid syllogisms, even if they can't label them.

Intuitive Love of Logic

You don't need a course in logic, or even to know that logic exists, in order to love the benefits of logic and live by it every day. Suppose the police say (premise #1), "A young man with brown hair and a red jacket robbed an old woman yesterday on Franklin Avenue at seven o'clock." And suppose your neighbor says to the police that (premise #2) your son, who has brown hair, was wearing a red jacket yesterday when he saw him on Franklin Avenue. And suppose the policeman says (conclusion), "Well, your son must, therefore, be the thief."

You don't need a degree in formal logic to rejoice in the clear (logical!) error of the policeman. No, that conclusion does *not* follow from the premises. It is strictly invalid. And, of course, you don't need to know any of these technical terms to rejoice in that awareness. Your mind is wired, at its best, to detect the fallacy. Other people have red jackets. My son always walks on Franklin Avenue. But, most of all, he was with me at seven o'clock last night!

Preaching necessarily involves thinking. Ideas and observations are being put together into a message. They are coherent or incoherent. Consistent or inconsistent. Logical or illogical. Thinking is either happening well or poorly. No preacher can claim exemption from thinking. And my plea is that we preach with clear, compelling, logical consistency—that none of our premises be false, and none of our inferences be invalid.

What Humility and the Authority of Scripture Require

Humility before the truth of Scripture, and before the authority of Christ, demands this kind of submission to logical consistency. If you abuse logic, what are you expecting your people to base their agreement on? You can't answer, "Scripture," unless you are committed to logically consistent explanations that your conclusions actually come from Scripture. Scripture will only have authority in your preaching if your appeal to Scripture can be seen to be a valid appeal.

If you draw invalid inferences from Scripture, it won't matter how loud you protest your belief in biblical inerrancy; you will not be helping your people base their lives on Scripture. You will be expecting them to base their lives on your faulty inferences from Scripture. That is not humble. It is proud. And it jeopardizes the authority of Christ, who speaks through true and valid inferences from Scripture.

But if we humble ourselves, and submit to the demands of logical consistency, we will be in the best of company. If our expositions are refreshingly free from non sequiturs,[8] and if we give clear premises and valid arguments for all our claims, we will join Jesus, who was scathing toward the Pharisees' truth-dodging strategies. And we will join Paul, who not only argued and persuaded that Jesus is the Christ (Acts 17:2, 4; 18:4, 19; 20:8–9, 26; 24:25; 26:28), but who wrote his own letters in a way that assumes we will use the clear, logical thinking to trace his arguments.[9]

How Natural Serves Supernatural

After all this emphasis on preaching as thinking, and preaching as logically consistent, you may be asking how all this relates to the supernatural effect of preaching that we are praying for. How does the natural act of thinking become the occasion for the supernatural experience of

---

8. A non sequitur (Latin for "it does not follow") refers to a conclusion that doesn't follow from the premises or evidence. The clearest kind of non sequiturs are strictly logical, like: "All horses have four legs. Fido has four legs. Therefore Fido is a horse." But countless others threaten careful, humble leadership and preaching, from logistical to theological: "Christmas occurs on Sunday this year; *therefore* it makes no sense to have a morning service." Or: "God controls all human behavior, *so* humans are not responsible." Or: "Humans *are* responsible; *therefore* God cannot decisively control all human behavior." Or: "God is kind in all his acts; *therefore* he is not a God of wrath." Or: "Salvation is by grace, *so* there can be no judgment according to works." Or: "Polygamy was permitted in Scripture; *therefore* it should be permitted in the church today." Or: "God promises to meet all our needs; *therefore* a believer will never go hungry." Or: "Christians are commanded to rejoice always; *therefore* it is a sin to feel sorrow over lost souls." Or: "God is merciful; *therefore* he could not have taken away my child." Or: "Jesus said to turn the other cheek; *therefore* it is wrong to spank children." Or: "Piper puts a high premium on being logically consistent; *therefore* he must think preaching is only an affair of the mind." And on and on. None of these inferences follow logically. They are all non sequiturs. Oh, what a blessing comes to a congregation when a preacher humbles himself under the liberating demand: "No non sequiturs!"

9. My thoughts about how we trace the argument of a biblical text are unfolded in chapters 25–29 of *Reading the Bible Supernaturally*, 350–90.

authentic worship—seeing and savoring and showing the beauty and worth of God? I will let the apostle Paul show the answer.

In Romans 5:3–5, Paul has just made the case for Christians to rejoice in suffering. His argument (and notice that it is indeed a logical argument!) goes like this: "We rejoice in our sufferings, knowing that suffering produces endurance, and endurance produces character, and character produces hope, and hope does not put us to shame."

Then come two arguments for why hope will not put us to shame. The relationship between these two arguments carries spectacular implications for preaching and for the way *natural means*, like rational thought and historical observation, become the occasion for *supernatural* experiences of the beauty and worth of God.

When I speak of natural means, I include not only logical argumentation, but also historical observation. The principle behind how God makes natural means serve supernatural experience is the same for both logic and history. In Paul's argument for why hope does not put us to shame, the intersection between the natural and supernatural is between historical observation and the work of the Holy Spirit in giving us a supernatural sense of the love of God.

> Hope does not put us to shame, because God's love has been poured into our hearts through the Holy Spirit who has been given to us. For while we were still weak, at the right time Christ died for the ungodly. (Rom. 5:5–6)

Supernatural Experience of God's Love

Paul's first argument for why hope will not put us to shame is that the Holy Spirit is present in us ("who has been *given to us*"); and what he does in us is make real to us the love of God. This is not a mere fact we learn from the Bible. It is a real experience that we have today. "God's love has been poured into our hearts through the Holy Spirit." It really happens in our hearts. It is a sensed and sure taste of the love of God for us, because God the Holy Spirit is in us giving us that taste of the love of God.

So Paul's first way of showing us why our hope will not disappoint us is to say that God gives us a real supernatural experience to confirm our hope. It is supernatural because it is given through the Holy Spirit, who is supernatural. This is what we are aiming at in our preaching—

real supernatural, radically transforming, empowering experiences of the beauty and worth of God, including his love for us. Our preaching is not aiming at mere information transfer, or mere persuasion of doctrinal truths, or mere human excitement about God. We are aiming at authentic, Spirit-given experience of God himself—in this case, as Paul calls it here, the pouring out of God's love into our hearts through the Holy Spirit (Rom. 5:5).

Natural Ground for Supernatural Experience

But then Paul does something in Romans 5:6 that has huge implications for preaching. He gives a *ground*, or basis, for supernatural experience. And it is a *natural* ground. A historical ground. We can see the ground in the word *for* (Greek *gar*) that begins verse 6. "God's love has been poured into our hearts through the Holy Spirit who has been given to us. *For* . . ." What makes the ground so striking is that it is a statement of historical fact along with a theological interpretation of the fact. "God's love has been poured into our hearts through the Holy Spirit who has been given to us. *For* while we were still weak, at the right time *Christ died for the ungodly*" (Rom. 5:5–6). "Christ died" is a historical fact. "For the ungodly" is a theological interpretation of the fact.

How are the natural and the supernatural related here? There is a supernatural experience of God's love given by the Holy Spirit in the heart, and there is the declaration that the ground—the foundation— of this experience of God's love in history ("Christ died") and theology ("for the ungodly"). The experience is *supernatural* (given by the Holy Spirit). The foundation is *natural* (a historical fact and a theological statement that even the Devil would agree with).

They relate like this: what it means to be loved by God is revealed by the historical and theological observation "Christ died for the ungodly." The Holy Spirit does not give this information to the heart. The Bible and the preacher give it to the mind. It is not the job of the Holy Spirit to describe the love of God to you. That is the job God has assigned to history and to Scripture, and to preaching.

Our people learn the nature and content of the love of God from the way that love acted in history in Jesus Christ. Then the Holy Spirit takes that natural truth—heralded by you, the preacher, with expository exultation—and he works a supernatural miracle with it. He causes their hearts to see God's love as supremely beautiful and to feel it as supremely precious. He gives them the real, heartfelt *experience* described in verse 5: "God's love has been poured into our hearts through the Holy Spirit."

Uniting Natural and Supernatural in Preaching

Both the *natural* fact of history with its interpretation and the *supernatural* work of the Holy Spirit are essential. If we make claims to have *experiences* of the love of God without solid foundations in history and its God-given meaning, we become cultic, emotionalistic, and fanatical. If we claim to *understand* what happened in history and its theological meaning, but we don't *experience* the love of God poured out into our hearts by the Holy Spirit, we become barren, impotent, and intellectualistic.

The place of preaching in this process is to be the mouthpiece of the historical and theological truth that "Christ died for the ungodly." We say all the wonderful things about the death of Christ that the text, and the reality behind it, give us to say—this is our *exposition*. And we *exult* over it with as much joy in it as the Spirit grants us to taste. That is our preaching—*expository exultation*.

But our aim is what only the Holy Spirit can do—the supernatural experience of the love of God in the hearts of our listeners. We aim for them to see and savor and show the beauty and worth of this love. The glory of preaching is that, even though we cannot make this happen by our own effort, since it is the work of the Holy Spirit, he will spare no effort to clarify the beauty and worth of the historical facts and the theological interpretations. Heralding that beauty and worth is our work. It is an indispensable and glorious work.

Strike the Match

The focus of this chapter has been on the fullest use of our human powers in preaching. The aim of such preaching is not less supernatural than was the aim in chapters 6 and 7, where the focus was on the power of the Holy Spirit. The premise here has been: supernatural grace does not replace *means* of grace.

More specifically, the focus has been on the importance of right thinking in our preaching. My plea has been that we preach with clear, compelling, logical consistency—that none of our premises be false, and that none of our inferences be invalid. I tried to show that this is an act of love and humility and submission to the truth and authority of Scripture. People are destroyed when language can be made to mean anything we want it to. Not submitting to the logic of biblical texts exalts ourselves and dethrones God.

I tried to show with Romans 5:5–6 how God makes the natural use of our powers serve his supernatural purposes. The *supernatural* experience of tasting the love of God in our hearts is made possible by Paul's use of the *natural* historical fact of Christ's death, and by the human theological statement that Christ did this for the ungodly. Preaching makes the fullest use of its natural powers to clarify history and its theological meaning. With that kindling in place, God lights the match and by his Spirit makes it burn in the hearts of his people.

In the next chapter, we shift the focus from right thinking and historical clarification to the actual composition of the sermon and the effort to choose words we hope will be effective in accomplishing supernatural purposes. Is that legitimate? Is there such a thing as spiritual Christian eloquence in preaching?

9

"Lest the Cross Be Emptied
of Its Power"

The Perils of Christian Eloquence

In part 4 I am focusing on the preacher's use of his natural powers in the effort to answer the question, How does preaching become a means of the miracle of worship? In the previous chapter, I argued that right thinking, clear logic, and the valid use of reason in preaching are essential to loving people well and humbly honoring the authority of Scripture. In this chapter, I move from the natural powers of thinking to the natural powers of writing and speaking. Should we use our natural powers in choosing words, with a view to making them as compelling as we can? Should we try to be eloquent?

"Not with Words of Eloquent Wisdom"

Should we even talk about *eloquence* in Christian preaching? The question is urgent first and foremost because the apostle Paul, writing under the inspiration of the Holy Spirit, says in 1 Corinthians 1:17, "Christ did not send me to baptize but to preach the gospel, and *not with words of eloquent wisdom*, lest the cross of Christ be emptied of its power." Christ sent Paul to preach, not with eloquence, lest the cross of Christ be gutted. That makes this an urgent issue.

Even if we cite other translations, the problem remains—the NIV ("not with wisdom and eloquence"), or the NASB ("not in cleverness of speech"), or the KJV ("not with wisdom of words"). There is a way to preach—a way of eloquence or cleverness or human wisdom—that nullifies the cross. We should dread nullifying the cross. We need to know what this eloquence-cleverness-wisdom of words is—and avoid it.

Consider a similar statement from Paul in 1 Corinthians 2:1: "I, when I came to you, brothers, did not come proclaiming to you the testimony of God *with lofty speech or wisdom.*" Or the NIV: "I did not come with *eloquence or human wisdom.*" Or the NASB: "I did not come with *superiority of speech or of wisdom.*" Or the KJV: "[I] came not with *excellency of speech* or of wisdom."

These passages are ominous for preachers. Most of us try to choose words and say them in a way that will have greatest impact. Should we? Should I choose words, or ways of putting words together, or ways of delivering them, with a view to increasing their life-giving, pride-humbling, God-exalting, Christ-magnifying, joy-intensifying, love-awakening, missions-mobilizing, justice-advancing impact? Am I usurping the role of the cross and the Spirit when I do that? Is Paul saying that the pursuit of impact on others through word selection, word arrangement, and word delivery preempts Christ's power and belittles the glory of the cross?

Is the Bible Eloquent?

Complicating the question is this: most Bible scholars throughout history have drawn attention to the fact that the Bible itself has many eloquent parts. For example, John Calvin said, "Let us pay attention to the style of Isaiah which is not only pure and elegant, but also is ornamented with high art—from which we may learn that eloquence may be of great service to faith."[1]

Similarly, the poet John Donne said, "The Holy Ghost in penning the Scriptures delights himself, not only with a propriety, but with a delicacy, and harmony, and melody of language; with height of Metaphors, and other figures, which may work greater impressions upon the Readers."[2] In other words, the Bible contains eloquent language, and some of its impact on readers is owing in some way to that eloquence.

---

1. Benjamin B. Warfield, "Calvin and the Bible," from *Selected Shorter Writings of Benjamin B. Warfield*, vol. 1, ed. John E. Meeter (Phillipsburg, NJ: Presbyterian & Reformed, 1970). Originally from *The Presbyterian*, June 30, 1909, pp. 7–8.

2. John Donne, *The Sermons of John Donne*, ed. George R. Potter and Evelyn M. Simpson (Berkeley, CA: University of California Press, 1953–1962), 6:55.

Spirit-Led Eloquence?

Consider what Martin Luther says on Galatians 4:6: "The Spirit makes intercession for us not with many words or long prayer, but only with a groaning . . . a little sound and a feeble groaning, as 'Ah, Father!' . . . Wherefore, this little word 'Father' . . . passes all the eloquence of Demosthenes, Cicero, and of the most eloquent rhetoricians that ever were in the world."[3] So, Luther says, the Holy Spirit himself leads us at times to a kind of eloquence—even in prayer.

If these observations of Calvin, Luther, and Donne are right, what did Paul mean when he said he renounced eloquence for the sake of the cross? Are Calvin and Luther and Donne missing something?

Eloquence of George Whitefield

Another way to feel the problem is to compare what was said about two giants of the First Great Awakening, George Whitefield and Jonathan Edwards. These two preachers were deeply unified theologically and significantly different in the way they preached.

In the spring of 1740, George Whitefield was in Philadelphia preaching outdoors to thousands of people. Benjamin Franklin attended most of these messages. Franklin, who did not believe what Whitefield was preaching, commented on these perfected sermons:

> His delivery . . . was so improved by frequent repetition, that every accent, every emphasis, every modulation of voice, was so perfectly well turned, and well placed, that *without being interested in the subject, one could not help being pleased with the discourse*: a pleasure of much the same kind with that received from an excellent piece of music.[4]

Here is preaching that is so eloquent you can like it without believing anything in it. That should make a preacher tremble. Whitefield's eloquence was pleasurable to Benjamin Franklin, who cared nothing for what Whitefield was trying to get across. Franklin loved Whitefield's eloquence and rejected his Savior. Was Whitefield emptying the cross of its power?

---

3. Martin Luther, *A Commentary on St. Paul's Epistle to the Galatians* (Westwood, NJ: Revell, 1953), 369–70.
4. Harry Stout, *The Divine Dramatist* (Grand Rapids, MI: Eerdmans, 1991), 104; emphasis added.

Eloquence in Our Day

But be careful. Some younger preachers may read this and think they are not bedeviled by this issue because they don't care about White-field's kind of eloquence. They have abandoned oratory the same way they abandoned coat and tie. Beware. It's not that simple. There is a kind of "eloquence" that consists not in traditional fluency of words but in the eloquence of hip and dress and slang and savvy and casual and the appearance of artlessness that can have the exact same mesmerizing effect in our day that Whitefield's eloquence had in his. People may love this contemporary, careless "eloquence" even if they care nothing for the truths the preacher is trying to get across. In other words, none of us escapes the urgency of this question. We all need an answer.

Eloquence of Jonathan Edwards

Jonathan Edwards, Whitefield's contemporary and friend, was very different. Edwards did not receive accolades for dramatic eloquence. But he did have another kind of eloquence. One eyewitness answered the question of whether Edwards was an eloquent preacher:

> If you mean, by eloquence, what is usually intended by it in our cities; he had no pretensions to it. He had no studied varieties of the voice. And no strong emphasis. He scarcely gestured, or even moved; and he made no attempt, by the elegance of his style, or the beauty of his pictures, to gratify the taste, and fascinate the imagi-nation. But, if you mean by eloquence, the power of presenting an important truth before an audience, with overwhelming weight of argument. And with such intenseness of feeling, that the whole soul of the speaker is thrown into every part of the conception and delivery; so that the solemn attention of the whole audience is riv-eted, from the beginning to the close, and impressions are left that cannot be effaced; Mr. Edwards was the most eloquent man I ever heard speak.[5]

In either case—Whitefield, the dramatic orator, or Edwards, the mo-tionless intense logician—the question remains: Were these forms of elo-quence an emptying of the cross of Christ? Were they following Paul's

---

5. Jonathan Edwards, *The Works of Jonathan Edwards*, 2 vols. (Edinburgh: Banner of Truth Trust, 1974), 1:*cxc*.

example when he said that he preached the gospel "not with words of eloquent wisdom, lest the cross of Christ be emptied of its power"?

Denney's Haunting Statement

James Denney (1856–1917), Scottish theologian and preacher, made a statement that haunts me as a preacher. Whether we are talking about the more highbrow eloquence of oratory or the more lowbrow, laidback, cool eloquence of anti-oratory, Denney's statement cuts through to the ultimate issue. He said, "No man can give the impression that he himself is clever and that Christ is mighty to save."[6] This has been one of the most influential sentences I have ever read regarding how to preach. Does this mean that any conscious craft or art in writing or speaking elevates self and obscures the truth that Christ is mighty to save?

Eloquence as an End in Itself?

In 2008, Denis Donoghue, professor of English and American letters at New York University, published *On Eloquence*. His contention is probably a modern expression of the kind of thing Paul was dealing with in Corinth. He argues that eloquence is a surprising, impacting style that is an end in itself. He says, for example:

> A speech or an essay may be eloquent, but if it is, the eloquence is incidental to its aim. Eloquence, as distinct from rhetoric, has no aim: it is a play of words or other expressive means. . . . The main attribute of eloquence is gratuitousness.[7]

> Eloquence does not serve a purpose or an end in action. . . . In rhetoric, one is trying to persuade someone to do something: in eloquence, one is discovering with delight the expressive resources of the means at hand.[8]

He agrees with E. M. Cioran that this notion of aimless eloquence began with the sophists, Paul's contemporaries, two thousand years ago:

> The sophists were the first to occupy themselves with a meditation upon words, their value, propriety, and function in the conduct of

---

6. Quoted in John Stott, *Between Two Worlds: The Art of Preaching in the Twentieth Century* (Grand Rapids, MI: Eerdmans, 1982), 325.
7. Denis Donoghue, *On Eloquence* (New Haven, CT: Yale University Press, 2008), 3.
8. Ibid., 148.

reasoning: the capital step toward *the discovery of style, conceived as a goal in itself, as an intrinsic end,* was taken [by the sophists].[9]

Eloquence, Donoghue says, is a style of speaking or writing that is intrinsically pleasing without any reference to other aims. It has no aim. It's gratuitous. That's what makes it eloquent. If it had an aim, it would be rhetoric and would stand in the service of some cause or ideology.

Donoghue says that the Bible—and Jesus in particular—put significant obstacles in the way of this view of eloquence, as aimless, gratuitous, pleasing language.[10] But one Christian reviewer, on the contrary, was effusive about how Donoghue's view shed light on the way God lavishes the world with superfluous, gratuitous eloquence:

> Is it really so hard to make the case for eloquence on Christian terms? What could be more eloquent, more blessedly superfluous, than Creation itself? All those beetles, those unseen creatures of the deep, those galaxies upon galaxies—all unnecessary. Shakespeare was unnecessary. My new grandson Gus is unnecessary.[11]

I don't think so. This is too cavalier about the purposefulness of God. Did God create this little boy Gus, and Shakespeare, and the galaxies, and the thousands of species of plants and animals we have yet to discover—whimsically or purposefully? If purposefully, they are not gratuitous. And they are not superfluous. Everything that is not God serves a purpose higher than itself.

Not Deep Enough

The problem with Donoghue and his reviewer is that they haven't gone deep enough into the implications for eloquence of the existence of a God who governs all things and does all things *purposefully*—indeed, with the purpose to magnify the glory of his Son. "All things were created through him and *for him*" (Col. 1:16). Galaxies and grandsons are not gratuitous or superfluous. They are created for the glory of Jesus Christ. Even the galaxies we have not yet seen will serve to magnify the greatness of Christ. From God's standpoint, nothing is superfluous.

---

9. Ibid., 136; emphasis added.
10. "The most forceful rejection of eloquence I am aware of is Christ's: 'Get thee behind me, Satan.'" Ibid., 143.
11. John Wilson, "Stranger in a Strange Land: On Eloquence," accessed September 29, 2008; www.christianitytoday.com/bc/2008/001/9.9.html.

What shall we make of all these varied witnesses to the goodness of eloquence in view of Paul's statement in 1 Corinthians 1:17, "Christ did not send me to baptize but to preach the gospel, and *not with words of eloquent wisdom*, lest the cross of Christ be emptied of its power"? What of 1 Corinthians 2:1, "I, when I came to you, brothers, did not come proclaiming to you the testimony of God *with lofty speech or wisdom*"?

Eloquence and the Sophists

An interesting link exists between Donoghue's reference to the sophists and the context of Paul's words to the Corinthians. Donoghue traces his view of eloquence back to the sophists. They were the first to treat style "as a goal in itself, as an intrinsic end." One of the most compelling books on the background of Paul's words about eloquence in 1 Corinthians is Bruce Winter's *Philo and Paul among the Sophists*. Winter's argument is that it is precisely the sophists and their view of eloquence that form the backdrop of what Paul says about his own speech and how he ministered in Corinth.[12]

Consider with me Paul's words in 1 Corinthians to see if he gives us enough clues to show what sort of eloquence he is rejecting and what sort he is not only not rejecting but using.[13]

Notice first in 1 Corinthians 1:10–12 that the Corinthian believers were forming divisions by lining up behind their favorite teachers, and the evidence is pretty good that the divisions had to do with the kind of eloquence the teachers had. It says in verse 12, "What I mean is that each one of you says, 'I follow Paul,' or 'I follow Apollos,' or 'I follow Cephas,' or 'I follow Christ.'"

We know from 2 Corinthians 10:10 that Paul's opponents mocked him as lacking eloquence. They said, "His letters are weighty and strong, but his bodily presence is weak, and *his speech of no account [ho logos exouthenēmenos]*." And we know that Apollos, one of the

---

12. "The wise, the well born, and the powerful epitomized the class from which the sophists came and which the latter helped perpetuate through an elitist educational system which emphasized the art of rhetoric. Given the great sin of the sophistic movement was it boasting . . . Paul made the Jeremiah prohibition against boasting about wisdom, status, and achievement a primary text in this critique of the Corinthian sophistic movement." Bruce Winter, *Philo and Paul among the Sophists: Alexandrian and Corinthian Responses to a Julio-Claudian Movement*, 2nd ed. (Grand Rapids, MI: Eerdmans, 2002), 253–54.

13. For example, 1 Cor. 1:25 is eloquent for its conscious shock value because it refers positively to "the foolishness of God" and "the weakness of God."

favorites at Corinth, *was* eloquent because Acts 18:24 says, "Now a Jew named Apollos, a native of Alexandria, came to Ephesus. He was an *eloquent* man, competent in the Scriptures." The fact that he is from Alexandria is significant. Philo worked in Alexandria and tells us how prominent the sophists were there in training people to be eloquent.[14]

Opposing the Sophists

We know from at least six sources that the sophists were present in Corinth as well.[15] They put a huge premium on style and form as evidence of education and power and wisdom. They likely had influenced some in the church to admire their kind of eloquence and look for it in Christian teachers. Apollos probably became their celebrity because he was so good with words. Bruce Winter says, "Paul deliberately adopts an anti-sophistic stance and thus defends his church-planting activities in Corinth against a backdrop of sophistic conventions, perceptions, and categories."[16]

The way Paul opposes the eloquence of the sophists is to show that it empties the cross. Why is that? Why does this view of eloquence empty the cross of power?

First Corinthians 1:18 gives part of the reason: "The word of the cross is folly to those who are perishing, but to us who are being saved it is the power of God." The reason the cross can't fit in with the eloquence of the sophists is that it is *folly* to them—that is, the cross is so destructive of human pride that those who aim at human praise through "rhetorically elaborated eloquence"[17] and "an elitist educational system"[18] could only see it as foolishness. The cross is the place our sin is seen as most horrible and God's free grace shines most brightly. Both of these mean we deserve nothing. Therefore, the cross undercuts pride and exalts Christ, not us, and that made it foolish to the sophists.

This is confirmed in verse 20: "Where is the one who is wise? Where is the scribe? Where is the debater of this age?"—the debater, the man

---

14. "There are . . . forty-two references to 'sophist' (*sophistes*) in Philo, apart from fifty-two references to cognates, and numerous comments on the sophistic movement." Winter, *Philo and Paul*, 7. "There can be no doubt . . . that sophists and their students were prominent in Corinth and played an important role in the life of the city." Ibid., 140.

15. Winter gives six sources for our knowledge of the sophist movement in Corinth. Winter, *Philo and Paul*, 7–9.

16. Ibid., 141.

17. Ibid., 144n16.

18. Ibid., 253.

who is so nimble with his tongue, he can take either side and win. He is smooth and clever and verbally agile. Truth and substance are not the issue; rhetorical maneuvering is. Paul says at the end of verse 20, "Has not God made foolish the wisdom of the world?" The wisdom in view is not any deep worldview over against Christianity; it's *the sophistry of using language to win debates* and show oneself clever and eloquent and powerful.

The eloquence Paul is rejecting is not so much any particular language conventions, but the exploitation of language to exalt self and belittle or ignore the crucified Lord. Notice the contrast again in 1 Corinthians 2:1–2: "I, when I came to you, brothers, did not come proclaiming to you the testimony of God with lofty speech or wisdom. For I decided to know nothing among you except Jesus Christ and him crucified." Paul's point is: "Whenever I meet scribes and debaters who bolster their ego with language jousting, and leave the cross in the shadows, I am going to bring it out of the shadows and showcase it fully. I will refuse to play their language games."

Two-Pronged Criterion

Notice one more detail in this context, which gives us the two-pronged criterion to distinguish good and bad eloquence. In 1 Corinthians 1:26–29, Paul turns the tables on the sophists' love affair with boasting.[19]

> Consider your calling, brothers: not many of you were wise according to worldly standards, not many were powerful, not many were of noble birth. But God chose what is foolish in the world to shame the wise; God chose what is weak in the world to shame the strong; God chose what is low and despised in the world, even things that are not, to bring to nothing things that are, so that no human being might boast in the presence of God.

First Prong: Self-Humiliation. God's design both in the cross and in election is "that no human being might boast in the presence of God." That is the first prong of our criterion to distinguish good and bad eloquence: *Does it feed boasting? Does it come from an ego in search of exaltation through clever speech?* If so, Paul rejects it. Then he continues in verses 30–31:

---

19. "The great sin of the sophistic movement was its boasting." Ibid.

And because of him you are in Christ Jesus, who became to us wisdom from God, righteousness and sanctification and redemption, so that, as it is written, "Let the one who boasts, boast in the Lord."

Second Prong: Christ-Exaltation. The second design of God, not only in the cross and in election, but also in the sovereign grace of regeneration (v. 30, "*Because of him* you are in Christ Jesus"), is that all boasting be boasting in the Lord Jesus—the one who was crucified and raised. "Let the one who boasts, boast in the Lord" (v. 31).

Therefore, the second prong of our criterion for distinguishing good and bad eloquence is: *Does it exalt Christ—especially the crucified Christ?*

Here is my understanding of Paul's two denunciations of eloquence. In 1 Corinthians 1:17, he says, ". . . *not with words of eloquent wisdom,* lest the cross of Christ be emptied of its power." And in 1 Corinthians 2:1–2, he says, ". . . [not] *with lofty speech or wisdom.* For I decided to know nothing among you except Jesus Christ and him crucified." The point of both is this: pride-sustaining, self-exalting use of words for a show of human wisdom is incompatible with finding your life and your glory in the cross of Christ. So let your use of words be governed by this double criteria: self-humiliation and Christ-exaltation.

If we put these two criteria in front of all our efforts to make an impact through word selection and word arrangement and word delivery—that is, if we put them in front of our attempts at *eloquence*—we will be guarded from the misuse of eloquence that Paul rejected. And now I see more clearly what was behind James Denney's dictum; precisely, these two criteria: "No man can give the impression that he himself is clever and that Christ is mighty to save."[20] Self-exaltation and Christ-exaltation can't go together.

The Bible Is Eloquent

When we go back to Calvin and Luther and John Donne—all of whom said that the Bible is filled with eloquence—I conclude they are right. *The Bible is filled with every manner of literary device to add impact to the language:* acrostic, alliteration, analogy, anthropomorphism, assonance, cadence, chiasm, consonance, dialogue, hyperbole, irony, meta-

---

20. Quoted in Stott, *Between Two Worlds,* 325.

phor, meter, onomatopoeia, paradox, parallelism, repetition, rhyme, satire, simile—they're all there, and more.

And it seems to me that God invites us to join him in this creativity of eloquence. He beckons us with words such as:

> To make an apt answer is a joy to a man,
> and a word in season, how good it is! (Prov. 15:23)

> A word fitly spoken is like apples of gold
> in a setting of silver. (Prov. 25:11)

> Like a lame man's legs, which hang useless,
> is a proverb in the mouth of fools. (Prov. 26:7)

> And whatever you do, in *word* or deed, do everything in the name of the Lord Jesus, giving thanks to God the Father through him. (Col. 3:17)

> Let your speech always be gracious, seasoned with salt, so that you may know how you ought to answer each person. (Col. 4:6)

In other words, give thought to the aptness and seasonableness and fitness and timing and appropriateness of your words. And make all of them honor the name of the Lord Jesus.

What Difference Does It Make?

I want to take up one last question. If we are permitted to pursue eloquence (powerful verbal impact)—indeed if we are invited to, and if the Bible is an abundantly eloquent book, and if we are guided in our pursuit of this impact by the double criteria of self-humiliation and Christ-exaltation—what would be our hope for our preaching if we succeed? Since only the Holy Spirit can perform the miracle of new birth and actually raise the spiritually dead, and since he can do it with mundane, pedestrian witnesses to the gospel or eloquent witnesses to the gospel, what difference does it make if we strive for any measure of eloquence or increased impact through language?

Five Hopes in Christian Eloquence

Here is a starter list of five hopes, which we apply knowing that anywhere along the way, God may step in and make our preaching instruments of salvation with or without eloquence. On any given Sunday, God may take the message we felt worst about and make it the means of a miracle. If so, why give any attention to maximizing the impact of our language?

1. Keep Interest

Artistic, surprising, provocative, or aesthetically pleasing language choices (that is, eloquence) may keep people awake and focused because they find it interesting or unusual or pleasing for reasons they cannot articulate. When the disciples fell asleep in Gethsemane, Jesus said, "The spirit indeed is willing, but the flesh is weak" (Matt. 26:41). We need to help people's weaknesses.

This is not conversion or even conviction or sanctification, but it is a serious means to those ends. Sleeping people or distracted people do not hear the word, and faith comes by hearing and hearing by the word. Therefore, eloquence is like a good night's sleep. It won't save your soul, but it might keep you awake to hear the word, which can save your soul. So a preacher's style may keep you interested and awake to the same end.

2. Gain Sympathy

Artistic, surprising, provocative, or aesthetically pleasing language may bring an adversarial mind into greater sympathy with the speaker. If the language is interesting and fresh enough, obstacles may be overcome—boredom, anger, resentment, suspicion—and replaced with respect and attraction and interest and concentration. These are not conversion, or conviction or sanctification, but they don't drive a person away like boredom does. In fact, they may draw a person so close to the light that Jesus says, "You are not far from the kingdom of God" (Mark 12:34).

For example, return to George Whitefield and Benjamin Franklin for a moment. Whitefield's eloquence overwhelmed Franklin. He did not think Whitefield was a sham. He admired him. He became one of Whitefield's closest friends. Whitefield biographer Harry Stout writes, "Franklin allowed himself to be drawn out on the subject of personal religiosity with Whitefield as with no one else, finding in Whitefield a listener he could trust—if not agree with."[21] Therefore, Whitefield could

---

21. Stout, *The Divine Dramatist*, 228.

speak to Franklin about Christ as no one else could. He defended his Christ-soaked correspondence to Franklin with a smile: "I must have something of Christ in all my letters."[22] Who knows how close Whitefield came to winning Franklin to the faith—and all this because Whitefield's eloquence and authenticity overcame, at least partly, Franklin's disdain for the revival.

C. S. Lewis once wrote a letter to a child who had asked for advice on how to write well.[23] Lewis's answer is so relevant for how preaching gains a sympathetic hearing that I am going to include his five suggestions here:

1. Always try to use the language so as to make quite clear what you mean and make sure your sentence couldn't mean anything else.

2. Always prefer the clean, direct word to the long, vague one. Don't *implement* promises, but *keep* them.

3. Never use abstract nouns when concrete ones will do. If you mean "More people died" don't say "Mortality rose."

4. In writing, don't use adjectives which merely tell us how you want us to feel about the things you are describing. I mean, instead of telling us the thing is "terrible," describe it so that we'll be terrified. Don't say it was "delightful"; make us say "delightful" when we've read the description. You see, all those words (horrifying, wonderful, hideous, exquisite) are only like saying to your readers "Please, will you do my job for me."

5. Don't use words too big for the subject. Don't say "infinitely" when you mean "very"; otherwise you'll have no word left when you want to talk about something *really* infinite.[24]

I think those pieces of advice for writing are exactly applicable to preaching.

3. Awaken Sensitivity

Fresh, surprising, provocative, aesthetically pleasing speech may have an awakening effect on a person's mind and heart that is short of

---

22. Ibid.
23. C. S. Lewis, *Letters to Children*, letter dated June 26, 1956, pars. 3–7, p. 64, quoted in Wayne Martindale and Jerry Root, *The Quotable Lewis* (Wheaton, IL: Tyndale, 1989), 623.
24. Ibid., 623–24.

regeneration but still important as an awakening of emotional and intellectual sensitivity for more serious and beautiful things. If a poetic turn of phrase can cause people to notice the magnificence of the sun, their next step might be to see that the heavens are telling the glory of God (Ps. 19:1), and then they might confess Christ as the great sun of righteousness (Mal. 4:2).

Is that not why David, the great poet of Israel, first says, "The heavens declare the glory of God" (Ps. 19:1), and then, more poetically, says, "In them he has set a tent for the sun, which comes out like a bridegroom leaving his chamber, and, like a strong man, runs its course with joy" (vv. 4–5)? Why compare the rising sun to a bridegroom and a runner? To help the dull mind awaken to the joyful beauty of the rising sun in the hopes that this natural kind of awakening might lead to the spiritual sight that nature is all about the glory of God.

4. Speak Memorably

Certain kinds of eloquence—cadence, parallelism, meter, rhyme, assonance, consonance—may not only interest and awaken the heart, but increase that impact by making what is said memorable, that is, easier to remember or memorize. In 2008 I delivered a version of this chapter to the Desiring God National Conference.[25] The name of the conference was "The Power of Words and the Wonder of God." I am very picky when it comes to cadence and consonance and assonance in titles. I worked on this title the same way I work on a poem. I wanted it to be pleasing and memorable. Notice a few things that I was conscious of:

- First is an intentional *cadence* or meter that I find pleasing. It's called iambic. The emphasis falls on every other syllable starting with the second: - / — / — / — /. TaDa tata Da tata Da tata Da. "The *Pow*er of *Words* and the *Won*der of *God*."

- Second is *consonance* or alliteration between the W's in *Words* and *Wonder*. Compare "The Power of Language and the Wonder of God" or "The Power of Words and the Majesty of God." To my ear, neither of these works. Both cadence and alliteration are lost.

---

25. That address was first published as "Is There Christian Eloquence? Clear Words and the Wonder of the Cross," in *The Power of Words and the Wonder of God*, ed. John Piper and Justin Taylor (Wheaton, IL: Crossway, 2009), 65–80. This chapter is an adapted version of that address.

- Third is *assonance*. Six of the nine words are dominated by the sound of the letter O: power, of, words, wonder, of, God. Contrast: "The Strength of Language and the Marvel of Deity." Great ideas. Weak language.

- Finally, I think the juxtaposition of "words" and "wonder" and "God" is unusual, provocative, and attractive.

All of that helps people remember the title, not because it is *dis*pleasing the way, say, the calamity of September 11, 2001, is memorable, but because it is aesthetically satisfying. The following year the conference title was, "With Calvin in the Theater of God"—iambic pentameter— so we can't add "John" to Calvin's name because that would wreck the meter. If you think this sort of thing is picky, I suggest you reconsider. It is not the most important thing in titling, or in preaching, but if you can choose between something arresting to the ear and something blah, why not arrest?

I presume that the mnemonic purpose of titling things so that they are pleasingly memorable is why some parts of the Bible are written in acrostics. For example, Psalm 119 is twenty-two stanzas of eight verses each, and each stanza begins with a different letter of the Hebrew alphabet, and all eight verses in each stanza begin with that letter. That is not careless, but intentional, artistic, eloquent.

5. Increase Power

The attempt to craft striking and beautiful language makes it possible that the beauty of eloquence can join with the beauty of truth and increase the power of your words. When we take care to create a beautiful way of speaking or writing about something beautiful, the eloquence— the beauty of the form—reflects and honors the beauty of the subject, and so honors the truth.

The *method* and the *matter* become one, and the totality of both becomes a witness to the truth and beauty of the message. If the glory of Christ is always ultimately our subject, and if he created all things, and upholds all things, then bringing the beauty of form into harmony with the beauty of truth is the fullest way to honor him in the crafting of our preaching.

Another way to think about this unity of truth and form is this: if a person sees and delights in the beauty of your language but does not yet see the beauty of the Lord Jesus, you have given the person not only a witness to Christ's beauty but an invitation. You have said, "It's like this, only better. The beauty of my words is the shadow. Christ, who created and sustains and mercifully accepts imperfect beauty, is the substance. Turn to him. Go to him." Of course, my assumption is that your prayerful, heartfelt aim is that your language will exalt not you but Christ. That motive matters to God. And people will discern what's behind your use of language.

Create Eloquence for His Name's Sake

Yes, Christian preaching may be eloquent. It is not the *decisive* factor in salvation or sanctification; God is. But faith comes by hearing, and hearing by the word. That word in the Bible is pervasively eloquent—words are put together in a way to give great impact. And God invites us to create our own eloquent phrases for *his* name's sake, not ours. And in the mystery of his sovereign grace, he will glorify himself in the hearts of others sometimes in spite of, and sometimes because of, the words we have chosen. In that way, he will keep us humble and get all the glory for himself.

Choose Compelling Words

The focus of part 4 has been on the use of the preacher's *natural powers* in the pursuit of the supernatural goal of preaching: authentic, heartfelt worship in all of life, forever. In chapter 8, I made the case that clear thinking, valid logic, the right use of reason, and the respectful, honest handling of words are utterly crucial for preaching faithfully and loving people. In the present chapter, I have argued that Paul's renunciation of "eloquent wisdom" in 1 Corinthians 1:17 does not rule out the preacher's use of his natural powers to choose words that he believes will compel attention and clarify truth and reflect the beauty (or sinful ugliness) of the reality in the text.

Putting parts 3 and 4 together, the picture we have is that the aims of preaching are supernatural. We labor and pray for the miracle in people's hearts that will wean them off the "fleeting pleasures" of sin and fill them with satisfaction in all that God is for them in Jesus. To that end, we seek to preach in the power of the Holy Spirit (part 3).

We must experience the miracle we hope for in our people. Preaching *pursues* worship and *is* worship. Paradoxically, we pursue the same supernatural goal of worship by using our natural powers of thinking and speaking—always in reliance on the Holy Spirit (part 4).

The question we turn to now in part 5 is, What does our reliance on the Holy Spirit and our use of thinking and speaking, actually look like in the act of preaching? The answer is that it looks like rigorous attention to the text of Scripture for the sake of radical penetration into reality. To that we now turn.

Rigorous Attention to the Text for the Sake of Radical Penetration into Reality

Making the Connection Manifest between Text and Reality

10

Text, Reality, and Sermon

Making the Connections Clear

The aim of part 5 is to make the case that preaching should give rigorous attention to the actual words of the biblical text for the sake of penetrating through those words to the reality the text aims to communicate. That rigorous attention should happen not only in the preparation to preach, but also in the preaching itself. The reason is so that the people can see the connections between text and reality. If they don't see this, the authority for believing the reality will shift away from the text. But, under God, only the text has divine authority. The effects of this shift are tragic for the life of the church and its mission in the world.

The Aim of Preaching Happens through the Words of Scripture

In this chapter, I will try to clarify this connection between text and reality and show why it is crucial that preachers help their people see that connection. To orient this chapter and the next in the wider scope of this book, recall that the ultimate goal of preaching is the same as the ultimate goal of Scripture: *that God's infinite worth and beauty would be exalted in the everlasting, white-hot worship of the blood-bought bride of Christ from every people, language, tribe, and nation.*[1] I am referring to *worship* not only as what one does in worship services, but also as every act of life in this age, and the age to come, that expresses

---

1. This was unfolded and supported in John Piper, *Reading the Bible Supernaturally: Seeing and Savoring the Glory of God in Scripture* (Wheaton, IL: Crossway, 2017), part 1.

the worth and beauty of God as our supreme treasure. Or we can say that the ultimate goal of preaching is that the hearers will see and savor the beauty and worth of God *through Scripture*, and show it in all of life forever.

In that last sentence, I emphasized the phrase "through Scripture"— "the hearers will see and savor the beauty and worth of God *through Scripture*." This is a momentous phrase. I have already tried to make the case that when Paul said to Timothy, "Preach the *word*" (2 Tim. 4:2), the term "word" referred to nothing less than all of Scripture, including both Old and New Testaments.[2] He had just said in 2 Timothy 3:16, "*All Scripture* is breathed out by God and profitable . . ." This, in general, is what he is referring to when he says in the next sentence (4:2), "Preach *the word*."

In pursuing the life-transforming worship of its hearers, preaching aims to be true to Scripture. Preaching and Scripture have the same goal. What the Scriptures aim to do, preaching aims to do. What the Scriptures aim to reveal, preaching aims to reveal. The assumption is that Scripture is inspired by God and therefore aims to communicate what human beings need, in order for God's purposes through Scripture to be realized. Preaching that brings out from Scripture what is really there joins God in bringing about his ultimate purposes.

Therefore preaching is expository. In chapter 3, I cited John Stott's extended definition of exposition: "To expound Scripture is to bring out of the text what is there and expose it to view." In other words, the content of preaching is "what is there." But what is really there? And where? Is it grammatical structures? Is it ideas in the author's head? Is it historical events? Is it God? Is it glory? Is it human affections? And is it *in* the text, *behind* the text, *through* the text?

Since "bringing out of the text what is there" is ambiguous, I clarified further what I mean by exposition. I argued that the content of preaching, in its essence, is not the biblical text (which, nevertheless, remains indispensable in all its details), but *the reality that the text is communicating*. For many preachers who take the text of Scripture seriously, this needs to be stressed. Otherwise, the preacher may think he has done exposition when he has only explained grammatical and contextual structures and patterns. The preacher may find so much

---

2. See chap. 3.

fascination with the logical and grammatical structures in the immediate context, and may be so captivated by canonical macrostructures of "biblical theology,"[3] that he thinks he has done his exposition when he has pointed these things out. And he may confuse his own aesthetic and intellectual and theological excitement, at spotting these things, with the spiritual *exultation* over the divine reality all of this is aimed to communicate.

Therefore, I am stressing *the reality factor* in the task of exposition. When Stott says the content of the sermon is "biblical truth," I want to make sure that the word "truth" refers not just to grammatical and historical propositions, or linguistic or thematic structures, but to *the reality* which is being referred to. So, if the text is, "God is love," the sermon "brings out and exposes to view" the *reality* of "God," the *reality* of "love," and the *reality* of the relationship between God and love expressed by the word *is*.

Essence of Preaching: Unveiling Reality

Suppose the preacher sees in his text—say, 2 Corinthians 6:16—that Paul calls the church "the temple of the living God," and that God promises, "I will make my dwelling among them and walk among them, and I will be their God, and they shall be my people." Suppose he points out to the people that this is part of an ancient stream of revelation beginning in the garden of Eden and ending with a similar promise of God's presence in the new heavens and the new earth. Suppose he uses ten or fifteen minutes of his message to point out four or five examples of this stream elsewhere in the Bible. My point is this: beware of thinking that all these observations about the overarching structures and patterns, along with a large dose of excitement at seeing such things, is the essence of preaching. It is not.

The essence is the reality factor. What reality are these texts and these structures and these patterns communicating? What is the nature of the reality? What is the value of the reality? What implications does

---

3. Lovers of biblical theology may feel picked on here. Don't. Your discipline is no more or less vulnerable to this problem than any micro or macro method of finding and describing meaning in Scripture—including any methods I might use. What I am emphasizing is that any *word* or *idea* such as *love* or *kingdom* or *covenant* or *temple* or *glory* or *God* may produce intellectual exhilaration in the micro discoveries of how they fit in clauses, or in the macro discoveries of how they fit in the patterns of biblical theology, and yet this exhilaration may not be a spiritual apprehension of the reality of love or kingdom or covenant or temple or glory or God.

the reality have for the lives of this congregation? Let the excitement deepen. Let excitement penetrate through the structures and the thrill of discovery to the reality itself. Or himself.

It requires no spiritual life to be excited about the discovery of grammatical relationships and linguistic structures and canonical patterns. This pleasure is real and good. But it may not be Spirit given, Christ exalting, or God centered. We share this pleasure with the fallen world. But only Spirit-given eyes of the heart (Eph. 1:18) can see and be thrilled at the God-centered, Christ-exalting reality communicated through the texts. Preachers do not aim to draw people into their excitement with the shape of literary windows, but with the reality seen *through* the windows. We aim to draw our people's minds and hearts to the world of glory, through the window of the Scriptures. The aim of preaching is that people experience the God-drenched reality perceived through the window of biblical words. Beware of making textual structures (whether microgrammatical structures or macrocanonical structures) the climax of preaching. Always keep before you the summons of *the reality factor*.

Rigorous Attention to Words, Radically Penetrating into Reality

What I am going to try to clarify and plead for in this chapter is that exposition includes both *rigorous attention* to the very words of the biblical text and a *radical penetration* into the reality the text aims to communicate. The text provides the path for discovering the reality, so we are not free to dream up our own reality and then highjack the text to give it authority. If we can't show the reality through the words of the text, we have no biblical authority for the reality.

This means that when Paul says, "Preach the word" (2 Tim. 4:2), he means, "Preach the word *for the sake of the reality it aims to communicate.*" I intentionally use the word *communicate* rather than *understand*. The word *understand*, for most people, would limit the aim of preaching to grasping the author's *ideas*. But when I call for a *radical penetration into the reality* that the text aims to communicate, I mean vastly more than understanding ideas. I mean perceiving the reality that gave rise to the ideas. And I mean the emotions awakened by the reality that the author wants us not only to understand but also to experience.

When the apostle Paul says, "Rejoice in the Lord" (Phil. 3:1), his intention is both that we *understand* his words, and that we *experience* joy. Therefore, to preach this text *for the sake of the reality it aims to communicate* means that preaching aims to embody and awaken joy through the exposition of these words. The reality factor presses the preacher on to his final aim—that God be glorified in his hearers' experience of what the biblical authors are aiming at—in this case, joy in the Lord.

Rigorous Attention to the Text for the Sake of Reality

My assumption in this chapter (which I defended and explained in *Reading the Bible Supernaturally*, chapter 20) is that the reality the biblical authors aim to communicate does not lurk in hidden places separate from the words and sentences of the biblical text. It is perceived in and through the right handling of those words and sentences. When we pray for God to show us his glory in the Scripture ("Open my eyes, that I may behold wondrous things out of your law," Ps. 119:18), we are not asking him to bypass the very words of the text. The psalmist prays, "Let me behold the wonders *'out of your law'* [*mittōwrātekā*]."

Similarly, when 1 Samuel 3:21 tells us, "The Lord revealed *himself* to Samuel at Shiloh *by the word of the* Lord," we take seriously the phrase "by the word of the Lord." The reality revealed is the Lord himself. Preaching will aim for people to perceive and reverence that reality—the Lord himself. But the Lord reveals himself "by the word of the Lord." Therefore, the preacher pays attention to the word—the very words of Scripture.

The preacher is not a psychic, or a medium, or a diviner. He does not conjure up divine reality for people to see apart from the words of Scripture. His work is "rightly handling the word of truth" (2 Tim. 2:15). The link between divine reality and the hearts of his hearers is the wording of Scripture and how he handles it—in the power of the Holy Spirit.

Therefore, in our quest to penetrate radically into the reality that the biblical authors aim to communicate, we don't just pray for the miracle of supernatural light; we also pray for God's help in construing the words of the text. The reality we are meant to perceive and experience does not hover over the text like a cloud to be divined somehow separately from what the authors wrote. The pathway to it is the right handling of the very words of the text. This is true of the preacher's private discovery in study, and it is true of his public explanation in preaching. The preacher unveils reality for his people by pointing to the very words of Scripture and helping the people see how those words fit together to reveal that reality.

One of My Greatest Burdens for Preaching

This is one of my greatest burdens for preaching today—that preachers point their hearers to the very words of God in Scripture. So many preachers endeavor to talk about biblical realities without making plain to the people the precise words through which they see the realities and how the words actually work together to make this reality clear. Notice, I am not at this point lamenting the failure to get the content of preaching from texts. That is an even more serious problem. But I am talking about the preachers who do, in fact, work hard to find the content of their preaching in and through the text of Scripture, but then in preaching do not help the people see the connection between the reality they are heralding and the very wording of the text.

I see myself as part of a long tradition of preaching that emphasizes not only that the reality we preach should come from the biblical text, but that it should be plain to the hearers that it does. We should show the hearers how we saw what we saw through the text. The Dutch theologian Peter Van Mastricht (1630–1706) was Jonathan Edwards's "favorite theologian," according to Douglas Sweeney. Van Mastricht wrote an essay on preaching as an appendix to a book that "Edwards cherished more than any but the Bible"—namely, Van Mastricht's masterpiece, *Theoretico-practica Theologia*.

In the essay Van Mastricht writes that when making any point from Scripture, two things must be observed.

> 1. That it should certainly be in the text, or be brought forth from it by invincible consequence, so that the preacher does not say just any word of God, but precisely the particular word that is in his text. 2. *That this also should be evident to his hearer, and the rationale of the deduction or consequence should be so plainly rendered that the hearers might not doubt what the doctrine is in the text.*[4]

---

4. Quoted from Douglas Sweeney, *Edwards the Exegete: Biblical Interpretation and Anglo-Protestant Culture on the Edge of the Enlightenment* (New York: Oxford University Press, 2016), 193–94; emphasis added.

I used to think the failure to do this was mainly owing to a desire not to sound pedantic or simplistic. Perhaps some preachers think that to tell people to look with them at the very words and phrases of the text as they make their points is academic or doctrinaire.

> NOTE: A quick parenthetical note of clarification that is too important to be in the footnotes: I am aware that millions of Christians around the world do not have Bibles in their laps or on their smartphones as they sit in worship. Some don't have them because they are too poor, some because they cannot read, some because there is no Bible translation in their language, some because they have been taught that you should just listen and not follow along in your Bible. I am not assuming that we can do serious exposition, as I am proposing, only where people have Bibles in front of them. I am pressing home a principle: show the people, *to whatever degree is possible*, that your claim to proclaim reality from God's word is, in fact, warranted by what the Bible actually says. This will be done differently in different settings, depending on the forms in which the Scriptures are available. But it needs to be done because the authority of our message lies in God's word, not in ourselves.

Now back to the point: Some preachers seem to think that to tell people to look with them at the very words and phrases of the text smacks of school and lectures that have boring connotations and so don't hold the attention or stir affections, let alone assist worship.

Besides that, we have all heard the term *proof-texting* used pejoratively. The proof-texting putdown is intended to suggest that the preacher is naive in his use of Scripture and does not pay close attention to the larger context. The criticism sometimes comes with the assumption that the Bible really can't be used as precisely as specific Scripture citation implies, but can be used only as a collection of thematic pointers to general insights. Behind some of this hesitancy to be explicit and specific about the basis of our insights in the very wording of Scripture is a loss of confidence in the Bible itself. Or a loss of confidence that the Bible really can be understood with authority and accuracy.

Two Unintentional Problems

I say I *used* to think the problem was mainly a desire not to sound pedantic or simplistic. But I have come to see that this is not the only, or perhaps even the main, problem among Bible-believing preachers. That explanation implies too much self-conscious effort to *avoid* referring to the text. But I have come to see that the preachers I have in mind are, by and large, not making conscious efforts to avoid referring to the wording of the text throughout their sermon. Rather, doing so simply does not come naturally, and they are not driven to do it by a strong conviction that it really matters. They are happy to make their points and hope their hearers see that the points come from the text, even though the preachers don't give the people the help they need.

This is a double problem. One has to do with *pedagogical gifting*. The other has to do with *conviction* about the importance of people seeing for themselves where and how the preacher found his insight into this biblical reality.

By "pedagogical gifting," I mean the intuitive ability to discern how people in the congregation follow your reasoning, and how they see in the Scripture what you see. This is at least part of what Paul was talking about when he said that the ministers of God's word in the congregation need to be skillful in teaching (*didaktikon*, 1 Tim. 3:2; 2 Tim. 2:24), and when he said that the word should be entrusted to those who are "sufficient" or "competent" or "able" to teach others (*hikanoi esontai kai heterous didaxai*, 2 Tim. 2:2). This "gift of teaching," which forms a significant part of what preaching is, includes the ability to discern how people grasp what you say, and whether they are with you, and what you can do to help them see what you see.

Not all preachers are equally gifted in this way. My plea here is that all of us pray for a greater gifting in our ability to help people see what we see through biblical texts. Many preachers assume people are following them when, in fact, the people are quite muddled in what they are hearing. The preacher proclaims an insight that he found in the text, and he assumes the people hear the insight and see where it comes from in the text. Perhaps he assumes this because the text was read at the beginning of the message ten or fifteen or thirty minutes earlier. But I can assure those preachers that the people do not remember the text well enough to know how you are getting your insights from it.

Sometimes the preacher will even mention what biblical verse his insight comes from, but the reference is so vague or so brief, and the pace of his preaching is such that it simply doesn't work for the listener to both look at the verse and keep on following the preacher as he moves on. The listener gets lost in trying to locate the wording of the text that supports the point, while the preacher is moving on to unpack the implications of his point.

What preachers should pray for is the pedagogical gift to sense when this is happening. Or better, to understand why it happens, and then, before it happens, help the listeners by referring more specifically and more precisely to the very words that make the insight clear and compelling. And if you think this implies a ponderous, lecture-like approach to preaching, I assure you, it doesn't have to. The tone of the preaching that points people to the word *therefore* at the beginning of a verse can be as lively and passionate as any emotion accompanying vague generalizations that never cite the text.

Turning to Illustrate

Whether it is owing to weakness in pedagogical gifting or to conviction that it doesn't really matter, there is a widespread disconnect between the points the preachers are making and the people's grasp of those points seen in the very words of Scripture. In the hopes of helping to close this disconnect, I will try in the next chapter to illustrate the kind of preaching I have in mind. I will give three examples of focusing on the words of Scripture for the sake of reality—and helping people see the connection.

11

Showing How Reality Shines through the Words of the Passage

Three Examples

In the previous chapter, I argued that the preacher should give rigorous attention to the actual words of Scripture, not for their own sake, but for the sake of penetrating through them to the reality which those words are intended to communicate. The words are an indispensable means to the spiritual sight of the glory of the reality. But the reality is the goal. I argued that the aim of preaching is to show this connection between text and reality. The key word was *show*. The people must see how the text communicates the reality. Otherwise, the opinion of the preacher replaces the authority of the text. The authority of preaching lies in the manifest correspondence between sermon and Scripture. Again, the key word is *manifest*.

In this chapter, I want to illustrate the kind of preaching I have in mind. My aim is to help overcome the disconnect between the point a preacher makes and the wording of the text as the people see it. What follows are three examples of focusing on the words of Scripture for the sake of reality—and helping people see the connection.

Example 1: Matthew 7:7–12

Ask, and it will be given to you; seek, and you will find; knock, and it will be opened to you. For everyone who asks receives, and the one who seeks finds, and to the one who knocks it will be opened. Or which one of you, if his son asks him for bread, will give him a stone? Or if he asks for a fish, will give him a serpent? If you then, who are evil, know how to give good gifts to your children, how much more will your Father who is in heaven give good things to those who ask him! So whatever you wish that others would do to you, do also to them, for this is the Law and the Prophets.

Suppose you were preaching through the Sermon on the Mount, and you were tremendously excited about something you saw in preparing to preach on Matthew 7:7–12. And suppose your heart filled up with joy over God's promise to answer our prayers like a good Father in verses 7–11 and the discovery that this joyful confidence is precisely what gives us the freedom and power to obey the incredibly difficult command in verse 12 ("Whatever you wish that others would do to you, do also to them"). And suppose you lingered over this truth for five or ten minutes, giving biblical examples and personal applications of how the promise of God's fatherly care in answering prayer helps us treat others the way we would like to be treated.

To this I would say, wonderful! Do that. But the entire thesis is hanging in the air—that is, the thesis that Jesus *really did say* that God's promise to answer prayer is the ground and power for obedience to the Golden Rule. You have not shown the people the *very word* that makes this crystal clear and gives it authority and power in their lives. You have stated the truth. You saw it in your preparation. It is really in the text. But you have not helped your people see what you saw *in the text*. This is a serious problem, because the people are left groping for some reason to believe what you say other than that you have said it. Do you want them to believe you because of *your* authority? Or because they see it in *Scripture*?

Show Them What's Really There

I am pleading that the preacher help the people see the beauty of this truth from the very wording of Matthew 7:12—the truth that God's promise to care for us through answered prayer is the *basis* of our ability to keep the Golden Rule. Verse 12 begins with *therefore* or *so*. "How much more will your Father who is in heaven give good things to those who ask him! *So* [=therefore] whatever you wish that others would do to you, do also to them."

This is what the people must see! They must. All the authority for your insight, all the warrant for your excitement, hangs on this. You are not making this up. Jesus actually said it! It is amazing. It is glorious! Jesus said, "*Because* your Father gives you what you need in answer to prayer, *therefore* . . . love others the way you want to be loved. Love others, no matter the cost, *because* your heavenly Father is far more committed to giving you what you need than any human father is committed to his child." This glorious and astonishing reality is in the word *therefore* at the beginning of verse 12! Show it to them! Make sure they see it for themselves.

When I say people need to see it, I mean they need for you to show it to them. They need more than a reading of the text at the beginning of the sermon. They need more than your saying that you saw this truth in the word *therefore*. Even that is not enough, because while you are going on talking about its implications, they are now (I hope) trying to see it for themselves. But they are getting lost and muddled as they try to see it while you are moving on. What they need is for you to *show* them the very word that supports your insight and your joy.

Take Them to the Text and Show Them

Take them to the verse and point to the word *so*. Ask them if they are seeing it. Ask them if they know what *so* means. Illustrate how *so* works in ordinary speech. ("My father bought me a fishing pole and taught me to fish when I was seven years old, *so* I've been an avid fisherman all my life.") Pray for the pedagogical gift to intuit whether what is so plain to you is or isn't plain to your people. They need wise, patient help to see and be amazed at what amazed you. And it *is* amazing. Show it to them. *Show* it to them. This is *exposition*. And you can do it with *exultation* over this magnificent reality of God's care and our love. It will not be boring! God's people love to see these things.

So (=therefore!) I am pleading that you not only say things that are in the text, and that you not only say *that* they are in the text, but rather that you *show* the people that they are in the text, and *how* they are in the text. And I am suggesting that you pray for an increased gifting in pedagogical intuitions about how your people listen and think.

Example 2: Romans 5:20–6:1

Our second example of how crucial it is to show the people your point from the very words and structures of the text is more complex. It is a great challenge to the preacher that some of the most glorious realities are revealed through some of the most complex texts. This is surely true in parts of the book of Romans. Let's consider, for example, Romans 5:20–6:1:

> Now the law came in to increase the trespass, but where sin increased, grace abounded all the more, so that, as sin reigned in death, grace also might reign through righteousness leading to eternal life through Jesus Christ our Lord. What shall we say then? Are we to continue in sin that grace may abound?

Suppose that you have come to the point in your message on this text where you are eager to make clear what Paul means by grace reigning "*through righteousness* leading to eternal life." You have already pointed out the *kingly* power of grace (implied in the word *reign*), more powerful than the king of death. You have shown that this king of grace will successfully bring us to eternal life.

Now you pose the question for your people, What did Paul mean by "through righteousness"? You urge them to think hard about this, because the inspired apostle gave us this phrase because he wants us to know *how* grace reigns to bring us to eternal life. It is not enough to know *that* grace will triumphantly bring us to eternal life. Paul wants us to know *how*. That's why he says it happens "through righteousness." Knowing this will be good for us. Good for our marriages. Good for our singleness. Good for our attitudes at work. Good for our dealing with sickness. Good for our children. Good for our endurance in faith to the end of life. God does not throw away words. He wants us to see *how* grace reigns to bring us to eternal life.

What Does "Righteousness" Mean?

At this point, you suggest to your congregation two possible meanings for "righteousness." One is the righteousness that Christ accomplished in his obedience and death—the "gift of righteousness" mentioned in Romans 5:17, the righteousness of Christ that is imputed to us through faith. And you clarify how different this is from righteousness that we perform by our good deeds.

But then you point out that some interpreters see the righteousness here in verse 21 as precisely the righteousness that *we* perform. Not legalism. Not self-righteousness. But the fruit of the Holy Spirit. You explain that this is not a straw man. Paul refers elsewhere to Christians being "filled with the fruit of *righteousness* that comes through Jesus Christ, to the glory and praise of God" (Phil. 1:11). You point out that those who see it this way agree that it is a "*gift of righteousness*"—not the righteousness of Christ *counted* as ours, but the righteousness which Christ *works in us* by the Spirit. But his free gift in any case.

Then you step back and clarify, as sharply and helpfully as you can, the two choices:

1. Grace reigns to bring us to eternal life. How? "Through righteousness." Meaning: *grace counts the righteousness of Christ as ours* and so keeps us in God's favor for Christ's sake till we are perfect in eternal life.

2. Grace reigns to bring us to eternal life. How? "Through righteousness." Meaning: *grace produces in us right attitudes and right behaviors* and so secures for us and in us the "holiness without which no one will see the Lord" (Heb. 12:14), and so brings us safely to eternal life.

Now what do you do at this point? Many preachers default to doctrinal standards—a confession of the church, or some Protestant tradition, or some respected theologian, or even some other biblical text to settle the question. They may try to set this up as a conflict between right and wrong doctrine, or between orthodoxy and heresy. But that will not work, since *both* these understandings of how salvation happens are true. Grace does count the righteousness of Christ as ours. And grace does produce in us right behavior. And both are necessary for eternal life, even if not in the same way. But only one of these interpretations is what Paul intends in *this* text. That's what matters here.

Don't Pull Rank—Do the Hard Thing, Show Them

You dare not pull rank here. You dare not tell your people, "Here's my view," and then proceed as if it were true just because you say so. No. You must *show* the people which is true—which of these interpretations is intended by Paul. So you say, "Let's look at the next verse to see if it sheds any light on the issue."

You point out the objection that someone raises to verse 21. Someone says, "Okay, if grace brings us to eternal life through righteousness, let's all sin that grace may abound!" Paul refers to this objection in Romans 6:1, "What shall we say then? Are we to continue in sin that grace may abound?" (Pause. Check. Did they just see verse 1? Do they see the objection it implies?)

Then you ask this question: "When the objector raises his protest ('If grace brings us to eternal life through righteousness, let's all sin that grace may abound!'), what meaning of *righteousness* is he assuming in order for his objection to make sense?" You admit to your people that this is complicated, and ask them to hang in there with you and think Paul's thoughts after him. Here is where the gift of teaching (which preachers are supposed to have, 1 Tim. 3:2; 2 Tim. 2:2, 24) becomes so crucial. How can you help the people follow your reasoning from the text? You must find a way. You will work very hard on this in your preparation.

You decide to say, "Let's try inserting each of the two meanings for righteousness into the objection to see which one makes it plausible." For surely Paul would not raise an objection that is a mere straw man with no plausibility and that no one ever really raised. So here they are. Which of these objections was the objector really raising?

1. "If grace brings us to eternal life through [*the imputed*] righteousness [*of Christ's obedience, not ours*], let's all sin that grace may abound!"

2. "If grace brings us to eternal life through [*producing in us our own real*] righteousness, let's all sin that grace may abound!"

You pause again. You ask them, "Does the second meaning make sense?" You answer: "No, it simply makes no sense." It amounts to this: if grace works in us to make us righteous and keep us back from sin, then let's all sin. That makes no sense. Let's sin because Paul just showed that grace keeps us from sinning? In other words, the objection behind Romans 6:1 would simply never have occurred to anyone if they thought the righteousness of verse 21 was a Spirit-given triumph over sin. No one would say: "If grace is keeping us from sinning, let's all sin that grace may abound." But if grace means counting *Christ's* righteousness as ours, then someone might indeed object, "Okay, let's all sin that grace may abound."

Then Take All That Reasoning and Show That It Matters

So you conclude (deep breath, are they still with you?), therefore, that we can be sure that what Paul meant in Romans 5:21 was that grace is reigning *through Christ's imputed righteousness* to bring us to eternal life. This is the meaning that makes sense out of the flow of his thought from verse 5:21 to 6:1. And then you spend the rest of the message digging into the *reality* of this imputed righteousness, and the *reality* of grace, and the *reality* of how Christ's righteousness relates to the power of grace, and the *reality* of eternal life, and the *real aspects* of our lives that are profoundly affected by these stupendous *realities*.

My point here is not to persuade you about any particular view of justification. My point is that preaching *gives rigorous attention to the very words and clauses of the text* as a means of penetrating into the reality the text is communicating. The preacher has only one definitive access point to the realities that matter infinitely—Christ, grace, righteousness, eternal life—and that is the inspired words of God in Scripture. This is the access our people have as well. The preacher does not take the place of Scripture. The preacher helps the people see the reality the Scripture aims to communicate. The preacher's job is to help his congregation see and savor the beauty and worth of these realities *through Scripture*.

I realize that this kind of preaching will be so utterly different from what many churches are accustomed to that the preacher will need great patience, and great wisdom, and pedagogical gifting to hold as many listeners as he can. But if his heart is full of joy over the practical and eternal value of what he has seen, and what he is showing, then those who know the Master's voice (John 10:4) will soar with him that at last "the voice" is sounding with clarity and power in the pulpit.

Example 3: Job 1–2

Suppose it has been several months since the nation just passed through a great earthquake followed by a terrorist attack. Hundreds of people died from the collapse of buildings during the earthquake and from the subsequent terrorist bombing. The weeks of grieving have given way to serious biblical and theological questioning. During that time you, the preacher, have modeled for your people what it means to lament and to grieve with those who grieve (Rom. 12:15). But now your church needs a word from their pastor on God's role in such disasters.

You choose for your text the first two chapters of Job. You have studied Job for years. You have preached on it before. You know where it goes. But you spend hours pondering and listening for a fresh word from the text. You know from past experience that one of the most common ways of evading what this book teaches is to say that Job's confidence in God's sovereignty through suffering is misguided. In other words, some say Job's affirmations of God's sovereignty in these tragedies is not the truth that the inspired author intends for us to believe—any more than the bad theology of Job's three friends is to be believed. Job is simply mistaken, they say. Don't join him in saying, "The Lord has taken away."

In your preaching, you may acknowledge with heartfelt, pastoral concern that some of the people find Job's experience, and what the book teaches, to be painful, perhaps even offensive. You express patience with that response because you know how you struggled with the sovereignty of God in your twenties. But you will remind your people that over the years many in this congregation (I am speaking out of my own experience here) have found the goodness and sovereignty of God to be the very rock they have needed, when tragedy came, to keep them from drowning in a sea of meaninglessness.

Job's Astonishing Trust and Worship

You devote the first part of the exposition to reconstructing the situation of chapters 1 and 2. God. Satan. The loss of Job's property and children. You read significant portions of each chapter as you lay out what happened. Then you draw their attention to Job's two responses to the waves of tragedy that broke over him. You make sure that as many of your people as have Bibles look with you at the very words you are about to focus on. For those who don't have Bibles, you tell them to listen very carefully, because you are going to cite Job's very words.

You point them one last time to the very place (Job 1:20–22). Then you read, in response to the death of his children:

> Job arose and tore his robe and shaved his head and fell on the ground and *worshiped*. And he said, "Naked I came from my moth-

er's womb, and naked shall I return. The LORD gave, and *the LORD has taken away; blessed be the name of the LORD.*" In all this Job did not sin or charge God with wrong.

Then you go back and ask them to look carefully at the very words. You say, "Notice the end of verse 20." You pause to let their eyes find it. You do not assume they remember what you just read—a mistake many pastors make. You show them again: "At the end of verse 20, it says that Job did what? He worshiped."

Then in the second part of verse 21 (I think the terms "first part" and "second part" of the verse is better than saying "verse 21a" or "verse 21b," which sounds too academic), we read the actual content of Job's worshiping soul (you pause to make sure they are with you in the second part of verse 21): "The LORD gave, and the LORD has taken away; blessed be the name of the LORD." Then you restate the obvious because it is so counterintuitive. You say, "In other words, 'God took my ten children.'" Then you expand that: "Job ascribed to God the ultimate control of the wind that collapsed the house and brought the death of his children. Then, instead of expressing anger toward the Lord, Job says [at the very end of verse 21, pause], 'Blessed be the name of the LORD.'"

You might say more at that point. But a significant pause may be in order. Likely, many of your people are wondering, at that moment, what losses in their lives this might apply to. Then you might say, "Before we apply this to our lives, let's finish listening to Job by going to Job 2:9–10." As the people are turning there, you remind them that Job has now been afflicted with horrible boils. This is the second wave of misery Satan has negotiated. In fact, you say to them, "Before we read Job's words in verse 10, let's notice that, whatever the role of Satan was in the death of Job's children, the text makes it explicit that Satan was indeed a cause of these loathsome boils. Verse 7 [pause, let them see it]: 'So Satan went out from the presence of the LORD and struck Job with loathsome sores from the sole of his foot to the crown of his head.' So we know that these boils are from Satan."

Second Wave of Sorrow

Now, you say, "Look at verse 9 [pause]. Job's wife says, 'Do you still hold fast your integrity? Curse God and die.' Job's calamities include not only the loss of property, the loss of children, and the loss of health, but also the loss of his wife's support. What will he say? Here's what he says. Notice verse 10 [pause]: 'You speak as one of the foolish women would speak. Shall we receive good from God, and shall we not receive evil?'"

Then you say, "Notice two things. First, Job says that his wife's suggestion that he curse God is the way a *foolish* woman speaks. It may seem reasonable. But cursing God because of our miseries is *foolish*." Then, second, you say, "Notice that the reason it is foolish to curse God is not that God has no hand in the miseries. Why then is it foolish to be angry at God? Job answers by asking a rhetorical question—a question without an answer, that he assumes we will answer in a certain way. He asks, 'Shall we receive good from God, and shall we not receive evil?' He assumes that we will answer: 'Yes, we shall receive evil (which means in this context, at least, *misery* and *trouble*) at the hand of the Lord.'"

What Does the Author Intend for Us to Believe?

Then you step back and ask: "Does the author of this inspired book want us to believe that Job is teaching us a right and godly way to respond to our sufferings? Or does the author want us to see Job's responses as wrongheaded, or even sinful?"

I want to stress here how tremendously important it is in preaching that you model good question asking and question answering. You can be sure that your people are quietly asking all the hard questions you asked as you studied your text. People can become greatly discouraged over time if a pastor does not answer the questions that they inevitably have as they are reading the sermon text. On the other hand, people love it when the pastor sees the questions they have, and asks those same questions, and shows the people how to answer them from the text. What tragedy when a people learn from the preacher's example that hard questions are not allowed in church.

People find it deeply satisfying when a pastor asks and answers their questions with good reasoning from the very words of the text. And they should. God gave them minds. Their minds think by asking and trying to answer questions. That is largely what thinking is. Unless they have been lulled into mental sleep by hundreds of sermons that don't ask and answer questions raised by the text, your people are brimming with questions as the text is read. Our job is to discern the most important questions that need to be answered and to show the people, by our exposition, how to answer them *from the text.*

You now say to your people that you believe Job is expressing a godly response to suffering, and you tell the people you are going to show them two reasons from the text of Job why you believe this. Believe me, people want to see what your reasons are.

Two Reasons from the Text That Job's Response Is Godly

First, you rivet their attention on Job 1:22 and read, "In all this Job did not sin or charge God with wrong." In other words, when Job said, "The LORD has taken [my children] away" (in v. 21), he was not attributing anything "wrong" to God. You point out that these are *not* the words of Job. These are the words of the inspired writer of this book who is answering our very question: Should we see Job's words as a godly response to suffering? Yes, he says, we should.

Then you do the same thing with Job 2:10. You ask the people to look at the end of verse 10. You say, "Job had just said, 'Shall we not receive evil at the hand of the Lord?'" (Pause.) Then you read, "In all this Job did not sin with his lips." The inspired writer wants us to understand that it is not sin to believe, and to say, that all things are from the hand of God, both good and evil, that is, both pleasant and painful. Both delight and disaster.

Then you say, "I'll mention one more place in Job that makes clear how the inspired writer sees the sufferings of Job." You ask your people to turn to Job 42:11. You give them time. Many of them remember that Job's fortunes take a wonderful turn for good and that God restores his wealth and health and gives him more children. But they may have missed one small comment from the writer. So you read verse 11: "Then came to him all his brothers and sisters and all who had known him before, and ate bread with him in his house. And they showed him sympathy and comforted him for *all the evil that the LORD had brought upon him.*"

This is not Job talking. This is the inspired writer. You rivet their attention on the last part of verse 11. You say the words slowly: *"All the evil that the LORD had brought upon him."* You pause. This is so clear that there is no need for any rough language or angry put-downs of those who deny this. You let the text do its work.

From Text to Reality

Then you step back and sum up your answer to the larger question. "Does this book teach us that God is in decisive control of the suffering of our lives and the things that cause it? Yes, it does. Even if Satan is real and has a hand in our misery—which he is and does—he is not in decisive control. God is. And he is wise and good. And we should say with Job, in the face of all loss and suffering, 'Blessed be the name of the LORD.'"

Then you take the rest of the message to deal with this reality. You will not leave it at the level of ideas that were taught in an ancient book. You will press through all this rigorous attention to the text. You will press through until you penetrate into the *reality* of suffering and divine sovereignty—the reality in this church and this nation. You will use examples and illustrations to bring this all home to the lives and families and hearts of your people. Some will hear and leave your church. Others will hear and weep for joy that nothing in their lives is random or meaningless or without a purpose in God's sovereign, fatherly plan.

You will not speak of the sovereignty of God as though it were a mere theological idea or textual inference. Your whole demeanor will be one of personal, painful, joyful exultation in the goodness, wisdom, and absolute sovereignty of God. You will not make light of the pain of your people—or of the nation. Instead you will glory in the fact that the goodness and grace and sovereignty of God are the only hope for help and meaning when all of life is caving in.

> His oath, His covenant, His blood
> Support me in the whelming flood;
> *When all around my soul gives way,*
> *He then is all my hope and stay.*[1]

Preaching I Am Pleading Against

The point of these three examples of preaching has been to show how and why preaching should not only find the reality communicated through the text, but should also show the people that it is really

---

1. William Bradbury, "My Hope Is Built: The Solid Rock," 1836, http://cyberhymnal.org/htm /m/y/myhopeis.htm.

there by helping them see it through the wording of the text. Exposition involves *rigorous attention* to the very words of the biblical text as a means of *radically penetrating* into the reality the text aims to communicate.

I am pleading against a widespread kind of preaching that is Bible based but not Bible saturated. I am pleading against the reading of a text followed by preaching that makes its points—sometimes very good points actually found in the text—without showing people the very words and phrases from which the points are taken. I am pleading against preaching that fails to help people see *how* the text actually takes us to the reality that is all important.

Why Preach Like This?

What are the underlying reasons for this conviction that a preacher should show the people from the very words of the text how they can see for themselves the realty he is heralding? I will discuss only two.

1. Manifest Correspondence of Sermon and Scripture

First, the authority of preaching lies in the manifest correspondence between what the preacher is trying to communicate with his words and what the biblical authors are trying to communicate through the inspired words of Scripture. The key word here is *manifest*. The correspondence between the points of the sermon and the meaning of the words of Scripture should *show*.

A preacher who does not care if his people believe what he says about the greatest matters in the world is a charlatan. He is playing language games in one of the most sacred places in the world. I assume most preachers who believe that the Bible is the word of God are not charlatans. That is, they take very seriously the calling to say things that people should believe. They want to be believed. They expect their people to believe what they say.

My First Sermon at Bethlehem

The basis for this astonishing expectation is the divine inspiration and complete truthfulness of Scripture.[2] The Christian preacher aims to

---

2. I explained how we can know the Bible is completely true, in John Piper, *A Peculiar Glory: How the Christian Scriptures Reveal Their Complete Truthfulness* (Wheaton, IL: Crossway, 2016).

speak the word of God. He wants to be believed because he is saying what God wants said. In the first sermon I preached as pastor at Bethlehem Baptist Church, at age thirty-four, I said,

> The source of my authority in this pulpit is not . . . my wisdom; nor is it a private revelation granted to me beyond the revelation of Scripture. My words have authority only insofar as they are the repetition, unfolding, and proper application of the words of Scripture. I have authority only when I stand under authority. . . . My deep conviction about preaching is that a pastor must show the people that what he is saying was already said or implied in the Bible. If it cannot be shown, it has no special authority.
>
> My heart aches for the pastor who increases his own burden by trying to come up with ideas to preach to his people. As for me, I have nothing of abiding worth to say to you. But God does. And of that word, I hope and pray that I never tire of speaking. The life of the church depends on it.

Tell Us What God Has to Say

I quoted W. A. Criswell (1909–2002), who pastored First Baptist Dallas for forty years. I said then, and I believe today, that his words are an admonition to pastors that I think is right on the money, and I take it as a great challenge:

> When a man goes to church, he often hears a preacher in the pulpit rehash everything that he has read in the editorials, the newspapers, and the magazines. On the TV commentaries, he hears that same stuff over again, yawns, and goes out and plays golf on Sunday. When a man comes to church, actually what he is saying to you is this, "Preacher, I know what the TV commentator has to say; I hear him every day. I know what the editorial writer has to say; I read it every day. I know what the magazines have to say; I read them every week. Preacher, what I want to know is, does God have anything to say? If God has anything to say, tell us what it is."[3]

This means that if the preaching is to claim authority to be believed, it needs to correspond to what the Scripture teaches. But here's the catch.

---

3. W. A. Criswell, *Why I Preach That the Bible Is Literally True*, Library of Baptist Classics (Nashville, TN: B&H, 1995).

The desire of the Christian preacher is not that the resting place of the people's confidence shift from the Scripture to the preacher. He wants them to believe what he says. He wants to have authority in that sense. But he wants the authority to remain in the Scripture itself, not in him and his words.

This implies, therefore, that the message must not only correspond to the meaning of Scripture but also *show* that it does. The authority of preaching lies in the *manifest* correspondence between what the preacher is trying to communicate with his words and what the biblical authors are trying to communicate through the inspired words of Scripture. If this were not so, then on what basis would the people believe that the meaning of the sermon is the same as the meaning of the Bible? They may discover on their own that it is, without any help from the preacher. But why would the preacher want to make it hard for the people to see the correspondence?

Why Don't More Preachers Show Meaning from Scripture?

It seems to me that a failure to *show* the people that the meaning of the sermon is there in the wording of Scripture is probably owing to incompetence, laziness, or presumption. *Presumption* that his words have enough authority on their own. *Laziness* because it is hard work not only to see what the text means but also to construct compelling explanations that show that the biblical text actually has this meaning. *Incompetence* because the preacher simply lacks the ability to show how the meaning of the message actually corresponds to the meaning of Scripture. These are traits that a preacher should not have.

Tragic Effects on the Church over Time

The tragedy that happens over time in a church where the preacher does not give rigorous attention to the words of Scripture to help the people penetrate into the reality it communicates is that the word of God ceases to exercise its power, and the people lose their interest in the Scriptures. When this happens, everything in the church shifts away from a joyful orientation on the Scriptures. The people cease to be a Bible-guided people. Without the saturation of Scripture, they become increasingly vulnerable to the winds of false teaching, and more subtly, the conditioning of unbelieving society. Their expectations become worldly, and they pressure the leadership of the church to make more and more concessions to what pleases unspiritual people. The preacher may wonder what the problem is, but he does not have to look far. He has not valued the word of God highly enough to make its glorious realities the content of his message while showing the people from the very words of the text how they can see these realities for themselves—and be thrilled.

That is the first reason for the conviction that the preacher should show his people from the very words of the text how they can see for themselves the realty he is heralding. It maintains the authority of Scripture as the manifest foundation for all that is preached.

2. Scripture Is God's Word for Wakening Faith

The second reason that a preacher should show the people from the very words of the text how they can see for themselves the realty he is heralding is that preaching aims to awaken and strengthen faith in Christ, which the Scriptures themselves are designed to do with greater effectiveness than any message of man that mutes their words and meaning.

The essence of saving faith is seeing the supreme beauty of Christ in the gospel and embracing him as Savior, and Lord, and the greatest treasure in the universe. I say this because, among other reasons, it is implied in 2 Corinthians 4:4: "The god of this world has blinded the minds of the unbelievers, to keep them from seeing the light of the gospel of the glory of Christ, who is the image of God." There is a spiritual *light* that shines through the gospel, and it is the light of *the glory of Christ*. Satan keeps unbelievers from seeing this. That is why they can't believe. This is the light and the glory of Christ that a person must see in order to believe and be saved. It is seen with the eyes of the heart (Eph. 1:18), when the Holy Spirit lifts the veil from our minds (2 Cor. 3:16).

The utterly decisive question preachers must answer is this: How will I preach so as to become an instrument of this miracle? How will I preach so as to awaken faith through a sight of the glory of Christ? My answer is that God has given the church a divinely inspired book, which is *the consummation of God's demonstration of the beauty and worth of Christ*. It is God's own complete portrait of the glory of his Son—the meaning of his work from eternity to eternity, and its implications for human life. This divine portrait of Christ is the God-ordained means of creating saving faith. The words of God are the best means of displaying the glory of God.

Therefore, preaching that we hope God will use to create saving faith will not assume that there is a more compelling portrait of the glory of Christ that a preacher can create while sidelining or muting the portrait of Scripture in the words of Scripture. Instead, the aim of the preacher will be to rivet people's attention on the words of Scripture and through them to reveal the reality of the glory of all that God is for us in Jesus. Scripture is the divine word where the glory shines. Our aim is to focus people's attention on that word in such a way that they see for themselves the glory. And believe.

Show the Connection between Text and Reality

I have been arguing in part 5 that the aim of preaching is to show the connection between text and reality. The key word has been *show*. Our aim is that the people see for themselves how the text communicates the reality. Otherwise, the inspired text ceases to clarify and verify the reality. People then are left to look elsewhere for solid foundations for their faith. Preaching aims to help people rivet such rigorous attention on the wording of the text that *through the text* they can see the reality the author aims to communicate.

The question this raises for us now is: What is that reality? Is it enough to say, "Preach the reality that the biblical author is trying to communicate"? Part 6 explains why this is not enough.

What Reality Shall We Preach?

Three Pervasive Emphases of All Expository Exultation

12

Preaching in the Light of an Author's All-Encompassing Vision of Reality

The aim of part 5 was to make the case that preaching should aim to penetrate *through the text* into the reality it aims to communicate, and help the congregation, by our exposition, to experience as much of that reality as the inspired author intends. I argued that penetrating *through the text* means that we aim to reveal this reality by a rigorous attention to the very wording of the biblical text. That is, we aim not only that what we proclaim be based on the wording of biblical texts, but also that our people see it for themselves. Preaching presses through texts into the reality being communicated and brings the congregation along, showing them how to get there. Now the point of part 6 is to answer, What reality?

Insufficient Answer

It is not sufficient to answer: the reality we preach is the reality that the biblical author is trying to communicate through the text. The reason this is insufficient is not that it is untrue. It is, in fact, wonderfully true. Gloriously true. Indeed, I pray that every preacher would make this his goal: by means of a rigorous attention to the wording of text, to explain and exult over the reality that the biblical authors are trying to communicate through what they write. The insufficiency of this answer is not that it is false. It is insufficient because it is too general and leaves unaddressed some critical questions that the preacher must answer about the scope of this reality and how to proclaim it.

Seeing the Text in the Light of His Larger Vision of Reality

In order to know what reality a biblical author intends to communicate, we have to know not only the immediate intentions he makes clear in the text, but also the all-encompassing vision of reality that governs the way the author thinks about everything. I am going to argue that handling the reality of most biblical texts in a way that the author would approve of requires that we know more of the author's view of life than is explicit in the specific sermon text. The only reason I say this is true of "most biblical texts" instead of "every biblical text" is that a preacher might choose to preach from a text that is so large (say, a whole book of the Bible) that everything we need to know about the author's vision of reality is in that text. But most of the time, that will not be the case. Most of the time, the author will expect us to handle his immediate communication in light of other crucial things he believes that are not explicit in this particular text.

We all write and speak this way. In fact, it's impossible not to. You can't make explicit in every sentence everything that is relevant for a full understanding of that sentence. Neither can the writers of Scripture. When we have a conversation, or write an email, there are the explicit sentences, *and* there are other things we take for granted that our friend knows about us. If I write to my son and say, "Live for the greatest thing!" I will assume he knows I mean, "Live for the glory of God." But I didn't say it. If he is going to know that part of my intention, he must know it from outside the immediate text. I am, in fact, assuming he will know it. And when he reads it that way, he will have correctly understood my intention *in the text*.

So it is with most of the biblical texts preachers use in their sermons. There are the immediate, prominent, explicit parts of the writer's intention, and there are the larger, unspoken parts that we must learn from other things the author has said, or from other reliable writers who share his view of reality. These "other things" may be revealed by the author a few sentences distant from our text, or a few chapters distant, or in other books that the author has written. Or, since we believe in the essential unity of the Scriptures,[1] we may learn necessary implications, or implicit dimensions of an author's meaning, from other authors of Scripture.[2]

---

1. For my foundation for believing this, as implied in the divine inspiration of Scripture, see John Piper, *A Peculiar Glory: How the Christian Scriptures Reveal Their Complete Truthfulness* (Wheaton, IL: Crossway, 2016).

2. For my discussion of "necessary implications" of an author's intention as part of an author's meaning, see John Piper, *Reading the Bible Supernaturally: Seeing and Savoring the Glory of God*

My Favorite Dessert

To illustrate that last point about learning from other authors, suppose you wrote to me and asked what dessert I would like for my birthday, and I wrote back, "I'd like my favorite." Suppose you then called my wife to ask what my favorite dessert is. If on my birthday you served me a Butterfinger Blizzard, I would say that you had correctly interpreted *my text*, even though the text said nothing about a Butterfinger Blizzard. In other words, there are aspects of an author's intention that are sometimes not explicitly included in the very words you are reading, but which you need to know in order to interpret him correctly, and which you may learn from other parts of Scripture, especially other things the same author has written.

Preaching on Hospitality

Suppose you are preaching your way through Romans and come to the command, "Seek to show hospitality" (Rom. 12:13). You believe that the church would benefit from a message on the practice of Christian hospitality, not only because you sense a deficiency in the people (and maybe yourself), and a growing insularity in society, but also because you see that Jesus puts a huge premium on taking in strangers (Matt. 25:35), and Hebrews tells the church to do it (Heb. 13:2), and Peter tells the church to do it (1 Pet. 4:9), and elders are supposed to be especially given to it (1 Tim. 3:2; Titus 1:8).

The immediate context of Romans 12:13 does not offer explicit explanations of hospitality. The command is part of a list:

> Let love be genuine. Abhor what is evil; hold fast to what is good. Love one another with brotherly affection. Outdo one another in showing honor. Do not be slothful in zeal, be fervent in spirit, serve the Lord. Rejoice in hope, be patient in tribulation, be constant in prayer. Contribute to the needs of the saints and *seek to show hospitality*. Bless those who persecute you; bless and do not curse them. (Rom. 12:9–14)

What are we to do? My point in this chapter is that we may not handle the reality of hospitality in a way that Paul approves if we do not take into account his larger, all-encompassing vision of reality. What

in Scripture (Wheaton, IL: Crossway, 2017), 318–19. The relevant section is titled, "Can an Author Mean More Than He Is Conscious Of?"

would that larger, all-encompassing vision include for the apostle Paul? What has Paul said that may shape the way you preach on the Christian duty of hospitality?

Hospitality's Larger Context

Here are some examples of what Paul has said that will shape how you preach on hospitality—how you help your people obey the command to be hospitable.

1. Practice hospitality *because God did not spare his Son.*

> He who did not spare his own Son but gave him up for us all, how will he not also with him graciously give us all things? (Rom. 8:32)

2. Practice hospitality *by the grace of God.*

> By the grace of God I am what I am, and his grace toward me was not in vain. On the contrary, I worked harder than any of them, though it was not I, but the grace of God that is with me. (1 Cor. 15:10)

3. Practice hospitality *as Christ has welcomed you.*

> Welcome one another as Christ has welcomed you, for the glory of God. (Rom. 15:7)

4. Practice hospitality *as dead to sin and alive to God in Christ.*

> Consider yourselves dead to sin and alive to God in Christ Jesus. (Rom. 6:11)

5. Practice hospitality *by looking to the glory of Jesus.*

> We all, with unveiled face, beholding the glory of the Lord, are being transformed into the same image from one degree of glory to another. For this comes from the Lord who is the Spirit. (2 Cor. 3:18)

6. Practice hospitality *as a new creation in Christ.*

> If anyone is in Christ, he is a new creation. (2 Cor. 5:17)

7. Practice hospitality *by the Spirit.*

> Walk by the Spirit. (Gal. 5:16)

8. Practice hospitality *with thanksgiving.*

> Give thanks in all circumstances; for this is the will of God in Christ Jesus for you. (1 Thess. 5:18)

9. Practice hospitality *prayerfully.*

> Pray without ceasing. (1 Thess. 5:17)

10. Practice hospitality *by faith.*

> We walk by faith, not by sight. (2 Cor. 5:7)
>
> The life I now live in the flesh I live by faith in the Son of God, who loved me and gave himself for me. (Gal. 2:20)

11. Practice hospitality *without anxiety.*

> Do not be anxious about anything, but in everything by prayer and supplication with thanksgiving let your requests be made known to God. (Phil. 4:6)

12. Practice hospitality *joyfully.*

> Rejoice in the Lord always; again I will say, rejoice. (Phil. 4:4; see also 1 Thess. 5:16)

13. Practice hospitality *without grumbling.*

> Do all things without grumbling or disputing. (Phil. 2:14)

14. Practice hospitality *as an act of love.*

> Let all that you do be done in love. (1 Cor. 16:14)

15. Practice hospitality *as an act of spiritual worship.*

> I appeal to you therefore, brothers, by the mercies of God, to present your bodies as a living sacrifice, holy and acceptable to God, which is your spiritual worship. (Rom. 12:1)

16. Practice hospitality *as beloved children of God imitating your heavenly Father.*

> Be imitators of God, as beloved children. (Eph. 5:1)

17. Practice hospitality *in the name of the Lord Jesus.*

> Whatever you do, in word or deed, do everything in the name of the
> Lord Jesus. (Col. 3:17)

18. Practice hospitality *to the glory of God.*

> Whether you eat or drink, or whatever you do, do all to the glory
> of God. (1 Cor. 10:31)

The preacher is regularly dealing with more than one context—the
distant ones that form his view of Paul's larger view of reality and
the nearer one here in Romans 12:13 that constitutes the immediate
preaching text. The preacher must be attentive to both contexts when
he brings something that Paul said in *another* place and applies it to *this
particular* sermon text. It is possible to misuse one passage in applying
it to another. But what I did in choosing the eighteen passages above is
to look for statements that were comprehensive enough to *necessarily
include* the practice of hospitality.

"All" Includes Hospitality

There is nothing arbitrary about saying that Paul *intends* for us to
practice hospitality on the basis of God's sacrifice of his Son, if God
graciously gives us "*all* things" on the basis of this sacrifice (Rom. 8:32).
There is nothing arbitrary about saying Paul *intends* for us to practice
hospitality with thanks, if he tells us to give thanks in *every* circum-
stance (1 Thess. 5:18); or to practice hospitality with prayer, if he tells
us to pray *without ceasing* (1 Thess. 5:17); or to do it with faith if *all
of life* is to be lived by faith (Gal. 2:20); or to do it without grumbling
or anxiety, if he tells us to do *all things* without grumbling (Phil. 2:14)
and without anxiety (Phil. 4:6); or to do it with love and joy, if he tells
us to do *all things* in love (1 Cor. 16:14) and joy (Phil. 4:4); or to do it
in the name of Jesus and for the glory of God, if he tells us to *do all* in
the name of Jesus (Col. 3:17) and to *do everything* for the glory of God
(1 Cor. 10:31).

Paul's All-Encompassing, Sermon-Shaping Vision of Reality

What all these texts (and hundreds of others) do is inform us about
Paul's all-encompassing vision of reality and how to live in the light of

this reality. Paul believes in God. He believes in sin and the necessity of God's sacrifice of his Son so that guilty people can be dealt with graciously (Rom. 8:32). He believes that the grace of God gives both pardon for sin and power to be godly (1 Cor. 15:10). He believes that Christ welcomes us before we are worthy (Rom. 15:7), and that in union with him we die to sin (Rom. 6:11). He believes that, as new creatures alive from the dead (2 Cor. 5:17), we now are being transformed by looking to the glory of Christ as our supreme treasure (2 Cor. 3:18).

Paul believes that this change, and all the good we do as Christians, is a work of the Holy Spirit (Gal. 5:16), and that, when we call out to God (1 Thess. 5:17) with thankfulness (1 Thess. 5:18) and faith (2 Cor. 5:7), the Spirit stills our anxiety (Phil. 4:6), fills us with joy (Phil. 4:4), overcomes our bent to grumbling (Phil. 2:14), and frees us for humble acts of love (1 Cor. 16:14)—like hospitality. Paul believes that these acts of love, done by faith and in the power of the Spirit, are genuine acts of worship (Rom. 12:1) that reflect the character of our heavenly Father (Eph. 5:1), adorn the name of Jesus (Col. 3:17), and glorify God (1 Cor. 10:31).

So we ask again: When the preacher makes it his goal to proclaim the *reality* that the biblical author is trying to communicate through the text (as I think he should), what reality does the preacher have in mind? With regard to Romans 12:13 ("Seek to show hospitality"), what is the preacher going to proclaim? It will probably include the nature and the ground and the goal and means of this hospitality. But all of that—anything that is truly Christian and truly significant about hospitality—the preacher will say on the basis of Paul's larger vision of reality. And he will learn this from careful attention to the immediate context, and, in this case, especially to the more or less distant contexts of Paul's writings.

Paul Wants Us to See the Very Words in Light of the Larger Vision
Owen Barfield, a friend of C. S. Lewis, once said of Lewis, "Somehow what Lewis thought about everything was secretly present in what he said about anything."[3] The more a person's thoughts are true and comprehensive, the more accurate that statement is about the person. The

---

3. Owen Barfield, "Preface," in *The Taste of the Pineapple,* ed. Bruce L. Edwards (Bowling Green, OH: Popular Press, 1988), 2.

biblical writings are the authors' God-breathed expressions of their true thoughts. How much more, then, shall such a statement be made of them: "What they thought about everything was secretly present in what they said about everything"? This really matters for preaching. Knowing an author's larger vision of reality will guide the preacher in handling particular texts in ways that are not contrary to the author's intention.

I am assuming that Paul would be displeased if we pulled his command, "Seek to show hospitality," out of the context of his overarching view of reality and made it serve a vision contrary to his own. He would not be pleased if we made it part of a secular "morals and manners campaign," or if we made it part of an ecumenical crusade to show how Hindus, Muslims, and Christians all really live the same way because they all practice hospitality; or if we made it serve a legalistic cult that taught us to earn our salvation by good deeds. In other words, I am suggesting that Paul *intends* for us to see all of his particular exhortations and observations in the light of his all-encompassing vision of reality.

Without the Larger Vision, We Will Distort the Text

So it is not enough to say (as true as this is) that the goal of preaching from Romans 12:13 ("seek to show hospitality") is to proclaim *the reality that the biblical author is trying to communicate through the text.* The scope of the reality informing this particular command is vast. What Paul wants us to take into account in obeying and proclaiming the command to be hospitable is greater than the mere practical performance of opening our home to others. In fact, the meticulous performance of that practice could deeply contradict Paul's intention. Not to do it from faith, not to do it by the Spirit, not to do it in the name of Jesus, not to do it for the glory of God—all these would, in Paul's mind, be a failure to see and savor and show the realities that matter most. It would not be faithful to his intention.

Two Mistakes to Avoid

How, then, do we answer the question, What reality are we supposed to preach when we have a limited and specific text in front of us? Before we press further into the answer, let me preempt two mistakes that are commonly made in preaching on a text such as, "Seek to show hospitality."

The first mistake is: Just do it!

The second mistake is: You can't do it, but Christ did it perfectly, so turn away from your doing to his doing, and enjoy justification by imputed righteousness.

1. Moralistic Preaching

The first mistake ("Just do it!") minimizes the larger, all-encompassing vision of Paul for *how* and *why* to do it. It deals with hospitality in limited, moralistic terms without reference to any of its deep *roots* in grace and Christ and faith, and without reference to any of its high *branches* in the glory of God. "Just do it" might seem helpful to some preachers because they think hospitality might provide enhancements for how to get along in the world, or it might earn some points with God, or it might make the church friendlier so more people will come, or it might inculcate some character traits of graciousness and generosity, or bring some unexpected rewards if you happen to welcome a wealthy person to your table. This is not faithful preaching. It ignores Paul's larger vision of reality: grace, Christ, Spirit, faith, joy, and the glory of God.

2. Reductionistic Doctrinal Preaching

The second mistake ("You can't do it; but Christ did it perfectly, so turn away from your doing to his doing, and enjoy justification by imputed righteousness") minimizes the seriousness of the command, diverts attention from the real necessity of the imperative, leads to a kind of preaching that oversimplifies the urgency and complexity of Christian obedience, and turns every sermon into a predictable soteriological crescendo that trains the people to tune out and start putting their coats on. It silences the specific riches of the text by preempting them with unwarranted applications of right doctrine.

Both Mistakes Silence the Text

Both mistakes have their own way of silencing what Paul intends to communicate. The first mistake mutes the reality of the text by a vacuous moralism. The second mistake mutes the reality by making every text lie in the procrustean bed of misused orthodoxy. To be sure, justification by faith alone on the basis of the imputed righteousness of Christ alone is a glorious and precious truth. But Paul does not use it in a way that diminishes the urgency of practical obedience.

Paul does not embrace an artificial law-gospel overlay that treats every imperative as a way of showing human impotence to be remedied only by minimizing obedience and maximizing divine imputation. As Paul writes to the churches, he treats his imperatives as real obligations to be obeyed *because* we are justified, and *because* we are loved by God, and *because* we have the Holy Spirit, and *because* grace is a transforming power, not just a pardon, and *because* justifying faith works by love. So the doctrine of justification is relevant—infinitely relevant!—but not in a way that minimizes the immediate and real concern with practical Christian hospitality.

Theological Concerns

My concern with these two kinds of preaching errors is both theological and homiletical. The theological concerns are the most serious. But the homiletical can be tragic. Theologically, both errors jeopardize salvation. The moralistic error ("Just do it!") does not lead to salvation, because moral behavior replaces the gospel of Christ crucified and risen for sinners. And it leaves untapped the only power that would make moral behavior acceptable to God, namely, the power of the Holy Spirit appropriated by faith in the blood-bought promises of God.

The second error ("You can't do it. But Christ did it perfectly, so turn away from your doing to his doing, and enjoy justification by imputed righteousness") jeopardizes salvation by giving people the impression that faith without works is *alive*—that it really can save (against James 2:17). It emphasizes Christ's obedience as a *replacement* for ours, rather than showing that it is an *empowerment* of ours. It thus tends toward the error of Romans 6:1, "Are we to continue in sin that grace may abound?" It leaves people utterly at a loss to grasp that there is a real, practical "holiness without which no one will see the Lord" (Heb. 12:14; also Gal. 5:21; 1 Cor. 6:9). This way of preaching, I fear, will be cursed on the judgment day by those who hear the Lord Jesus say, "Not everyone who says to me, 'Lord, Lord,' will enter the kingdom of heaven. . . . I never knew you; depart from me, you workers of lawlessness" (Matt. 7:21, 23).

Homiletical Concerns

My homiletical concerns are that the first kind of preaching ("Just do it!") trains people not to see what is really in the Bible. It reduces the Bible to a handbook of good morals and manners endorsed by God. It marginalizes the gospel. As a result, such preachers do not lift burdens but, as Jesus said, "tie up heavy burdens, hard to bear, and lay them on people's shoulders, but they themselves are not willing to move them with their finger" (Matt. 23:4). Therefore, their preaching leads to despair or pride. A bit of moral success leads to pride. A bit of moral failure leads to despair. Grace is not there as a ground. The glory of God is not there as a goal. Preaching shrivels up to become a pep talk for positive thinking. Therefore, preaching ceases to be expository *exultation*. It is no longer part of worship.

My homiletical concerns about the second way of preaching ("You can't do it, but Christ did it perfectly, so turn away from your doing to his doing, and enjoy justification by imputed righteousness") are that it simply does not take seriously the very words of the text, and therefore teaches the congregation bad habits about how to read the Bible. It is controlled by a theological scheme that, instead of illuminating the riches that are resident in the text, short-circuits the discovery of those riches. There are some kinds of overarching theological convictions that cloud the specifics of a text, and there are some that impel us deeper into the specifics (I will deal with these in chapters 13–18). Finally, this kind of preaching has the lamentable effect of dulling a congregation's hope of discovery, because instead of finding fresh specifics in the text, a monotonous "discovery" of the doctrine of justification by faith apart from works is made again and again. The tragic result is that one of the most glorious truths in the world becomes commonplace in the name of preaching Christ.

How Shall the Preacher Choose from the Vastness of an Author's Vision?

The question we are trying to answer in this chapter is, What reality are preachers supposed to proclaim as we do our exposition of the text at hand? We said that it does not suffice to answer, "Proclaim the reality that the biblical author is trying to communicate through the text." The reason this doesn't suffice is not that it is untrue, but that it is too general. It doesn't make clear that almost every sermon text demands that we know something of the author's larger, all-encompassing vision of reality in order to handle the limited revelation of reality in the text. Once we concede that, we are left wondering, *What aspects of that larger vision should I include in my sermon?*

The scope of the biblical author's larger vision is so vast, and so multifaceted, that the preacher cannot proclaim it all in one sermon but must make choices. In the example I gave above about preaching on Romans 12:13 ("Seek to show hospitality"), I cited eighteen aspects of Paul's all-encompassing vision of reality that shape the way he wants people to be hospitable. There are many more than eighteen. How is a preacher to decide what aspects of Paul's vision of reality should shape this particular sermon on hospitality?

Three Illuminating Questions

I am going to commend three approaches to answering that question. Or to put it another way, I'm going to suggest three questions that shed light on how the preacher decides what aspects of the author's intention he will proclaim. (1) What is the ultimate goal of the biblical author in the sermon text? (2) How does the sermon text relate to Jesus Christ and his saving work? (3) What is the way of life that leads to final salvation rather than destruction?

These three questions correspond to the three persons of the Trinity, because the answer to the first one will focus mainly on the glory of God the Father, the answer to the second on the saving work of God the Son, and the answer to the third on the empowering application of Christ's work by God the Holy Spirit. What we will find is that the answers to these three questions are all interlocking. That is, if we answer them correctly, each answer will include the answers to the other two.

As I try to show why these three questions are biblically helpful in guiding the preacher, I will use the writings of the apostle Paul to illustrate. What are Paul's answers to these three questions and how do they help us preach from his writings and from the rest of Scripture? Chapters 13–18 deal with these three questions one at a time.

13

Expository Exultation and the Glory of God, Part 1

As the Ultimate Goal of All Things

What we saw in chapter 12 is that the biblical authors intend for us to take into account their overarching vision of reality when we interpret and apply their particular texts. Therefore, the preacher is always faced with the question, How much, and which parts, of the author's larger vision should be included in a sermon on any particular text?

I suggested three questions that I think shed light on how the preacher decides what aspects of the author's intention he will proclaim: (1) What is the ultimate goal of the biblical author in the sermon text? (2) How does the sermon text relate to Jesus Christ and his saving work? (3) What is the way of life that leads to final salvation rather than destruction? In this chapter, we will address the first question.

What Is the Ultimate Goal of the Biblical Author?

By "ultimate goal" I mean the goal that *all* other goals are intended to lead to. So there may be a chain of cause and effect that has ten thousand links in it, but the last link, beyond which there are no higher goals, is the "ultimate goal"—the one that the author intends for everything else to lead to. The reason I even raise this question about the author's ultimate goal is that biblical authors write this way, especially Paul (who uses the Greek word *hina*, "in order that," which usually means "purpose to attain a goal," 246 times). Hundreds of times the biblical authors encourage us by their language to take note of purposes that lead to goals, and finally to the ultimate goal.

God's Glory Is Ultimate

In fact, the biblical authors so pervasively point to *the glory of God* as the ultimate goal of all things that I came to the conclusion decades ago, as my life of preaching was beginning, that no biblical text is distorted if we say that part of the author's intention is to help us enjoy and display the glory of God. If that is true—if the ultimate goal of all Scripture (and every text) is that God be glorified—this will have a significant effect on how a preacher chooses what to say about his text. My assumption is that the more ultimate a goal is, the more important it is for our people to see and savor and seek. Therefore, if the glorification of God is the ultimate goal, preaching will seek to be as effective as it can be in *clarifying* the people's understanding of the glory of God and *enflaming* their hearts to love it.

Foundations for Thinking God's Glory Is the Ultimate Goal of Every Text

But that is a huge claim to make. So let me provide some biblical basis for it. For the most compelling case, I refer you to Jonathan Edwards's essay "The End for Which God Created the World." I read this in my early twenties and found it totally compelling, theologically revolutionary (Copernican-like), and homiletically explosive. The essay has a philosophical part, which is impressive (but not decisive), and a biblical part that for me proved to be mind-boggling (and decisive). After piling text upon text about the glory of God, Edwards concludes:

> All that is ever spoken of in the Scripture as an ultimate end of God's works is included in that one phrase, *the glory of God.* . . . The refulgence shines upon and into the creature, and is reflected back to the luminary. The beams of glory come from God, and are something of God and are refunded back again to their original. So that the whole is of God, and in God, and to God, and God is the beginning, middle and end in this affair.[1]

---

1. Jonathan Edwards, *The Dissertation Concerning the End for Which God Created the World*, ed. Paul Ramsey, vol. 8, *The Works of Jonathan Edwards* (New Haven, CT: Yale University Press, 1989), 526, 531.

I don't have the space or time to duplicate Edwards's whole-Bible display of this truth. But it may be helpful to pull the curtain back a little on Paul's vision of the glory of God as the ultimate goal of all things. Here is a nonexhaustive sampling of how he thinks about the glory of God.

> The essence of the evil of all humans apart from saving grace is that we have "exchanged the glory of the immortal God for images" (Rom. 1:23).

> This is how Paul defines sin: We "all have sinned and fall short of [literally "lack," because we have exchanged it] the glory of God" (Rom. 3:23).

> Even when the covenant people lie about God, "God's truth abounds to his glory" (Rom. 3:7).

> Abraham's faith is held up as the model because "he grew strong in his faith as he gave glory to God" (Rom. 4:20).

> Because of justification by faith alone, "we rejoice in hope of the glory of God" (Rom. 5:2).

> The endpoint of our adoption into God's family is that we are "fellow heirs with Christ, provided we suffer with him in order that we may also be glorified with him" (Rom. 8:17, cf. v. 30; 1 Cor. 2:7).

> The glory we will one day see face-to-face, and be drawn into, is so great it will outweigh all our suffering in this world, "for I consider that the sufferings of this present time are not worth comparing with the glory that is to be revealed to us" (Rom. 8:18; cf. 2 Cor. 4:17).

> God shows his power and wrath "in order to make known the riches of his glory for vessels of mercy, which he has prepared beforehand for glory" (Rom. 9:23).

> All glory will be given to God because he is the source, the sustaining, and goal of all things: "From him and through him and to him are all things. To him be glory forever. Amen" (Rom. 11:36).

> "Christ has welcomed you, for the glory of God" (Rom. 15:7).

Christ became a servant to the Jewish people not only to confirm God's faithfulness to the patriarchs but also "in order that the Gentiles might glorify God for his mercy" (Rom. 15:9).

The final reason you have a body as a physical creation of God is so that you would "glorify God in your body" (1 Cor. 6:20).

Glorifying God is the reason everything should be done: "So, whether you eat or drink, or whatever you do, do all to the glory of God" (1 Cor. 10:31).

Since all the promises of God find their "Yes" in Christ, "that is why it is through him that we utter our Amen to God for his glory" (2 Cor. 1:20).

The heart of the gospel is "the light of the gospel of the glory of Christ, who is the image of God" (2 Cor. 4:4, cf. v. 6).

The gospel is spreading so that "as grace extends to more and more people it may increase thanksgiving, to the glory of God" (2 Cor. 4:15).

Paul gives several climactic doxologies that seem to point to the glory of God as the great goal: "To whom be the glory forever and ever. Amen" (Gal. 1:5). "To our God and Father be glory forever and ever. Amen" (Phil. 4:20). "To him be the glory forever and ever. Amen" (2 Tim. 4:18). "To him be glory in the church and in Christ Jesus throughout all generations, forever and ever. Amen" (Eph. 3:21).

We are predestined for adoption "to the praise of the glory of His grace" (Eph. 1:6 NASB).

In Christ we have obtained an inheritance, having been predestined according to his will, so that we "might be to the praise of his glory" (Eph. 1:12).

The Holy Spirit is "the guarantee of our inheritance until we acquire possession of it, to the praise of his glory" (Eph. 1:14).

Paul prays that we will be "filled with the fruit of righteousness that comes through Jesus Christ, to the glory and praise of God" (Phil. 1:11).

God has highly exalted Christ and "bestowed on him the name that is above every name, so that at the name of Jesus every knee should bow, in heaven and on earth and under the earth, and every tongue confess that Jesus Christ is Lord, to the glory of God the Father" (Phil. 2:9–11).

Christ is going to return someday "to be glorified in his saints, and to be marveled at among all who have believed" (2 Thess. 1:10).

Keep in mind that this list is based only on the word *glory* or *glorify* but does not include any of the dozens of texts that make the same impact using the word *name* or *honor* or *praise*. Nor have I taken the time to point out the numerous ways that the glory of God is not just mentioned but actually embedded in the structure of Paul's thought so as to make explicit that it is the ultimate goal of God's work (e.g., Rom. 11:36; Eph. 1:6; Phil. 1:11; 2:11; and others). I conclude, therefore, that, for Paul, the ultimate goal in all that God *does* and all that God *says* (every text of Scripture understood according to the author's Scripture-shaping vision of reality) is that God's glory be seen and savored and shown as the greatest beauty and treasure of the universe.

Other Candidates for What Is Ultimate?

If someone should raise the question as to whether there are other dimensions of God's greatness, besides his glory, that might be shown to be the ultimate end, my response would be this: each of those candidates will be seen, on careful examination, to be *part* of the glory of God or as performed *for the sake of* the glory of God.

For example, I was once challenged that *the love and mercy of God* are more ultimate than God's glory. After all, "God *is* love" (1 John 4:8). My response was to point to Romans 15:8–9 where Paul says that Christ came "in order that the Gentiles might *glorify God for his mercy*." Mercy is penultimate; glory is ultimate. Paul explicitly says that mercy is shown for a higher goal—that the Gentiles might glorify God.

But I am not eager to draw a line between the love of God and the glory of God. That may turn out to be like drawing a line between apples and fruit. I am happy to affirm that the glory of God consists in the beauty of the whole panorama of God's perfections. I have no desire to minimize any of God's attributes. All of them are facets in the diamond that is the glory of God. If God lost any of his divine attributes, he would be less glorious—indeed he would not be God. The glory of God is the Bible's shorthand way of referring to the reality of the greatness and beauty and worth of God. The beauty and worth of all that he is, shining forth through creation (Ps. 19:1) and through the history of his saving works (Ps. 79:9) and through his inspired word (1 Sam. 3:21; 2 Cor. 4:4), is his glory.

What Does It Mean to Glorify God?

One matter concerning the glory of God that we have not sorted out yet demands clarifying at this point. Till now I have spoken at least three ways about the ultimate goal of Paul's intention in biblical texts. I have sometimes called it "the glory of God." But other times I have said that the ultimate goal is "glorifying God." And still other times I have been more specific and said the ultimate goal is that "this glory be seen and savored and shown as the greatest beauty and treasure of the universe." Why this multiplicity and imprecision?

The reason is that the Bible itself speaks in all these ways about the ultimate goal of reality. It says, "Do all to *the glory of God*" (1 Cor. 10:31). It says the Lord Jesus is coming "on that day *to be glorified*" (2 Thess. 1:10). And it describes the soul's satisfaction in that glory: "One thing have I asked of the LORD, / that will I seek after / . . . to gaze upon *the beauty of the* LORD" (Ps. 27:4). "O LORD, I love . . . / the place where *your glory* dwells" (Ps. 26:8).

The shorthand expressions of the goal ("to the glory of God" and "that the Lord be glorified") are ambiguous. This is why the Bible says so much more about *how* this is to happen. The ambiguity is that "to the glory of God" and "that he may be glorified" do not, in themselves, make clear whether *glorify* means "make" glorious or "display" as glorious. The difference is a matter of life and death. If we think that what we do *makes* God glorious, we blaspheme. If we aim in what we do to *display* God's glory, we worship.

What Heart Responses Glorify God?

This is why the Bible presses forward to make explicit the kind of heart responses that display the glory of God for what it really is, namely, infinitely beautiful and precious. The Devil and all the world of unrepentant humans will one day serve to glorify God through the just and holy divine wrath that they endure (Rom. 2:4; 9:22), but their heart's response will not see or celebrate the beauty and worth of God.

But that kind of unwilling glorification of God is not the ultimate goal of all things. In fact, Paul makes this explicit in saying that the glory of God, revealed in his wrath, serves a higher purpose. He has "endured with much patience vessels of wrath prepared for destruction, *in order to* [achieve the highest purpose, which is to] make known the riches of his glory for vessels of mercy, which he has prepared beforehand for glory" (Rom. 9:22–23).

Therefore, in describing the ultimate goal of the biblical authors in what they write, it is not enough to say, "The goal is the glory of God," or even to say, "The goal is to glorify God." We must *show* how this happens. We must join the Bible in saying that the goal is to glorify him by *seeing* and *savoring* and *showing* him as the greatest beauty and treasure in the universe. The word *seeing* implies a right perception or knowing of the glory that God reveals. The word *savoring* implies all the positive affections of the Spirit-filled heart in response to the beauty and worth of God (praise, admiration, delight, love, satisfaction, joy, wonder, desire, awe, and more). The word *showing* implies the profound, visible life transformation that this seeing and savoring produce for God and men and angels to see, now and forever.

We Glorify God *by* Enjoying Him

The implications of this understanding of glorifying God are incalculably great for life and preaching. It elevates the heart and the affections to a place of essential importance in glorifying God. It implies, as I have tried to show in many places,[2] that God is most glorified in us when we are most satisfied in him. It implies that when the Westminster Catechism says that the chief end of man is "to glorify God and enjoy him

---

2. We have already made the case for this in chap. 4. The fuller explanation and defense is found in John Piper, *Desiring God: Meditations of a Christian Hedonist*, rev. ed. (Sisters, OR: Multnomah, 2011); *When I Don't Desire God: How to Fight for Joy*, rev. ed. (Wheaton, IL: Crossway, 2013); *God Is the Gospel: Meditations on God's Love as the Gift of Himself* (repr. Wheaton, IL: Crossway, 2005); and *God's Passion for His Glory: Living the Vision of Jonathan Edwards* (Wheaton, IL: Crossway, 2006).

forever," the word *and* may be clarified with the word *by*. The chief end of man is "to glorify God *by* enjoying him forever." It does not say, "Man's chief *ends* . . ." It says, "Man's chief *end* . . ." Glorifying and enjoying are one, because the glorifying happens through the enjoyment. Jonathan Edwards put it like this:

> God is glorified not only by His glory's being seen, but *by its being rejoiced in*. When those that see it *delight in it*, God is more glorified than if they only see it. His glory is then received by the whole soul, both by the understanding and *by the heart*.[3]

If this is true, no preaching can be content to inform the mind about the glory of God. Preaching that is faithful to the ultimate goal of Scripture must also seek, by the power of the Spirit, to waken and sustain the heart's deep and unshakable satisfaction in the glory of God. This is not minor or marginal. It is not icing on the cake of Christianity or preaching. It is the heart and essence of what glorifies God.

See, Love, and Show His Glory

In chapters 13 and 14, I am trying to answer the first of three questions designed to shed light on how a preacher decides what aspects of an author's intention—including this larger, all-encompassing vision of reality—should shape a particular sermon. That question is, What is the ultimate goal of the biblical author in the sermon text? My assumption is that the more ultimate a goal is, the more important it is for our people to see and savor and seek.

To answer the question, I have been focusing on the apostle Paul and his all-encompassing vision of reality. My understanding of the unity of Scripture leads me to believe that the ultimate goal for Paul is the ultimate goal for the rest of Scripture. Therefore, I conclude that the ultimate goal of all biblical truth, and therefore every text, is that God be glorified by our *seeing* and *savoring* and *showing* him as the greatest beauty and treasure in the universe.

Therefore, preaching will seek to be as effective as it can be in clarifying the people's *sight* of the glory of God, and in enflaming their

---

3. Jonathan Edwards, The "Miscellanies," ed. Thomas Schafer, vol. 13, *The Works of Jonathan Edwards* (New Haven, CT: Yale University Press, 1994), Miscellany #448, 495; emphases added. See also Miscellany 87, pp. 251–252; Miscellany 332, p. 410; Miscellany 679.

hearts to *love* it, so that the people of God will be profoundly and pervasively and practically transformed to *show* the supreme beauty and worth of God.

Now I turn to be more specific. How does this aim of preaching to glorify God, in accord with every text of Scripture, shape our preaching of specific texts? In the next chapter, I will suggest six answers to this question.

14

Expository Exultation and the Glory of God, Part 2

How It Shapes Every Sermon

In chapter 13, I concluded that the *ultimate* goal of all biblical truth, and therefore every text, is that God be glorified by *seeing* and *savoring* and *showing* him as the greatest beauty and treasure in the universe. This implies then that preaching will seek to be as effective as it can be in clarifying the people's *sight* of the glory of God and in enflaming their hearts to *love* it. The biblical expectation is that seeing and savoring the glory of God in this way will bring to pass in God's people ways of life that show the supreme beauty and worth of God.

The purpose of this chapter is to offer six suggestions that show how the aim to glorify God from every text of Scripture shapes our preaching of specific texts.

1. Be Confident in Finding the Glory of God in Every Text

We should have a strong confidence that it is not arbitrary, but biblically warranted, to bring the reality of the glory of God to light through our text as we preach. The simple but all-encompassing statement of 1 Corinthians 10:31 should give us a great zeal for this: "Whatever you do, do all to the glory of God." If all of life is about the glory of God, how much more all of preaching. Over time our people should find themselves at home seeing and savoring the glory of God in all of Scripture.

2. Authentically Embody God's Glory in Expository *Exultation*

The presence of the reality of the glory of God in our preaching is one of the main reasons that our preaching will be expository *exultation*. We will do as much harm as good if we weave the glory of God into our messages without any manifest wonder or joy. Presenting the glory of God in a way that communicates its minimal value to the preacher is slander against God. It communicates a lie—that God is not supremely beautiful and valuable. To be sure, as we argued in parts 4 and 5, rational *exposition* of every text is essential. But just as essential is a pervasive spirit of authentic and serious joy, suffusing the service, the sermon, and the preacher inside and outside the pulpit.

If the glory of God seems to the people to be the preacher's shtick, or a brand, or a rhetorical device, or a mere tradition, no oratorical decorations will be able to conceal the hypocrisy. The very nature of this all-embracing beauty and value means either that it will shine through the preaching for what it is, or it will sound like an empty slogan. Expository exultation is an authentic *elucidation* and *embodiment* of the glory of God.

3. Aim to See and Show Glory to Encourage Attention to Detail

Seeing the sermon text in the light of its ultimate purpose to glorify God will not mute the concrete details and particular intentions of the text. It will not deflect interest in, or attention from, the rigorous textual analysis that digs into the realities specific to this text. Instead, careful, detailed observation, analysis, and reflection are encouraged because the riches of the glory of God do not hover above or outside the realities of the text but are found in and through them.

I warned in chapter 12 about overarching theological convictions that we bring to texts that may obscure rather than brighten the specifics of the text. I warned against artificial theological overlays that mute the particular realities of the text by making every passage of Scripture lie in the procrustean bed of a misused doctrine.

Conceivably, the glory of God in the hands of a lazy, undiscerning, or unreal preacher could be used this way. But my experience over four decades of preaching is that the all-encompassing, all-pervading beauty and worth of God have not disinclined me, or disabled me, from the most rigorous attention to the details and intentions of the biblical text.

On the contrary, knowing that every newly discovered nuance of meaning and reality would provide another glimpse of God's glory has been a motivation to spare no effort of analysis in study, or effort in exposition.

4. Be Mindful That God's Glory Enlarges and Brightens Everything

Keeping the glory of God in mind, as the ultimate goal of all biblical truth, does not result in reductionism but *superductionism* (to coin a term). Reductionism comes from *reduce*, which comes from the Latin *re* (back) + *ducere* (to lead)—to lead back. The idea in reductionism is that the wonderful diversity and specificity and concreteness of thousands of Scripture passages may be reduced (led back) to a bland theological scheme that robs them of their particularity and replaces them with a colorless abstraction. I flee this like the plague. I love concreteness and specificity and hate vague, boring abstractions.

But reduction is *not* what happens when we see specific, concrete realities in relation to the glory of God. *Superduction* is what happens. Specific, concrete realities are not led *back* and *down* to less, but led *forward* and *upward* to more. *Superductionism* does not boil things down; it blows them up. They get bigger, not smaller; clearer, not murkier; sharper, not duller; brighter, not darker. Divine radiance does not make reality dull. The glory of God makes all concreteness, all specificity, all ordinariness radiant with the greatness of God.

Therefore, preaching that skillfully and wisely and beautifully brings specific textual realities into connection with the glory of God enlarges and brightens everything. Things that we once thought small and insignificant in life take on a beauty and preciousness they did not have till they were touched by the glory of God. In the process, the hearts of the people in the congregation are enlarged. "You enlarge my heart!" (Ps. 119:32). The people are made to feel that they walk among wonders—in God's world and in God's word. This will have a direct effect on how they view the call to practice hospitality, for example, which we focused on in chapter 12—and every other biblical command (as we will see below).

5. Keep in View That Preachers Are Workers for Joy *in God*

Preaching that keeps in view the ultimate goal of all biblical texts as seeing, savoring, and showing the beauty and worth of God will always be seeking to awaken the enjoyment of the glory of God. Such preaching will never settle for informing or persuading. It will relentlessly pursue the joy of God's people in God. In *God*. That is the key. Many preachers would say they aim at the joy of their people. But there is a world of difference between the joy that treasures *God himself* above all things, and the joy that comes from an entertaining service and a likeable preacher.

Preaching for the glory of God realizes that God is not glorified in the hearts of people who delight in his gifts more than in him. This is ultimately why the joy of Christians was such a high apostolic priority. Paul said, "Not that we lord it over your faith, but *we work with you for your joy*" (2 Cor. 1:24). He also wrote, "I know that I will remain and continue with you all, for your progress and *joy in the faith*" (Phil. 1:25). Joy in God was Paul's reason for life and ministry. This joy is not marginal in the Bible. It is an essential means of glorifying God. Therefore, if every text aims at the glorification of God, every text is an invitation to find fullest satisfaction in him in relation to what this text is about. This is woven into the way God has made the world and how he is saving it.

6. Show the Glory of God through Preaching Because It Is God's Path for Transforming Christians

Finally, preaching that hopes and prays and aims toward glorifying God in every exposition of every text rejoices that the revealing of the glory of God through his word is the way congregations are conformed to the image of Christ. Preaching never forgets the needs of the people. Those needs are a thousand times more diverse and more complex than we could ever know. Therefore, we cannot specifically address all those countless needs directly.

But God has not designed the church to experience transformation by means of every need of every member being explicitly addressed— not by the preacher or by anyone. It is impossible. We don't even know the innumerable needs that we ourselves have. So there is no way we or anyone else could address them all specifically. Instead God has designed that *some* of our needs be addressed specifically by preachers or other believers, but that *most* of our needs be met in ways that we never planned, and often before we even know that we have them.

One way to describe how God has designed for his people to be changed into the image of Christ is to say that they are changed by seeing the glory of God revealed in the reading and preaching of his word. In *Reading the Bible Supernaturally* (chapters 3–5), I discussed how this works.[1] The chapters are together called "Reading to See Supreme Worth and Beauty." Everything said there applies to how the preacher sees the glory of God in Scripture and how he helps the people see it by his preaching.

The most important text to show this design of God through reading and preaching is 2 Corinthians 3:18:

> We all, with unveiled face, beholding the glory of the Lord, are being transformed into the same image from one degree of glory to another. For this comes from the Lord who is the Spirit.

The main point is that people's needs for transformation are met by "beholding the glory of the Lord." I argued in *Reading the Bible Supernaturally* that beholding happens through the Spirit-illumined Scripture. And now I would add, for the same reasons—through the Spirit-anointed preaching of those Scriptures.

This means that a pastor who loves his people, and wants to meet their needs and bring them ever closer to the holiness of Christ, will not make the common mistake of becoming less God-centered and more pragmatic. That strategy backfires. It has a short-term appeal because people like it—at first. It seems to scratch where they itch. But most people don't realize that the itch is a symptom and not the disease. Part of the disease is that we don't know the nature of it. But God does. And the realities of his word are the remedy. And Paul says this means seeing the glory of the Lord *through the word*, as we showed by the connection between 2 Corinthians 3:18 and 4:4–6.[2]

Preaching the Glory of God in Relation to Hospitality

Since in chapter 12 we introduced the challenge of preaching on hospitality from Romans 12:13 ("Seek to show hospitality"), it may be helpful to circle back to that issue and end this chapter by suggesting how

---

1. John Piper, *Reading the Bible Supernaturally: Seeing and Savoring the Glory of God in Scripture* (Wheaton, IL: Crossway, 2017), 65–97.
2. See chapter 4, pp. 83–84. (dealing with 2 Cor. 3:18 and how preaching is implied in 4:5).

the glory of God frees people to show hospitality, and how the glory of God becomes more visible through hospitality.

In preparing to preach, we try to keep in mind the kinds of human obstacles that lie between the text and obedience. In this case, what are the obstacles to hospitality? From Scripture, from conversations with our people, and from our own hearts, we know these obstacles include: (1) It will cost extra money to have people over for dinner, and the budget is tight. (2) Our house, or our apartment, is not very nice compared to what some people have. (3) We are having marriage troubles, and it feels phony to put up a good front. (4) The conversation might lag, and that will be really awkward. (5) This will require a lot more work with housecleaning and shopping and cooking.

Pragmatic preaching might simply take these one at a time and give a smart and entertaining motivational talk on how to get over those obstacles. The supposed aim is to help people feel good about themselves and get into the lives of other people. As time goes by, this kind of preaching starts to feel thin. Because it is. Discerning people start to wonder what the difference is between these gatherings and other motivational conferences, even non-Christian ones.

But what I am suggesting in chapter 13 and this chapter is that the ultimate goal of every text, including the particular command to show hospitality (Rom. 12:13), is to display the glory of God as supremely beautiful and satisfying. We realize that the people need to see the glory of God as their all-satisfying treasure. Beholding the glory of the Lord this way will change them. So in our sermon, we decide to relate the glory of God to the five obstacles to hospitality. A sketch of the points may look something like this:

Obstacle #1: It will cost extra money to have people over for dinner, and the budget is tight.

> We point the people to Philippians 4:19: "My God will supply every need of yours *according to his riches in glory* in Christ Jesus." We point out the context of Philippians 4 where Paul is thanking the Philippians for showing him a kind of hospitality at a distance. They sent him gifts through Epaphroditus to help meet his needs. He encourages them not to worry about the strain this generosity may have put them under financially, because the riches of God's glory

ensure that God can supply every need they have. So Paul himself brings the glory of God into connection with the hospitable generosity of God's people, and God's readiness to take care of them.

Obstacle #2: Our house, or our apartment, is not very nice compared to what some people have.

> Here we could take them to John 5:44 where Jesus rebukes people for seeking glory from men over the glory of God. The fear of man, and his disapproval of our house, is rooted in a failure to be satisfied in the approval we have in Christ and the glory we enjoy in God.
>
> Or we might take them to Romans 15, which begins, "Let each of us please his neighbor for his good, to build him up" (v. 2). In other words, take your eyes off yourself and seek the good of the folks you are inviting to your house. Seek how to bless them with your encouragements.
>
> Then Paul motivates this welcoming attitude in verse 7: "Therefore welcome one another as Christ has welcomed you, *for the glory of God.*" In other words, lift your eyes off your small worries of disapproval and think of the glorious welcome you have from Christ, and that this welcome was *to glorify God.* He bids you join him in that welcoming ministry for the glory of God.

Obstacle #3: We are having marriage troubles, and it feels phony to put up a good front in showing hospitality.

> It may seem counterintuitive, but you might say this to your people: "Maybe one of the reasons you have marriage problems is that your eyes are too much on yourselves, and perhaps the most life-giving thing you could do right now is take a deep breath and try to serve others while putting your own marriage concerns on hold. Hospitality is not about you. It's about others. Paradoxically, then, maybe God will show up with surprise resources for *your own* healing, while you are pouring your energies into serving others. Jesus said, 'It is more blessed to give than to receive' (Acts 20:35). Maybe part of that blessedness will come to your marriage as you turn away from your own failures and look to his all-glorious, all-supplying resources. Besides, the greatest purpose for marriage is to display *the glory of Christ's covenant-keeping faithfulness* in relation to his church. That covenant—even between Christ and his

church—is often troubled. Really troubled. But he keeps on showing his glorious patience and all-sufficiency. So go ahead and put him on display in your weakness."

Obstacle #4: The conversation might lag, and that will be really awkward.

Perhaps you may remind the people that Moses objected to being God's servant in Egypt because he could not speak well. "Oh, my Lord, I am not eloquent, either in the past or since you have spoken to your servant, but I am slow of speech and of tongue." It is absolutely astonishing what God said to Moses. He took the conversation to a whole new level and described his absolute (*glorious!*) sovereignty over all disease and disability: "Then the LORD said to him, 'Who has made man's mouth? Who makes him mute, or deaf, or seeing, or blind? Is it not I, the LORD?'" And then from that breathtaking point of sovereign power, he says, "Now therefore go, and I will be with your mouth and teach you what you shall speak" (Ex. 4:10–12).

Obstacle #5: This will take a lot more work with housecleaning and shopping and cooking.

Lack of energy is one of the common reasons Christians don't do the good deeds that would show the glory of God. We feel too tired to take on anything else. God often comes to his people who are weary with things for them to do, and he bases his command not on their strength but on his. The reason Peter gives for this is that it gives more glory to God. "Whoever serves, [let him serve] by the strength that God supplies—*in order that in everything God may be glorified* through Jesus Christ. To him belong glory and dominion forever and ever. Amen" (1 Pet. 4:11).

Priority of God's Glory

We have been trying to answer the question, What reality do preachers proclaim to their people from any given text? Even though it is a true answer, it is not enough to say, "Preach the reality that the biblical author is trying to communicate through the text." This is inadequate because, as we saw, the reality that the biblical author intends for us to take into account is so vast and diverse, we could not say it all in one sermon. Therefore, we must choose from this all-embracing vision of reality what aspects of it we will bring to bear on the specifics of this text.

So our question became, How is a preacher to decide which aspects of an author's vision of reality to bring into the sermon to shed light on the present text? In addition to the immediate and explicit demands of the wording of the text itself, I suggested three questions that shed light on how the preacher decides what aspects of the author's overarching vision of reality he will proclaim: (1) What is the ultimate goal of the biblical author in the sermon text? (2) How does the sermon text relate to Jesus Christ and his saving work? (3) What is the way of life that leads to final salvation rather than destruction?

Chapters 13 and 14 have proposed an answer to the first question. My assumption is that the more ultimate a goal is, the more important it is for our people to see it and savor it and seek it. I concluded that the ultimate goal of all biblical truth, and therefore every text, is that God be glorified by our *seeing* and *savoring* and *showing* him as the greatest beauty and treasure in the universe. Therefore, preaching will seek to be as effective as it can be in clarifying people's understanding of the glory of God and in enflaming their hearts to love it and show it. How this priority of the glory of God in preaching works out in practice I tried to sketch above in six steps.

In the next two chapters, we continue our attempt to shed light on how the preacher decides what aspects of the author's intention he will proclaim. The second question that sheds such light is: How does this text relate to Jesus Christ and his saving work?

15

Expository Exultation and Christ Crucified, Part 1

Boasting Only in the Cross in Every Sermon

In trying to discern what reality we should preach, I turn now from the question of the previous chapter (What is the ultimate goal of the biblical author in the sermon text?) to the question, How does the sermon text relate to Jesus Christ and his saving work? There is a reason for posing this question, just as there was a reason for the first one. Each follows from an assumption. The assumption behind the first question was that the more ultimate the goal of an author's meaning, the more important it is that our preaching should prioritize that goal. The assumption behind the second question is that what the apostle Paul says is indispensable to his preaching should be indispensable to ours.

Trinitarian: Goal, Ground, Means

I am trying to answer the overarching question, What reality shall we preach? In pursuit of the answer, I am asking three subordinate questions, each related primarily, though not exclusively, to one of the persons of the Trinity. First, What is the ultimate goal of the biblical author in the sermon text? This relates finally to the glory of God the Father. Second, How does the sermon text relate to Jesus Christ and his saving work? This relates, of course, to God the Son. Third, What is the way of life that leads to final salvation rather than destruction? This relates to the

Holy Spirit and how he enables us to embrace and obey the Scripture in a saving way. Thus our guiding questions relate to the *goal*, the *ground*, and the *means* of Christian existence—and, therefore, of preaching.

Jesus Christ: Crucified, Risen, Full of Riches

As in chapters 13 and 14, we will let the apostle Paul guide us. Paul does not leave us uncertain about the question, What reality shall we preach? The ultimate goal of life is the glorification of God. Every meal we eat, every cup we drink, every text we preach, is for the glory of God (1 Cor. 10:31). To miss that reality in preaching is like a spaceship bound for Mars missing the goal and flying into empty space. In this chapter and the next, another reality takes center stage—Jesus Christ, crucified, risen, and full of riches for his people.

The statements of the apostle that govern my thinking in this chapter and the next are more specific than his sweeping statement in 2 Timothy 4:2, "Preach the word." "Preach the word," as we argued in chapter 3,[1] mandates that our texts for preaching come from Scripture. But "preach the word" does not tell us what aspects of an author's overarching vision of reality should be prominent in our preaching. Paul, however, makes at least five statements that elevate one reality to a central prominence in his preaching—and ours:

> To them God chose to make known how great among the Gentiles are the riches of the glory of this mystery, which is Christ in you, the hope of glory. *Him we proclaim,* warning everyone and teaching everyone with all wisdom, that we may present everyone mature in Christ. (Col. 1:27–28)

> To me, though I am the very least of all the saints, this grace was given, *to preach to the Gentiles the unsearchable riches of Christ,* and to bring to light for everyone what is the plan of the mystery hidden for ages in God, who created all things, so that through the church the manifold wisdom of God might now be made known to the rulers and authorities in the heavenly places. (Eph. 3:8–10)

> Since, in the wisdom of God, the world did not know God through wisdom, it pleased God through the folly of what we preach to save

---

1. See pp. 63–65.

those who believe. For Jews demand signs and Greeks seek wisdom, but *we preach Christ crucified*, a stumbling block to Jews and folly to Gentiles, but to those who are called, both Jews and Greeks, Christ the power of God and the wisdom of God. (1 Cor. 1:21–24)

I, when I came to you, brothers, did not come proclaiming to you the testimony of God with lofty speech or wisdom. For *I decided to know nothing among you except Jesus Christ and him crucified*. (1 Cor. 2:1–2)

Far be it from me to boast except in the cross of our Lord Jesus Christ, by which the world has been crucified to me, and I to the world. (Gal. 6:14)

Boiling these passages down to the minimal statements of focus in preaching:

- "Him [Christ] we proclaim" (Col. 1:28).

- We "preach . . . the unsearchable riches of Christ" (Eph. 3:8).

- "We preach Christ crucified" (1 Cor. 1:23).

- "I decided to know nothing among you except Jesus Christ and him crucified" (1 Cor. 2:2).

- "Far be it from me to boast except in the cross of our Lord Jesus Christ" (Gal. 6:14).

The last two (1 Cor. 2:2 and Gal. 6:14) are the ones with the most surprising and staggering implications for preaching. The other three do not say explicitly that Christ crucified is what Paul *always* and *only* preaches. But that is what Galatians 6:14 and 1 Corinthians 2:2 seem to say.

What does Paul mean by saying that he decided to know *nothing* among the Corinthians *except Jesus Christ and him crucified*? And what did he mean by saying he would not boast in *anything but the cross* of the Lord Jesus Christ? Together with the other three statements, what do these two sweeping statements imply for our preaching?

Strategy of Preaching for All Churches

Paul's statement about his preaching at Corinth—that he decided to know nothing "among you" except Jesus Christ crucified (1 Cor. 2:2)—

could be taken to be a special strategy of preaching for Corinth that we should not generalize as a rule for all preaching. But I doubt that is the case. The problem of pride and boasting that plagued the church at Corinth, and prompted Paul's emphasis on the pride-destroying, crucified "Lord of glory" (1 Cor. 2:8), is not unique to Corinth. It is a human problem, not a Corinthian problem.

There is another reason why we should not limit Paul's emphasis on Christ crucified to the Corinthian situation—or any one situation. Paul says essentially the same thing in Galatians 6:14, and we know that Paul's letter to the Galatians was a circular letter to numerous churches. He says he is writing "to the *churches* of Galatia" (Gal. 1:2). To *all* of these churches, he wrote, as his own settled way of life and preaching, "Far be it from me to boast except in the cross of our Lord Jesus Christ, by which the world has been crucified to me, and I to the world" (Gal. 6:14). So we need to know what Paul means by this amazing emphasis on knowing "nothing among you except Jesus Christ and him crucified" (1 Cor. 2:2) and boasting only "in the cross" (Gal. 6:14). We need to understand what this implies for our preaching.

Boasting Only in the Cross

Paul's negative statement in Galatians 6:14 can be stated positively: "Boast only in the cross of Jesus Christ." The word for *boast* (*kauchasthai*) can be translated "exult in" or "rejoice in." *Exult* only in the cross of Christ. *Rejoice* only in the cross of Christ. This is shocking for two reasons.

One is that it's like saying, "Boast only in the electric chair." "Exult only in the gas chamber." "Rejoice only in the lethal injection." "Let your one boast and one joy and one exultation be the lynching rope." No manner of execution that has ever been devised is more cruel and agonizing than to be nailed to a cross. It was horrible. We probably would not have been able to watch it—not without groaning and pulling our hair and tearing our clothes. Let *this* be your only boast!

The other shocking thing about Paul's statement is the implicit word *only*. Let the cross be your *only* boast. "Far be it from me to boast *except* in the cross." Let Christ crucified be your only boast, your only exultation, your only joy. What does he mean by this? No other boast? No other exultation? No other joy except the cross of Jesus—the death of Jesus?

The main problem here is that Paul uses various forms of this same word (*kauchasthai*) to say that he boasts or exults in other things.

- "We exult in hope of the glory of God" (Rom. 5:2 NASB).

- "We . . . exult in our tribulations" (Rom. 5:3 NASB).

- "Most gladly . . . I will . . . boast about my weaknesses" (2 Cor. 12:9 NASB).

- "Who is our hope or joy or crown of exultation? Is it not even you?" (1 Thess. 2:19 NASB).

So, if Paul can boast (or exult or rejoice) in all these things, what does Paul mean—that he would not "boast except in the cross of our Lord Jesus Christ"?

Let Every Boast Be a Boast in the Cross

Paul is not inconsistent. He is not guilty of double-talk. He has a profound reason for saying that all exultation, all rejoicing, all boasting in anything should also be a rejoicing in the cross of Jesus Christ. That's what I take him to mean—that, for the Christian, all other boasting should also be a boasting in the cross. All exultation in anything else should also be exultation in the cross. If you exult in the hope of glory, you should be exulting in the cross of Christ. If you exult in tribulation, because tribulation works hope, you should be exulting in the cross of Christ. If you exult in your weaknesses, or in the people of God, you should be exulting in the cross of Christ.

Preaching must affirm this. It must be based on this. Every sermon that offers anything good to believers in Christ, or that helps believers see that God will turn for good everything bad in their lives, must be a sermon that exults in Christ crucified.

Logic of Heaven—Romans 8:32

Why must every Christian sermon exult explicitly in Christ crucified? For this reason: for redeemed sinners, every good thing—and every bad thing that God turns for good—was secured for us by the cross of Christ. Every heaven-bound breath that a believer takes was bought by the blood of Christ. What could be more pervasively significant in preaching? Paul gives the foundation for this claim in Romans 8:32: "He who did not spare his own Son but gave him up for us all, how will he not also with him graciously give us all things?" This is one of the most important verses in the Bible, both for living and for preaching.

What puts Romans 8:32 in a class by itself is the logic that gives rise to the promise and makes it as solid and unshakable as God's love for his infinitely admirable Son. I call it the logic of heaven. Romans 8:32 contains a foundation—a guarantee—that is so strong and so solid and so secure that there is absolutely no possibility that the promise could ever be broken. Whatever else gives way, whatever else disappoints, whatever else fails, this all-encompassing promise can never fail.

Heavenly Logic, Part 1

Romans 8:32 has two parts: the foundation and the promise. The first part is the foundation: "He who did not spare his own Son but gave him up for us all . . ." If this is true, says the logic of heaven, then God will most surely give *all things* to those for whom he gave his Son. God did not spare his own Son. He handed him over to death. Many in our day—as in every day—scorn the truth of God's ordaining the death of his own Son. They call it primitive, pagan, divine child abuse, etc. The Bible calls it love. And the Bible makes explicit that the death of Christ was the will of his Father.

"This Man [was] delivered over by the predetermined plan and foreknowledge of God" (Acts 2:23 NASB). "We esteemed him stricken, *smitten by God*. . . . It was *the will of the* LORD to crush him; he [his Father!] has put him to grief" (Isa. 53:4, 10). "*God* displayed [him] publicly as a propitiation in His blood" (Rom. 3:25 NASB).

Why did he "not spare his own Son"? The answer is given in the very assertion: God "did not spare his own Son but gave him up *for us all*." For us. In another place, Paul says, "[God] made him to be sin who knew no sin, so that in him we might become the righteousness of God" (2 Cor. 5:21). Or, as Isaiah saw it hundreds of years before it happened (Isa. 53:5–6),

> He was pierced *for our transgressions*;
>   he was crushed *for our iniquities*;
> upon him was the chastisement *that brought us peace*,
>   and with his wounds *we are healed*.

All we like sheep have gone astray;
> we have turned—every one—to his own way;
and the LORD has laid on him
> *the iniquity of us all.*

God did not spare his own Son, because it was the only way he could spare *us* and still be the all-holy, all-just God that he is. The guilt of our transgressions, the punishment of our iniquities, and the curse of our sin would have brought us inescapably to the destruction of hell. Except for Christ crucified.

But now the logic of heaven begins. Paul reasons like this: *Since* God did not spare his own Son, *then* surely he *must* and *will* freely give us all things with him. Why is that? How does this all-important logic work? The technical name for this kind of reasoning is *a majori ad minus*. This refers to an argument "from the greater to the lesser."

Suppose two tasks are motivated by the same desire, but one is very improbable because the cost is so high, and one is more probable because the cost is less. If I have the desire for both tasks and somehow manage to accomplish the costly one, then it is virtually assured the less costly one will be accomplished. Overcoming the greater obstacles assures you that I will overcome the lesser ones. That's an argument *a majori ad minus*.

Paul is reasoning in Romans 8:32 from the impossibly hard to the relatively easy, or from the greater to the lesser. God did not spare his own Son but gave him up—that's the hard thing, the great thing, the unthinkable thing. The reason it's the greater thing is that God loved his Son *infinitely*. His Son did not deserve to be killed. His Son was worthy of worship by every creature. He did not deserve spitting and whipping and scorn and torture. To hand over "his beloved Son" (Col. 1:13) was the incomparably great thing.

Heavenly Logic, Part 2

In doing this greatest and most difficult of all things, God showed that he most certainly would give *all things* to the people for whom he gave his Son. Giving us "all things" may sound to us like a stupendously great thing. It is. But compared to not sparing his own Son, it is, in God's mind, a relatively easy thing. Astonishing. This is the logic of heaven. "He who did not spare his own Son but gave him up for us all, how will he not also with him graciously give us all things?"

The great promise, guaranteed in the logic of Romans 8:32, is that God will give us "all things." What does that mean? In a context that includes Romans 8:36 ("We are being killed all the day long"), I take this to mean that God will give us everything that is good for us, and that he will turn everything bad in our lives—like being killed for Christ's sake—for good.

John Flavel, a Puritan pastor from over three hundred years ago, exulted in Romans 8:32:

> Surely if [God] would not spare this own Son one stroke, one tear, one groan, one sigh, one circumstance of misery, it can never be imagined that ever he should, after this, deny or withhold from his people, for whose sakes all this was suffered, any mercies, any comforts, any privilege, spiritual or temporal, which is good for them.[2]

Every Blessing Calls for Boasting in the Cross

Now we can see why Paul would say that all his boasting, all his exultation, all his joy is in the cross. I take him to mean that every single blessing in the Christian life, including every hard thing God turns for the good of his people, is owing to the cross. It is one of the "all things" that Romans 8:32 says was secured by God's not sparing his Son. This is why I said that every sermon that offers anything good to believers in Christ, or that helps believers see that God will turn for good everything bad in their lives, must be a sermon that exults in Christ crucified.

There simply can be no benefits, offered to us as God's dear children, apart from the cross of Christ. But *every* sermon offers some benefit to God's children. *Every* text, Paul says, is "profitable" (2 Tim. 3:16). And the only way that anything finally "profitable" can come to a hell-deserving, fallen human being is because of the cross. Therefore, every profit, every blessing, every gift, every promise, every gracious warning, and every helpful glimpse of God's glory in every sermon are blood bought. They are owing to the cross—to Christ crucified. To boast or exult or rejoice in any benefit, offered in any sermon, will also

---

2. John Flavel, *The Works of John Flavel*, vol. 6 (Edinburgh: Banner of Truth; repr., 1988), 418. In the preceding paragraphs, I have adapted parts of chap. 8 of John Piper, *Future Grace: The Purifying Power of the Promises of God* (Colorado Springs, CO: Multnomah, 2012), 109–16.

be a boasting in the cross. For we would not have anything but wrath without the cross.

Nothing but Christ Crucified

To confirm that we are tracking with the apostle Paul, consider again 1 Corinthians 2:2: "I decided to know nothing among you except Jesus Christ and him crucified." We know from the rest of 1 Corinthians that Paul did not mean that he would not talk about other issues. It is clear that he did "know" and talk about lots of issues: church divisions (1:10–17; 3:1–4), church discipline (5:1–5), sexual immorality (6:12–20), lawsuits (6:1–11), marriage and singleness (chapter 7), food offered to idols (8:1–6), head coverings (11:1–16), spiritual gifts (chapters 12–14), and more. So if Paul did not mean, in 1 Corinthians 2:2, that he knows and talks only about Christ crucified, what did he mean when he said that he would "know nothing among you except Jesus Christ and him crucified"?

My answer is that Paul meant that whatever else he knew, whatever else he spoke about, and whatever else he did, he would know it and say it and do it in relation to Christ crucified. Paul makes tents in the shadow of the cross. He preaches in the shadow of the cross. He disputes with opponents in the shadow of the cross. Christ crucified is related to everything he does and says because any good Paul can do for anyone in words or deeds is possible only because of the death of Jesus. Without Christ crucified, Paul had nothing hopeful to offer anyone. Or to put it positively, every good that Paul does, or any good news that he preaches, is owing to Christ crucified. Therefore, he will think ("know") of things only that way. He will preach only with that assumption.

Christ Secured Every Good

What we have seen so far, then, is that to proclaim Christ (Col. 1:28), or to preach with the aim of boasting only in the cross (Gal. 6:14), or to preach with the aim of knowing only Christ crucified (1 Cor. 2:2), or to preach the unsearchable riches of Christ (Eph. 3:8) is to preach every biblical reality in relation to the death of Jesus. More specifically, knowing only Christ and him crucified in our preaching means making clear that every good thing offered to God's people in every text (whether a warning, a rebuke, a trait of God, a command, or a promise) is secured for them by the blood of Jesus. Apart from the cross, every divine goodness would compound our deserved condemnation (Rom. 2:4). Therefore, the cross is the foundation in every sermon of every good offered in every text.

We turn now in chapter 16 to the question, How then shall we preach with this understanding of boasting only in the cross and knowing only Christ and him crucified?

16

Expository Exultation and Christ Crucified, Part 2

"That We Might Live to Righteousness"

As we wrestled in the previous chapter with Paul's amazing claim to boast only in the cross (Gal. 6:14), we concluded that this does not mean that Paul boasted in nothing else, but that in all other boasting, he was also, foundationally and supremely, boasting in Christ. Christ made all other legitimate boasts possible and, therefore, became part of them. And as we wrestled with Paul's claim to know nothing except Christ and him crucified (1 Cor. 2:2), we concluded that this does not mean Paul never discussed other topics, but that the death of Christ secured everything hopeful that he had to say about every other topic. Without Christ crucified, there would be nothing hopeful that he could offer anyone. Any good news for God's people that Paul preached on any topic is owing to Christ crucified.

Impact on Preaching May Not Be What You Think

Understanding Paul's focus on Christ crucified in this way has an effect on preaching that is different from what some have thought. The effect it has is to encourage the preacher to take all the details of his text with great seriousness, and to spend time opening their meaning and their application with all the specificity that the words imply. When I say it this way, I am distinguishing this kind of preaching from the kind that deals superficially with the details of the text only to move on to talk about the atoning work of Christ crucified. I am offering an alternative to those who think "preaching Christ" means giving a nod to the subject matter of the text and then moving to the real concern by ending every sermon with a rehearsal of what Christ did on the cross.

I don't think that is what "preaching Christ" means in the week-in, week-out work of the preacher among the gathered people of God. I say this for several reasons. First, there are *secondary* reasons: (1) That kind of preaching tends to dull the expectations of the people with a predictable homiletical path. (2) It tends to treat the actual words and phrases and logic of the text as having minor significance by giving the impression they need not be treated with care and depth, but only as preparations for the Christ-crucified crescendo. (3) It tends to train people in bad habits of how to read their Bibles, by diminishing the rigor and earnestness with which they meditate on the very words of Scripture. (4) It tends to weaken the seriousness of biblical imperatives on how to live the Christian life by inserting the substitutionary atonement at critical moments when the emphasis should be falling on the urgency of obedience.

But here's the *primary* reason for my concern with this way of understanding "preach Christ." I said above that I am trying to offer an alternative to a way of "preaching Christ" that treats the details of the text superficially and then moves to the real concern by ending with a rehearsal of what Christ did on the cross. But I ask, What *did* Christ do on the cross in regard to the reality of this particular sermon text? Take 1 Peter 4:7–9, for example:

> The end of all things is at hand; therefore be self-controlled and sober-minded for the sake of your prayers. Above all, keep loving one another earnestly, since love covers a multitude of sins. Show hospitality to one another without grumbling.

What did Christ do on the cross with regard to the reality of this text? Did he die for sinners so that this text about self-control and sober-mindedness and love and hospitality and grumbling would be in the Bible simply to remind us that he died for sinners? Or did he die for sinners precisely to make this text, in all its amazing specificity, possible for redeemed people? Did he die for us so that when we come to this text we would dig deeply into the details of this kind of blood-bought life, and how to live it? When Peter says that Christ "bore our sins in his body on the tree, *that we might die to sin and live to righteousness*" (1 Pet. 2:24), did he mean: "Glory in the might of the cross, and the method of God through the cross, to empower Christians to do what biblical texts call them to do"?

Beeline to the Cross?

When we preach 1 Peter 4:7–9, should our mind-set be: Make some general comments about the details, and then make a "beeline to the cross"? That phrase comes from a quote attributed (by hundreds of people) to Charles Spurgeon: "I take my text and make a beeline to the cross." To my knowledge, no one has cited the place Spurgeon said this, and those who know Spurgeon best don't seem to be able to show he said it.[1] But the quote has been used to cultivate a kind of preaching that I am discouraging.

Of course, the quotation itself need not be misleading, any more than Paul is misleading when he says he knows nothing but Christ crucified. But the quotation certainly may mislead preachers. So back to my question: As we read and preach 1 Peter 4:7–9, should our mind-set be to give some general comments, and then make a beeline to a rehearsal of the death and resurrection of Jesus, with a grand crescendo that Christ died for our sins? Is that what preaching "the unsearchable riches of Christ" (Eph. 3:8) means when we are preaching 1 Peter 4:7–9?

Turning the Aim of the Cross Upside Down

I don't think so. In fact, I think that mind-set turns the cross and the realities revealed in Scripture upside down. What did Christ do on the cross with regard to the reality of this text? He purchased the Christian life described and commanded in this text. Let me say that again: When Christ died for us on the cross, he obtained for us the glory of Christ-permeated obedience to 1 Peter 3:7–9. The realities revealed and demanded in this text do not exist for the sake of the cross. The cross exists for the sake of these realities!

---

1. "Christian George and a team of guys at the college had also dedicated some time over the summer to finding this citation. They came up empty handed too. If they can't find it, I'm not sure anyone can." Joel Littlefield, "I Can't Believe Spurgeon Didn't Say That," The Blazing Center website, accessed March 14, 2017, https://theblazingcenter.com/2016/08/i-cant-believe-spurgeon -didnt-say-that.html.

This is the glory of the cross! The cross leads to this kind of life of love. Not the other way around. The cross bought this. Christ died for this—namely, that we, with all our sins forgiven, might enjoy the presence and power of the living Christ as he works in us blood-bought self-control and sober-mindedness and love and hospitality without grumbling. This is the miracle life—the glory of Christ-filled godliness that he died to bring about.

Therefore, the *primary* reason for rejecting preaching that makes "a beeline to the cross" (as we have described it) is that it *diminishes* the glory of the cross. It thinks it is doing just the opposite. It thinks the cross is more magnified by bringing the sermon to a crescendo every week with a celebration of substitutionary atonement. That is not the way to make much of the glories of the cross. By all means, make sure that the congregation knows the details of the greatest event in the history of the world—the death and resurrection of Jesus. But then spend most of your time preaching the glorious *achievements* of the cross, which fill the pages of Scripture.

And what we have seen is that every beneficial thing in the Bible—every blessing, every gift, every promise, every gracious warning, every helpful glimpse of God's glory in every sermon—is blood bought. It is owing to the cross—to Christ crucified. Every undeserved benefit, every grace, expressed in any text anywhere in the Bible (whether a revealed beauty or ugliness, warning or promise) is a blood-bought grace—including all those in the Old Testament (Rom. 3:25; 2 Cor. 1:20).

Beeline from the Cross

The beeline in the Bible is in the other direction. Christ died so that we would make a beeline *from* the cross to the resurrection to the outpouring of the Holy Spirit to the giving of Scripture to the blood-bought miracle of new birth to the mystery of *Christ in you, the hope of glory*, to the beauties of Christ-permeating, Christ-exalting self-control and sober-mindedness and love and hospitality without grumbling.

This means that if you want to glorify the cross in your preaching, give a stunning exposition of the wonders of self-control, and the rare beauties and benefits of sober-mindedness, and the preciousness and painfulness of brotherly love, and the powerful graces at work in practical hospitality, and the world-shaking rarity of a person who never grumbles. And create a constant and joyful awareness in your people that every one of these—the seeing of every truth, the savoring of every glory, and the obedience to every command—is a Christ-exalting, blood-bought gift.

Good Tree Glorified by Its Fruit

A good tree bears good fruit. Christ died so that his body—the church— would be the tree where this beautiful and luscious fruit grows. We will magnify the success of his sacrifice if we make a beeline in every text to the concrete, detailed, specific realities that the text is truly dealing with, and what they look like, and how they come to pass by the power of the Spirit unleashed by the blood of Jesus. Jesus did not die so that a Bible would be written with a thousand pages describing only Calvary. He went to Calvary so that a thousand glories would be described in the Bible for us to see and savor and show through a crucified life.

Christ Died to Give Us Riches of Enjoying God in All of Life

Let me try to say it another way. I wrote a book called *God Is the Gospel: Meditations on God's Love as the Gift of Himself*.[2] Here is the key to what I am saying about preaching and the cross: "Christ also suffered once for sins, the righteous for the unrighteous, that he might bring us to God" (1 Pet. 3:18). Forgiveness, imputed righteousness, escape from divine wrath, rescue from hell, resurrection of the body, eternal life—these are glorious achievements of Christ crucified. But they are not the main gift of God's love—not the ultimate gift that Jesus bought with his blood. They are all means, not the end. The end is seeing God in all his beauty, and enjoying personal friendship with him, and being conformed to his likeness in every way that maximizes our enjoyment and reflection of his greatness. Christ died mainly for this.

All the Scriptures are written to advance this experience of God. Every revelation of his character and ways, every description of Christ, every word he spoke, every rebuke of our sin, every promise of his grace, every practical command to walk in love and holiness, every warning against unrighteousness—all of these are blood-bought means of walking in joyful fellowship with God. This is what Jesus died for.

---

2. John Piper, *God Is the Gospel: Meditations on God's Love as the Gift of Himself* (Wheaton, IL: Crossway, 2005).

Therefore, to preach Christ crucified, as Paul implied in 1 Corinthians 2:2 and Galatians 6:14, is not to turn every sermon into a message that climaxes with a rehearsal of the atonement. Rather, it is to treat seriously and carefully every word and every clause and every logical connection in the text in order to show how Christ—crucified, and risen, and present by the Spirit—empowers and shapes the new way of life described in the text.

Preaching the "Unsearchable Riches of Christ"

Paul was stunned that God would call him "to preach to the Gentiles the unsearchable riches of Christ" (Eph. 3:8). We will not succeed in glorifying these "unsearchable riches of Christ" in our preaching if we train people to move away from the rigorous and detailed attention to biblical texts in order to make a beeline to familiar facts about the atonement (glorious as they are!). Look at the context of Ephesians 3:8. Here is why Paul preached the unsearchable riches of Christ:

> . . . to bring to light for everyone what is the plan of the mystery hidden for ages in God, who created all things, so that through the church the manifold wisdom of God might now be made known to the rulers and authorities in the heavenly places. (Eph. 3:9–10)

Preach Christ. Unfold the mystery of God for the world. Create by his power a new people of God called "the church." And by that people— how they come into being, and worship, and live—show the angels and demons the manifold wisdom of God, the wisdom of how God creates a people by the cross. The glorious wisdom of the cross is seen in the church. And God gave the church a book filled with concrete, specific teachings. These are the instrument that the Spirit uses to shape the church into a Christ-exalting presence in the world.

Preaching takes hold of those concrete, specific teachings and wrings from them every drop of stunning, life-transforming wisdom. No apologies for dealing with the details of the text and pressing them home on the hearts of the people. No impatience to leave the text and get to more cross-explicit texts. You have made clear to your people over and over: the cross is already here. Always here. It is the foundation of everything. No good without it. So let us dig down deep into the beauties of the fruit of life and worship. This is what Christ died to achieve. This is preaching the unsearchable riches of Christ.

"Him We Proclaim"

We see the same thing from a different angle in Colossians 1:27–28:

> To them God chose to make known how great among the Gentiles are the riches of the glory of this mystery, which is *Christ in you, the hope of glory. Him we proclaim*, warning everyone and teaching everyone with all wisdom, that we may present everyone mature in Christ.

"Him we proclaim." Yes! In front of Paul's declaration "Him we proclaim" is "Christ in you, the hope of glory." Proclaiming Christ means making gloriously clear and beautiful all the implications of the blood-bought reality of Christ in you *now*. The death of Christ, two thousand years before you existed, purchased the presence of Christ in you today. Texts that deal with how to experience this living Christ, and how to be transformed by him in the specific attitudes and behaviors of life, are in the Bible not to send us on a beeline to the cross. The cross is in the Bible to send us on a beeline to dig deep into those texts and discover the wonders of blood-bought, obedient life in Christ. That does not happen by treating those texts quickly and superficially before we leave them in the name of preaching Christ crucified.

Then, on the backside of Paul's declaration "Him we proclaim," is Paul's elaboration of what's involved in this proclamation: ". . . warning everyone and teaching everyone with all wisdom, *that we may present everyone mature in Christ*." The aim of preaching Christ is maturity in the living Christ. This involves warnings and teachings and wisdom. These are the kinds of things we find filling the pages of Scripture. "Proclaim Christ" does not mean turning from the specific and detailed warnings and teachings and wisdom of Scripture to repeat the gospel story. Instead "proclaim Christ" spares no effort to see deeply into what is really there in the text—all the wonders in truth and life that Christ died to make ours.

The Interlocking Reality of God's Glory and the Son's Work

I mentioned in chapter 12 that the three answers to our overarching question, "What reality do we preach?" are interlocking: (1) the glory of God the Father, (2) the saving work of the Son, and (3) the sanctifying and keeping work of the Spirit. Here we see the interlocking of the Father's and the Son's glory.

Preaching Christ, according to the apostle Paul, not only includes heralding his sacrificial purchase of every good thing believers ever experience, and the transforming power of his presence in our lives; it also includes the aim to bring Christ glory because of his work for us and in us. It is true that the glory of the Father has a kind of ultimacy. We see it in Philippians 2:11 where the Father exalts the Son above every name so that "every tongue [would] confess that Jesus Christ is Lord, *to the glory of God the Father*." Nevertheless, the glory of the Father and the Son is one glory. The glory of Christ that streams from his cross, and from the resurrection, and from his work in his people—this glory is the very glory of God. We see this most clearly in 2 Corinthians 4:4–6:

> In their case the god of this world has blinded the minds of the unbelievers, to keep them from seeing the light of the gospel of *the glory of Christ, who is the image of God.* . . . For God, who said, "Let light shine out of darkness," has shone in our hearts to give the light of the knowledge of *the glory of God in the face of Jesus Christ.*

Paul makes the point clear and explicit. As soon as he refers to the glory of *Christ*, he says Christ is the image of *God*. And as soon as he mentions the glory of *God*, he says this glory is in the face of *Christ*. In other words, these are not two glories. The glory of Christ is the glory of God.

Not surprisingly then, Paul makes the glory of Christ the goal of creation and the goal of the Christian life. "He is the image of the invisible God. . . . All things were created through him and *for him*" (Col. 1:15–16). That is, all things were created for Christ's glory. Therefore, when we preach Christ, we aim to display his glory.

This is the goal of all preaching because the faith and power of believers that Christ died to obtain, and we preach to awaken, exist for the glory of Christ. This is what Paul said in 2 Thessalonians 1:11–12: "We always pray for you, that our God may make you worthy of his calling and may fulfill every resolve for good and every work of faith by his power, *so that the name of our Lord Jesus may be glorified in you*."

Enjoy the Living Christ

We have now answered two of our three questions designed to show what biblical realities should be woven into all our preaching.

1. What is the ultimate goal of the biblical author in the sermon

text? We answered: The glorification of God. Our people should see all things with ever greater brightness because of their relation to the glory of God. The glory of God shines not instead of what is in the text, but rather in and through the concrete realities of the text. The more rigorously we attend to what God put in the text, the more radiantly will his glory shine out of the text.

2. How does the sermon text relate to Jesus Christ and his saving work? We answered: To proclaim Christ (Col. 1:28), or to preach with the aim of boasting only in the cross (Gal. 6:14), or to preach with the aim of knowing only Christ crucified (1 Cor. 2:2), or to preach the unsearchable riches of Christ (Eph. 3:8) is to preach the reality that the blood of Christ purchased for his people. Preaching magnifies the glory of that purchase not by leaving the text and making a beeline to the cross, but by making a beeline *from* the all-providing cross to the details of every text and the wonders of Christ-saturated, Christ-exalting, blood-bought worship and obedience. Thus Christ crucified becomes the foundation of every sermon. There would be nothing to offer in preaching if he had not died for sinners.

Let me clarify once more in closing this chapter that calling the cross the "foundation" of every blood-bought blessing must never obscure, but only magnify, the truth that the greatest of those blessings is Christ himself in all his glory. Christ in us. Christ over us. Christ before us. Christ behind us. Christ befriending us, sustaining us, and satisfying us with his own glorious presence. The glory of Christ that the cross enabled us to enjoy is the glory of his love in sorrow revealed in the cross, the glory of his justice in mercy revealed in the cross, the glory of his power in weakness revealed in the cross.

Therefore, the cross is not "foundation" the way the cement blocks in your basement are foundation—out of sight, out of mind. It is foundation the way fire is the foundation of light. The way paint is the foundation of portraits. The way love is the foundation of relationships. The way lilacs are the foundation of the aroma that fills the air. The way the sacrifice is the foundation of the eternal song of the Lamb. The glory of this "foundation" lingers in all that it secures and sustains. Christ crucified did not purchase Christ-forgetting obedience, but Christ-cherishing, Christ-exalting obedience.

Since Jesus himself is also the capstone of every blood-bought blessing, the experience of God's people, pursued in every sermon, is incomplete without the enjoyment of the living Christ. Every sermon, therefore, seeks to glorify Christ in the joyful, Christ-exalting, text-shaped obedience of his people.

In the next two chapters, we turn to our third question: What is the way of life that leads to final salvation rather than destruction? This too will lead us to a reality that will shape every sermon.

17

Expository Exultation and the
Obedience of Faith, Part 1

The Path of Love That Leads to Life

I have suggested three questions that guide us in how to choose which aspects of a biblical author's larger vision to include in our preaching of specific texts: (1) What is the ultimate goal of the biblical author in the sermon text? (chapters 13 and 14). (2) How does the sermon text relate to Jesus Christ and his saving work? (chapters 15 and 16). (3) What is the way of life that leads to final salvation rather than destruction? (the present chapter and the following one).

In this chapter, we deal with the third question, which assumes that if there is a way to pursue holiness (and eternal life) that succeeds and a way that fails, preaching should make clear the way that leads to life and warn against the way that fails. I assume, further, that the human heart may respond to *any* text in a way that leads to destruction or to glory. Therefore, whatever the text, preaching should point the way to life and glory.

One way to see the relationships among these three questions is that the first dealt with the glory of God as the *goal* of the Christian life, the second dealt with the cross of Christ as the *ground* of the Christian life, and now the third deals with the *way* we live the Christian life—the only viable way that leads to final salvation. If preaching succeeds in making the goal clear, and making the ground clear, but fails to make the way between them clear, it fails totally. Jesus said, "The way is hard that leads to life, and those who find it are few" (Matt. 7:14). The task of preaching is to help people get on that path and stay on it.

Preaching and Perseverance

It is possible to know the goal of the Christian life, and to know the ground, and yet perish. Judas knew all the same teachings that Peter knew. The Pharisees spent more time in the Scriptures than any other group, and they were full of deadness (Matt. 23:27). Before his conversion, Paul was so expert in the law of God that he could be called "blameless," but was so blind and dead that he persecuted the church (Phil. 3:6). Peter said that there were professing Christians for whom "it would have been better for them never to have known the way of righteousness" (2 Pet. 2:21). And the book of Hebrews says that it is possible to misuse "the knowledge of the truth" in such a way that "there no longer remains a sacrifice for sins" (Heb. 10:26).

In spite of these flashing yellow lights in Scripture, there is a view of the Christian life that minimizes the need for perseverance in faith and holiness. It has no place for the exhortation, "Be all the more diligent to confirm your calling and election" (2 Pet. 1:10). This view sees our initial profession of faith as imparting a kind of security that does not need ongoing confirmation through persevering faith and holiness.

There is a kind of preaching that goes with this view of salvation. It aims to get people to make that first profession of faith, and after that, salvation is never at stake in the congregation. For professing believers, such preaching has no implications for their eternal life. Perseverance in faith and holiness are not essential to their security, and therefore the ongoing preaching of the word of God is not essential for sustaining faith for eternal life.

This is a perilous view of salvation, with an eviscerating effect on the depth and urgency of preaching. The biblical truth is that perseverance in faith and holiness are indeed required for final salvation, and preaching is one of God's gracious means of making sure it happens for all who are truly his. Therefore, every week in corporate worship, salvation is at stake—not just because unbelievers are present who need to be saved, but because God's plan is to preserve his people for final salvation through the ministry of the word. Nothing weighed heavier on me in my thirty-three years of pastoral ministry than the knowledge that I was God's instrument in helping my people get safely home.

Every Sermon Appointed to Save Saints

Preachers must settle this matter in their minds in order to understand their calling and feel the urgency of every sermon. I have heard many people talk about the urgency created by the possible presence of one unbelieving person in the congregation who may die before he hears the gospel again. But it seems that far fewer people speak of a similar urgency created every week, not by what *may* be the case, but what definitely *is* the case: any of the professing believers present could perish if they fail to press on in faith and obedience. And your preaching on this very Sunday may be God's instrument to rescue them in the coming week from apostasy in the face of some horrific suffering. Every week your sermon is appointed to empower some person to escape temptation that otherwise might be the decisive step into a path of irretrievable wickedness. Every sermon is a salvation sermon for every believer.

Holiness without Which We Will Not See the Lord

You need to settle this matter in your mind. It will make a huge difference in the urgency with which you preach. Consider the implications of the following passages of Scripture. As you read them, ask, Do these passages teach that real, practical, lived-out holiness is the only path that leads to final salvation?

> *If you do not forgive others their trespasses*, neither will your Father forgive your trespasses. (Matt. 6:15)

> On that day many will say to me, "Lord, Lord, did we not prophesy in your name, and cast out demons in your name, and do many mighty works in your name?" And then will I declare to them, "I never knew you; depart from me, *you workers of lawlessness*." (Matt. 7:22–23)

> The one who *endures to the end* will be saved. (Mark 13:13)

> Do not marvel at this, for an hour is coming when all who are in the tombs will hear his voice and come out, *those who have done*

good to the resurrection of life, and those who have done evil to the resurrection of judgment. (John 5:28–29)

To those who *by patience in well-doing* seek for glory and honor and immortality, he will give eternal life. (Rom. 2:7)

Now I would remind you, brothers, of the gospel I preached to you, which you received, in which you stand, and by which you are being saved, *if you hold fast to the word I preached to you—unless you believed in vain.* (1 Cor. 15:1–2)

If you live according to the flesh you will die, but *if by the Spirit you put to death the deeds of the body, you will live.* (Rom. 8:13)

The one who sows to his own flesh will from the flesh reap corruption, but the one who sows to the Spirit will from the Spirit reap eternal life. And let us not grow weary of doing good, *for in due season we will reap [eternal life], if we do not give up.* (Gal. 6:8–9)

[Christ] has now reconciled [you] in his body of flesh by his death, in order to present you holy and blameless and above reproach before him, *if indeed you continue in the faith*, stable and steadfast, not shifting from the hope of the gospel that you heard. (Col. 1:22–23)

We ought always to give thanks to God for you, brothers beloved by the Lord, because God chose you as the firstfruits to be *saved, through sanctification* by the Spirit and belief in the truth. (2 Thess. 2:13)

Christ is faithful over God's house as a son. And we are his house, *if indeed we hold fast our confidence* and our boasting in our hope. (Heb. 3:6)

We have come to share in Christ, *if indeed we hold our original confidence firm to the end.* (Heb. 3:14)

We are not of those who *shrink back and are destroyed*, but of those who have faith and preserve their souls. (Heb. 10:39)

Strive for peace with everyone, and *for the holiness without which no one will see the Lord.* (Heb. 12:14)

Blessed is the man who remains steadfast under trial, for *when he has stood the test he will receive the crown of life*, which God has promised to those who love him. (James 1:12)

Faith by itself, *if it does not have works, is dead.* (James 2:17)

If we walk in the light, as he is in the light, we have fellowship with one another, and the blood of Jesus his Son cleanses us from all sin. (1 John 1:7)

Whoever says "I know him" but *does not keep his commandments is a liar*, and the truth is not in him. (1 John 2:4)

We know that we have passed out of death into life, *because we love the brothers*. Whoever does not love abides in death. (1 John 3:14)

Be faithful unto death, and I will give you the crown of life. (Rev. 2:10)

If this were a book on sanctification and perseverance, I would need to linger over all those verses and show their meaning and implications in context.[1] But this is a book on preaching, and my main aim here is not to defend this view of salvation, but to show its implications for preaching. To do that, I must at least clarify the biblical issues.

What those texts teach is that there is a holiness—a real childlike, Christ-dependent, God-glorifying, joyful way of life—that leads to eternal life, and without which we will perish. Or to put it another way, saving faith is of such a nature that it is authenticated in a life of holiness. Not perfection. But a real change of heart and attitude and action that shows Christ has become the Savior and Lord and treasure of one's life.

Holiness and Eternal Security

This necessity for holiness does not undermine our assurance or our eternal security, because God has committed himself to hold fast to all those who are his. We are secure not because perseverance is optional, but because the omnipotent, covenant-keeping God is the one who decisively makes it happen. Which means that the following passages are just as important and precious as the ones above. These are the ones that show God's total commitment to preserve our faith and holiness:

---

1. See John Piper, *Future Grace: The Purifying Power of the Promises of God* (Colorado Springs, CO: Multnomah, 2012).

I will make with them an everlasting covenant, that I will not turn away from doing good to them. And *I will put the fear of me in their hearts, that they may not turn from me.* (Jer. 32:40)

My sheep hear my voice, and I know them, and they follow me. I give them eternal life, and *they will never perish, and no one will snatch them out of my hand.* My Father, who has given them to me, is greater than all, and no one is able to snatch them out of the Father's hand. (John 10:27–29)

Those whom he predestined he also called, and those whom he called he also justified, and *those whom he justified he also glorified.* (Rom. 8:30)

[He] will sustain you to the end, guiltless in the day of our Lord Jesus Christ. God is faithful, by whom you were called into the fellowship of his Son, Jesus Christ our Lord. (1 Cor. 1:8–9)

And I am sure of this, that *he who began a good work in you will bring it to completion* at the day of Jesus Christ. (Phil. 1:6)

Not that I have already obtained this or am already perfect, but I press on to make it my own, because Christ *Jesus has made me his own.* (Phil. 3:12)

Consequently, *he is able to save to the uttermost* those who draw near to God through him, since he always lives to make intercession for them. (Heb. 7:25)

By God's power [you] are being guarded through faith for a salvation ready to be revealed in the last time. (1 Pet. 1:5)

They went out from us, but they were not of us; for *if they had been of us, they would have continued with us.* But they went out, that it might become plain that they all are not of us. (1 John 2:19)

Now to him who is *able to keep you from stumbling* and to present you blameless before the presence of his glory with great joy, to the only God, our Savior, through Jesus Christ our Lord, be glory, majesty, dominion, and authority, before all time and now and forever. Amen. (Jude 24–25)

Confirm Your Calling and Election

God has promised to be our keeper. To the end. Nothing can snatch us out of God's hand. Therefore, we know that when the Bible tells us to "be all the more diligent to confirm your calling and election" (2 Pet. 1:10), this does not mean *our* action of confirmation is decisive in preserving us for heaven. *God's* action of preservation is decisive. Our action is dependent and essential. God's is foundational and causal. It brings ours about. Our perseverance in faith is a supernatural miracle. God causes the miracle. We act the miracle.[2] Both are essential. This is evident in the following passages.

> By the grace of God I am what I am, and his grace toward me was not in vain. On the contrary, I worked harder than any of them, though it was not I, but the grace of God that is with me. (1 Cor. 15:10)

> For this I toil, struggling with all his energy that he powerfully works within me. (Col. 1:29)

> As you have always obeyed, so now, not only as in my presence but much more in my absence, work out your own salvation with fear and trembling, for it is God who works in you, both to will and to work for his good pleasure. (Phil. 2:12–13)

> May the God of peace who brought again from the dead our Lord Jesus, the great shepherd of the sheep, by the blood of the eternal covenant, equip you with everything good that you may do his will, working in us that which is pleasing in his sight, through Jesus Christ, to whom be glory forever and ever. Amen. (Heb. 13:20–21)

So our people's security as God's chosen and called and adopted children is not in question. They will persevere. If anyone does not persevere, he shows that he did not belong to God in the first place. That is what 1 John 2:19 makes plain—"If they had been of us, they would have continued with us." But what the preacher must be especially clear about is the fact that God holds on to his people—he preserves their faith and obedience—*through the agency of his word.* The preaching of that word to the people of God is one way God wields the word to save his people.

---

2. See John Piper and David Mathis, *Acting the Miracle: God's Work and Ours in the Mystery of Sanctification* (Wheaton, IL: Crossway, 2013).

Preaching Saves the Saved

This means, strange as it may sound, that the task of the preacher is to save the saved. That is not rhetorical overstatement or meaningless. It is exactly the truth. God can save his people any way he pleases. And the way he saves them is first by converting them to Christ (Acts 18:27; Eph. 2:5, 8), and then by "working in us that which is pleasing in his sight" (Heb. 13:21). And he does both by the word of God. Conversion happens by the word—"Faith comes from hearing, and hearing through the word of Christ" (Rom. 10:17). And ongoing faith and obedience happen by the word of God—"You received the word of God . . . which is at work in you believers" (1 Thess. 2:13).

So it should not surprise us that Paul describes the unstoppable word of God as the means by which he *saves the elect*: "The word of God is not bound! Therefore I endure everything *for the sake of the elect, that they also may obtain the salvation* that is in Christ Jesus with eternal glory" (2 Tim. 2:9–10). That's what the preacher does every week: he heralds the unstoppable word of God "for the sake of the elect, that they also may obtain . . . salvation"—not just initial conversion, but final salvation at the end of the age.

Salvation through Sanctification

Now the question is this: If they are already saved, how does preaching help them attain final salvation? What do the people need to hear, week in and week out, in order to experience the miracle of "holiness without which no one will see the Lord" (Heb. 12:14)? How does the preacher preach in order to sustain saving faith and bring about the sanctification through which his people will be saved? For indeed the preacher knows from 2 Thessalonians 2:13 that his people are "saved, *through sanctification* by the Spirit and *belief* in the truth." This is the preacher's mission: to be God's instrument to save his people *through* Spirit-wrought *sanctification* and persevering *faith*.

How then are sanctification and belief strengthened and sustained by preaching?

Holiness and Love

First, let's clarify that the essence of sanctification is genuine, sacrificial, Christ-exalting love—for God and other people. Don't limit sanctification, or holiness, to personal acts of devotion or to personal abstinence from bad behavior. It is that. But that is not the essence of it. The essence of it is being set free from the old powers of selfishness for the service of love to others.

We see the connection between holiness and love in 1 Thessalonians 3:12–13: "May the Lord make you increase and abound in *love* for one another and for all, as we do for you, *so that* he may establish your hearts blameless in *holiness*." The heart of Christian holiness is to be so radically distinct from the old ways of self-exaltation, and the old bondages to defiling pleasures, that we are free to "look . . . to the interests of others" (Phil. 2:4)—that is, freed and empowered to love.

Holiness and Justification

Next, let's make sure that we are on the same page concerning justification by faith alone. Few things are more important for the preacher's life and preaching than to be clear about the reality of justification by faith alone and its biblical relationship to sanctification. Every congregation needs to be clear about justification by faith. And every congregation needs to be clear about how justification relates to a life of faith and holiness. This is one of the great aims of preaching: to keep the congregation clear about such things.

Nothing I have said above about the necessity of holiness for final salvation implies that we are justified on the ground of faith *plus* works. We are justified on the ground of Christ alone, through the means of faith alone, apart from works. "By the *one man's obedience* the many will be made righteous" (Rom. 5:19). "We hold that one is justified *by faith apart from works* of the law" (Rom. 3:28). Not justified "from works" but for works, as Paul shows in Ephesians 2:8–10:

> By grace you have been saved through faith. And this is not your own doing; it is the gift of God, not a result of works, so that no one may boast. For we are his workmanship, created in Christ Jesus for good works, which God prepared beforehand, that we should walk in them.

Here Paul makes wonderfully clear how "works" are related to our first experience of salvation (including our justification): it is not "*a result of* works." Rather, it happened "*for* good works." Justification doesn't *rest on* good works; it *results in* good works.

We have seen that the works of this new creation are *essential* for final salvation because "faith apart from works is dead" (James 2:26). But the works are not the *ground* of our justification. Christ is the ground (Rom. 5:9, 18–19; 2 Cor. 5:21)—his blood and righteousness. Neither are good works the *instrument* or *means* by which this ground becomes ours. The means is faith alone. "We know that a person is not justified by works of the law but *through faith in Jesus Christ*, so we also have *believed in Christ Jesus*, in order to be justified *by faith in Christ* and not by works of the law, because by works of the law no one will be justified" (Gal. 2:16).

Every Good Tree Bears Good Fruit

But, while "good works" are not the ground or the instrument of our justification, they are the necessary *fruit* of justifying faith. Every good tree bears good fruit (Matt. 7:17). This means that justification and sanctification always go together. The Westminster Confession of Faith, chapter 11, puts it like this:

> Faith, thus receiving and resting on Christ and his righteousness, is the alone instrument of justification; yet it is not alone in the person justified, but is ever accompanied with all other saving graces, and is not dead faith, but works by love.

So the Westminster authors believed that saving faith "works by love." That is, faith is of such a nature that it brings about a changed life of love. This is the teaching of Galatians 5:6: "In Christ Jesus neither circumcision nor uncircumcision counts for anything, but only *faith working through love*." This is how I understand James 2:22 ("You see that faith was active along with [Abraham's] works, and faith was completed by his works"). That is, faith comes to its fulfilled aim in producing good works. Otherwise, it is dead and does not unite us to Christ, and therefore does not save.

Saving Faith Is Sanctifying Faith

When Paul says that the aim of his preaching is "obedience," he calls it the "obedience of faith," which I take to mean, the obedience *that comes from faith* (cf. Rom. 15:18; 16:26). And when he relates our "labor of love" to faith, he calls it a "work of faith" (1 Thess. 1:3; 2 Thess. 1:11). Which means that the works Paul aims to bring about by his preaching are the works of love coming from a heart of faith. He says this explicitly in 1 Timothy 1:5: "The aim of our charge [our preaching!] is *love* that issues from . . . sincere *faith*." So the reason the Westminster Catechism says that saving faith is "ever accompanied with" the good works of love is that the apostle Paul says it is. It belongs to the very nature of saving faith to produce love—"faith working through love" (Gal. 5:6).

Heart of Saving Faith: Being Satisfied in God

But the preacher asks, Why does faith produce love? That is, what is it about faith that inevitably produces the works of love? The preacher wants to know this, because he sees that it will have a huge effect on how he preaches in order to pursue the love and holiness without which his people will not get to heaven. I wrote the book *Future Grace: The Purifying Power of the Promises of God* in order to answer this question. The answer that I see in Scripture is this: The reason faith produces love is that the essence of saving faith means *being satisfied in all that God is for us in Jesus*, and this superior satisfaction in God severs the root of sin and seeks to expand by including others with us in our joy in God, even if it costs us our lives. We call that impulse to expand our joy by including others in it *love*.

Another way to say it is that faith means receiving Christ (John 1:12) not simply as Savior and Lord, but as *treasured* Savior and *treasured* Lord (Matt. 13:44; Phil. 3:8). Or, more simply, it means embracing all that God is for us in Christ as our supreme treasure. Which means embracing him gladly—receiving him as the deepest satisfaction of our souls. This soul satisfaction defeats the deceitful pleasures of sin by the power of a superior pleasure. This joy is the key to love.

The implication this has for preaching is that the preacher constantly seeks to portray, from every text, that God in Christ is supremely and everlastingly satisfying. This is the goal of his *exposition*. It is the ground of his *exultation*.

Joy in God Produces Love

In the next chapter, my aim is to illustrate the way satisfaction in God actually produces the kind of love that is necessary for final salvation.

My hope is that preachers will be strengthened and encouraged by these illustrations in their resolve to preach for their people's joy—a joy in God that gives rise to love, and thus confirms faith and election. That is, I pray that these illustrations will empower us to preach the *all-satisfying* greatness and grace of God.

18

Expository Exultation and the Obedience of Faith, Part 2

The Pursuit of Joy, Love, and Eternal Life

The main point of this chapter and the previous one is that woven into all our preaching must be the relentless illumination of the way of life that leads to final salvation, seeking always to provide protections against the way of life that leads to destruction. Specifically, I have tried to show that there is a holiness without which our people will not see the Lord (Heb. 12:14). Paul calls it the "obedience of faith" (Rom. 1:5). It is urgent that our people see the necessity of how this obedience is maintained. They need to see how it relates to justification by faith alone, and how persevering faith, in the power of the Holy Spirit, produces a life of sacrificial love.

I argued that the reason faith produces love (Gal. 5:6; 1 Tim. 1:5) is that the essence of saving faith is *soul satisfaction in all that God is for us in Jesus*. This superior satisfaction in God dethrones the deceitful allurements of sin. Not only that, but something about satisfaction in God seeks to expand by including others in it. We call that *love*.

Since the preacher knows that such love is necessary for final salvation (1 John 3:14), he will be vigilant in all his preaching to portray God in Christ as supremely satisfying to the souls of his people. That is, he will seek to awaken and sustain faith. The aim of this chapter is to give specific illustrations, from history and from the Scripture, of how finding delight in God is essential to our becoming holy, and why preaching should aim at that delight.

What Brainerd Discovered Preaching to Natives

I begin with an encounter that I had with David Brainerd's preaching to Native Americans in the 1740s. It turned out to be a remarkable discovery about the way preaching gives rise to genuine contrition and repentance. This is relevant to our question because contrition is the *beginning* of all genuine obedience, holiness, and love. So the way contrition comes about is crucial for the way love comes about.

David Brainerd was a missionary in colonial America. Jonathan Edwards published his *Diary*, which became a missionary classic. As I read some portions of Brainerd's *Diary*, I was amazed at the effect of his preaching on the Native Americans. On August 9, 1745, he preached at Crossweeksung, New Jersey, and made this observation:

> There were many tears among them while I was discoursing publicly, but no considerable cry: Yet some were much affected with a few words spoken to them in a powerful manner, which caused the persons to cry out in anguish of soul, *although I spoke not a word of terror, but on the contrary, set before them the fullness and all-sufficiency of Christ's merits*, and his willingness to save all that come to him; and thereupon pressed them to come without delay.[1]

He had said earlier on August 6, "It was surprising to see how their hearts seemed to be pierced with the tender and melting invitations of the Gospel, when there was not a word of terror spoken to them."[2]

Again on November 30, he preached on Luke 16:19–26 concerning the rich man and Lazarus:

> The Word made powerful impressions upon many in the assembly, especially while I discoursed of the blessedness of Lazarus "in Abraham's bosom" [Luke 16:22]. This, I could perceive, affected them much more than what I spoke of the rich man's misery and torments. And thus it has been usually with them. . . . *They have almost always appeared much more affected with the comfortable than the*

---

1. Jonathan Edwards, *The Life of David Brainerd*, ed. Norman Pettit, vol. 7, *The Works of Jonathan Edwards* (New Haven, CT: Yale University Press, 1985), 310; emphasis added.
2. Ibid., 307.

> *dreadful truths of God's Word.* And that which has distressed many
> of them under convictions, is that they found they wanted [lacked],
> and could not obtain, *the happiness of the godly.*[3]

This points to something remarkable about the spiritual cause of true
contrition, which is the beginning of all acceptable obedience. But before we analyze what that spiritual cause is, let's consider a biblical
example similar to Brainerd's experience with Native Americans.

Grace Broke Peter's Heart

The same dynamic seems to occur in Luke 5:1–10. After teaching the
crowds from a boat off land in the lake of Gennesaret, Jesus told the
fishermen to push out into the deep and let down their nets for a catch.
Simon protested, "Master, we toiled all night and took nothing! But at
your word I will let down the nets" (v. 5). The nets filled with so many
fish that they started to break. Both boats were filled and started to sink
from the catch.

Peter's response was remarkable, very unlike our modern, self-
esteeming response to grace. Verses 8–9:

> When Simon Peter saw it, he fell down at Jesus' knees, saying, "De-
> part from me, for I am a sinful man, O Lord." For he and all who
> were with him were astonished at the catch of fish that they had
> taken.

What is remarkable here is that a miracle of grace, not a word of judgment, broke Peter's heart and brought him to contrition and repentance.
It was the same with the natives of Crossweeksung under Brainerd's
preaching.

Tasting God's Goodness Gives Regret for Not Drinking

Genuine contrition for sin is a *sorrow for not having holiness.* But we
have to be careful here. Not all sorrow over sin is godly sorrow. It is
possible to weep over not having holiness *not* because you love God
and want to enjoy all that he is for you in Christ, but because you fear
the punishment that comes from not having holiness. Many a criminal
will weep when his sentence is read, not because he has come to love

---

3. Ibid., 342; emphasis added.

righteousness, but because his freedom to do more unrighteousness is being taken away. That kind of weeping is not true repentance. And it does not lead to Spirit-given obedience and love.

The only true sorrow for not having holiness comes from a *love* for holiness, not from a fear of the consequences of not having it. Or a more precise way to say it is this: true remorse over not having holiness is remorse over not enjoying God as our supreme treasure, and not living by the impulse of that joy. To cry over the punishment one is about to receive for wrongdoing is no sure sign of hating wrong. It may be a sign only of hating pain. For crying and contrition to be real, it must come from *the brokenhearted feelings we have for lacking a life of joy in God*, not just from the fearful feelings of being threatened with pain. True contrition is to be brokenhearted that God has been so boring and insignificant to us.

But now think what this implies. In order to cry over not having something, you must really *want* to have it. And the more you *want* to have it, the more you feel distressed over not having it. This means that true contrition, true repentance, must be preceded by falling in love with God—by the wakening of a taste for his glory. To truly weep at not having holiness, you must long for holiness. To truly weep over not possessing it, it must be attractive to you.

Perhaps you see how strange this seems at first: God and his way of holiness must become our *joy* before we can *weep* over not having it. We must fall in love before estrangement truly hurts. Our eyes must be opened to the superior treasure that God is, before we will be brokenhearted for how long we have scorned him as worthless.

Preaching That Leads to Genuine Contrition—and Love

What kind of preaching is needed to produce such genuine repentance— both for unbelievers and backsliding Christians? Brainerd found that a message about the winsome attractiveness of God produced more brokenheartedness than did a message of warning. Warning has value in stirring us up to take the glories of holiness and heaven seriously so that perhaps we might come to see them for what they are, and delight in them. But it is the delight in them that causes the true grief when we fall short. No one cries over missing what they don't *want* to have.

Peter saw in the miracle of the fish catch a glimpse of how valuable and amazing and beautiful Jesus was. He saw a person so wonderful that he was overwhelmed with how out of sync his life was with such a treasure. Is not this your experience? It is mine. If this much power and this much goodness is there in Jesus for those who trust him, then, oh, how different would be my life if I truly believed. How radical would be my obedience! What abandon I would feel in living for such a Christ! What freedom from petty grievances and from fleeting pleasures of sin I would enjoy!

What I saw in Brainerd's preaching was that true contrition—and all the holiness and love that grow from that root—comes into being by the awakening of satisfaction with all that God is for us in Jesus. Until God is our treasure, we will not grieve over falling short of being satisfied in God. Which means we will still be in bondage to the deceitful pleasures of this world.

Preaching Lures with the Beauty of God

So preaching that aims to produce true gospel contrition must continually aim to make God and his holiness look alluringly attractive so that, by the work of the Spirit, people will come to delight in it so much that they feel intense remorse over falling short of it. That is the beginning of all true holiness and love. To say it another way, we must preach in a way that awakens joy in the glory of God if we hope to produce true grief over falling short of the glory of God.

But we are not just interested in contrition. We want that bud to open as the flower of holiness and love. What the preacher discovers is that the same taste of God's glory that causes grief over our failures to be satisfied in him, also produces a life of holiness and love when that taste grows into (or explodes into) a deep satisfaction in God.

Drawing the Language of Joy from the Well of the Psalms

Once the preacher sees from the Scripture that holiness and love flow from a deep soul-satisfaction in God, he knows that from then on, every sermon, even those that deal with the evils of sin and the horrors of judgment, must portray God and all that he is for us in Christ as supremely satisfying. The preacher will lower his bucket into the well of the Psalms and draw up the language of soul-satisfaction. And it will begin to permeate his sermons, even though it may be foreign to his people.

O God, you are my God; earnestly I seek you;
    my soul thirsts for you;
my flesh faints for you,
    as in a dry and weary land where there is no water. . . .
My soul will be satisfied as with fat and rich food,
    and my mouth will praise you with joyful lips. (Ps. 63:1–5)

They feast on the abundance of your house,
    and *you give them drink from the river of your delights.* (Ps.
        36:8)

As for me, I shall behold your face in righteousness;
    when I awake, *I shall be satisfied with your likeness.* (Ps. 17:15)

Satisfy us in the morning with your steadfast love,
    that we may rejoice and be glad all our days. (Ps. 90:14)

He satisfies the longing soul,
    and the hungry soul he fills with good things. (Ps. 107:9)

The preacher will drink from this well—from the river of God's delights—until his *exposition* of God's word overflows with *exultation* in the all-satisfying glories of God. These glories are indeed in every text. He will realize that he is always handling the word of *God*. The very word *of God*. If a word is in the mouth of God, it cannot be commonplace. It cannot be boring. It cannot be insignificant. It cannot be monotonous or tiresome or dull. The very fact that it comes from the mouth of the Creator of the universe makes it astonishing. The souls of our people do not live by bread alone. They live by this astonishing, soul-awakening, soul-satisfying word of God. To touch the fire of this word with *exposition* is to be enflamed with *exultation*.

But Does All Holy Love Flow from Joy in God?

All Christ-exalting, God-glorifying, Spirit-empowered obedience and holiness and love flow from this God-besotted soul satisfaction. This fact transforms preaching. So let me go just a few steps further in making sure that all the preachers who read this book will see this amazing truth. Here are three glimpses into the way our satisfaction in God sets us free from sin, and expands into love. These are glimpses of what every faithful preacher longs to see in his people. This is what he aims at through his preaching.

Glimpse #1: 2 Corinthians 8:1–2

First, consider the Macedonian Christians that Paul holds up to the Corinthian church as an example of what love looks like and how it comes about:

> We want you to know, brothers, about the grace of God that has been given among the churches of Macedonia, for in a severe test of affliction, *their abundance of joy* and their extreme poverty have *overflowed in a wealth of generosity* on their part. (2 Cor. 8:1–2)

We know Paul sees this Macedonian generosity as an act of genuine *love* because in verse 8 he explains, "I say this . . . to prove by the earnestness of others that your *love also* is genuine." What then is love, according to 2 Corinthians 8:1–2? And how did it come about in the lives of the Macedonians?

First, the grace of God was shown (v. 1). The Macedonians were converted and profoundly joyful over the grace of God. This joy was the source of the generosity that Paul calls love. "Their abundance of joy . . . *overflowed* in a wealth of generosity." You could even say that their generosity *was their joy expanding to include others in it.*

And what was their joy in? Not in greater wealth, because Paul said they were acting from "extreme poverty." Not in comfort, because Paul said they were acting "in a severe test of affliction." This is simply astonishing. The grace of God was so satisfying to these people that in spite of poverty and affliction, their joy was unstoppably expansive. It overflowed in generosity. Paul calls this "love." And he said in the next chapter that God loves this way of loving: "God loves a cheerful giver" (2 Cor. 9:7).

Effect on Preaching

This sacrificial love is the holiness without which we will not see the Lord (Heb. 12:14). This is the love without which we abide in death (1 John 3:14). This is the narrow gate and the hard way that leads to life (Matt. 7:14). This is the path between the cross of Christ (chapter 15–16) and the glory of God (chapters 13–14). This is the reality we preach. We aim to show that the grace and glory of God are so satisfying to the heart that our joy overflows to meet the needs of others. Therefore, we preach and pray that God will be seen in every text as all-satisfying.

Glimpse #2: Hebrews 10:32–35

After the conversion of the Christians to whom the book of Hebrews was addressed, a serious persecution arose. Some were put in prison. The rest faced a crisis of whether to publicly identify with the prisoners and risk reprisals. They took that risk. With extraordinary love, they became "partners with those so treated" (Heb. 10:33). It cost them dearly. How did they do it? Where did this love come from? Here's the answer:

> Recall the former days when, after you were enlightened, you endured a hard struggle with sufferings, sometimes being publicly exposed to reproach and affliction, and sometimes being partners with those so treated. For you had compassion on those in prison, and you *joyfully* accepted the plundering of your property, *since you knew that you yourselves had a better possession and an abiding one*. Therefore do not throw away your confidence, which has a great reward. (vv. 32–35)

They *joyfully* embraced the cost of love. Again this is simply amazing. I am rebuked and inspired every time I read it. The glimpse of love in 2 Corinthians 8:1–2, together with this glimpse in Hebrews 10:32–35, forms for me a composite picture of *the path of life that leads from cross to crown*—from the foundation of Christ's cross to the consummation of God's glory. This is the answer to our third question, which this chapter and the previous one are devoted to: What is the way of life that leads to final salvation rather than destruction? This astonishing, supernatural love sustained by joy through suffering is the reality I was aiming at in my preaching for thirty years—to show a God so satisfying that joy would overcome all selfishness and unleash the most authentic kinds of love.

Where did this joy come from that freed the Hebrew Christians to risk their property and lives for the sake of Christian prisoners? The writer says they *joyfully* accepted the plundering of their property, "*since* you knew that you yourselves had a better possession and an abiding one" (v. 34). The essence of this supremely better and eternally abiding "possession" is God himself.

To be sure, in the age to come we will have resurrection bodies with consummate enjoyments for body, mind, and soul. But if we are not to be idolaters in that day, the essence of our delights will be God himself. "In your presence there is *fullness* of joy [a *better* possession]; at your right hand are pleasures *forevermore* [an *abiding* possession]" (Ps. 16:11). "I will go to the altar of God, to *God* my exceeding joy" (Ps. 43:4)—or as the Hebrew reads literally, "to *God* the joy of all my joys." That is what freed this astonishing act of love in Hebrews 10:32–35.

Effect on Preaching

This is what our people must see in the word of God week in and week out through our *expository exultation*. This is our calling—by rigorous attention to the words of the text to penetrate though the text to the reality of the all-satisfying God. Every preacher should ask, Are my people so deeply satisfied in God that their joy overflows in generosity to the poor in the midst of their own suffering? Are my people so deeply satisfied in God that they joyfully risk losing their property? How is my preaching, and how is my life, helping them experience the miracle of seeing and savoring God in Scripture?

Glimpse #3: Hebrews 11

In our third glimpse, what becomes clear is that the obedience that flows from soul satisfaction in God is the *obedience of faith*. We see this in Hebrews 11. It begins, "Now faith is the assurance of things hoped for, the conviction of things not seen" (v. 1). The word translated "assurance" (*hupostasis*) is used two more times in Hebrews. First, in Hebrews 1:3, "He [Christ] is the radiance of the glory of God and the exact imprint of *his nature* [*hupostaseōs autou*]." Second, in Hebrews 3:14, "We have come to share in Christ, if indeed we hold our original confidence [*hupostaseōs*] firm to the end." So, as in Hebrews 1:3, this Greek word can mean "nature" or "substance" or "essence." And, as in Hebrews 3:14, it can mean "confidence" or "assurance."

Based on what comes in the rest of Hebrews 11, which shows people acting "by faith," I think both these meanings are part of Hebrews 11:1: "Faith is the *hupostasis* of things hoped." The meaning "confidence" or "assurance" is fairly easy to see: "Faith is the *assurance* of things hoped for." When we have faith, we feel *confident* in God's promises. The other meaning is less easy to grasp. Faith is the "substance" or "nature" and "essence" of what we hope for. In what sense is that true?

Faith Is the Substance of Things Hoped For

The essence of what we hope for is the perfected experience of joy in God when we meet him at the last day. What does it mean, then, to say that faith is the *substance* or *essence* of that? I think it means that faith tastes that future joy now. Faith is the beginning of that satisfaction in God now. Some degree of that future experience of seeing and savoring God is experienced now. That advance experience of seeing and savoring God's beauty in Christ is called faith. It is only a taste by comparison to what it will be. Since faith sees the glory of God now only as "in a mirror dimly" (1 Cor. 13:12; cf. 2 Cor. 5:7), our present experience of the substance and essence of future joy with God is embattled and varying. Faith can be weak or growing or strong (Luke 17:5; Acts 16:5; 1 Thess. 3:10; 2 Thess. 1:3). But the essence of faith is that it tastes the all-satisfying glory of what God is for us in Christ. Thus it participates in the "substance" or "nature" of what is hoped for.

How Faith Produces Obedience

We see this as we watch faith at work in Hebrews 11. Verse 6 says, "Without faith it is impossible to please [God], for whoever would draw near to God must believe that he exists and that [he is the rewarder (*misthapodotēs*) of] those who seek him" (Heb. 11:6). God's greatest reward is the gift of himself to be enjoyed forever. The essence of faith is that it tastes and sees the substance (or the nature or the essence) of this reward *now*. Not perfectly. But profoundly. So profoundly that it unleashes extraordinary acts of costly obedience.

We see this joy at work in Moses in Hebrews 11:24–26. And it is called acting "by faith":

> By faith Moses, when he was grown up, refused to be called the son of Pharaoh's daughter, choosing rather to be mistreated with the people of God than to enjoy the *fleeting pleasures* of sin. He considered the reproach of Christ *greater wealth than the treasures of Egypt, for he was looking to the reward.*

This is a picture of self-sacrificing love just like the one in Hebrews 10:32–35. There the believers risked their property to visit those in prison. Here Moses chooses mistreatment with the captives rather than hiding in the comfort and security of Pharaoh's court. The Christians did it because they "knew that [they] had a better possession and an abiding one" (10:34). Moses did it because "he was looking to the reward" (Heb. 11:26). The added insight here in chapter 11 is that this liberating joy of hope is called "faith."

Aim of Paul's Preaching—and Ours

This leads us back to Paul's all-encompassing statements about the aim of his ministry and preaching that we saw at the end of the previous chapter. "We have received grace and apostleship *to bring about the obedience of faith*" (Rom. 1:5). "The aim of our charge is *love that issues from . . . sincere faith*" (1 Tim. 1:5). These two phrases—"the obedience of faith" and "love that issues from . . . sincere faith"—sum up the kind of life that leads to final salvation. This obedience of faith and love from faith are the "holiness without which no one will see the Lord" (Heb. 12:14).

But not just any obedience and any love are required of Christians. Only the obedience and love that come *from faith* count with God. "In Christ Jesus neither circumcision nor uncircumcision counts for anything, but only *faith* working through *love*" (Gal. 5:6). This faith has joy in God as its essence. Which is why Paul not only makes all-inclusive statements about pursuing love *through faith*, but also makes all-inclusive statements about pursuing the *joy* of his people—the joy of faith. "I know that I will remain and continue with you all, for your progress and *joy in the faith*" (Phil. 1:25). "Not that we lord it over your *faith*, but we work with you for your *joy*" (2 Cor. 1:24). This is the way that leads to life.

Therefore, all preaching should aim, in every sermon and in every text, to help people experience the reality of the text in such a way that they will not turn it into a kind of obedience or a kind of love or a kind of holiness that leads to death. We know this is possible because the Bible gives us a stark example of it happening. "Israel who pursued a law that would lead to righteousness did not succeed in reaching that law. Why? Because they did not pursue it by faith" (Rom. 9:31–32). It is possible to perish pursuing obedience to the word of God.

The Way That Leads to Eternal Life

Preaching must know this. This is why we have devoted two chapters to our third question, "What is the way of life that leads to final salvation rather than destruction?" We have seen in this chapter the way of life that leads not to destruction, but to life. Every text of Scripture is related in some way to the new life of the Spirit called "walking by faith" (see 2 Cor. 5:7; Gal. 2:20). Every text in some way helps us "walk by faith." Every text nurtures in some way the "obedience of faith." Preaching either sees this aim of Scripture and helps people on the way to eternal life, or gives stumbling blocks.

What we have seen is that walking by faith—obeying by faith, being holy by faith—means walking in the freedom and power of satisfaction in all that God is for us in Jesus. Our people's satisfaction in God—treasuring God over all things—is either being nurtured by our preaching or neglected. Therefore, every sermon is a salvation sermon—salvation for the saints. For the love that flows from this satisfaction in God is necessary for final salvation. "Whoever does not love abides in death" (1 John 3:14).

Preaching Backward for the Joy That Gives Assurance

Preaching that draws out the all-satisfying glories of God through every text works backward and forward. It works *backward* by sustaining and confirming the faith that alone unites us to Christ in whom is our perfect righteousness. Christ alone is the ground of the truth that God, here and now and forever, is one hundred percent for us. We do not love people in order to get God to be for us. We love people because God *is now, already, because of Christ*, 100 percent for us. This is part of his glory that satisfies our souls. Thus the preaching that weaves the all-satisfying glories of God into every sermon honors and applies the indispensable doctrine of justification by faith alone.

Preaching Forward for the Joy That Leads to Love

Such preaching works *forward* by sustaining and confirming the faith that is the *effect* and the *reception* of the Holy Spirit. Thus the Spirit produces in us all his fruit through this faith (Gal. 3:5; 5:5, 22; Eph. 2:8; Phil. 1:29). All our future acts of love, all our experiences of holiness, are the work of the Spirit through faith. Or they are worthless. The Spirit's great mission in the world, Jesus said, is to glorify the Son of God (John 16:14).

This is how the Spirit brings about the beauty of holiness in us. He enables us to see the all-satisfying glory of Christ (2 Cor. 3:18). The joy that comes from this sight frees us from the "fleeting pleasures of sin" and transforms us into humble servants who rejoice to meet the needs of others. Spirit-given joy in the glory of God is expansive. It seeks to enlarge itself by including others in it—even, if necessary, at the cost of property and life.

What Reality Do We Preach?

Therefore, the reality that pervades our preaching week in and week out is the all-satisfying glory of God. Our aim is eternal life for our people. Spirit-produced holiness, rooted in the cross of Christ, and lived for the glory of God, is the only path that leads to eternal life (Rom. 6:22; Heb. 12:14). This holiness is the obedience of faith (Rom. 1:5). It is the love that comes from faith (1 Tim. 1:5). Therefore, it comes from being satisfied with all that God is for us in Jesus. Therefore, the reality we preach is the path of life sustained by a sight of the all-satisfying glory of God.

PART 7

Expository Exultation and
the Old Testament

The Glory of God, the Cross of Christ, and the Obedience of Faith

19

Expository Exultation and the Old Testament, Part 1

Preaching the Glory of God

The upshot of part 6 (What Reality Shall We Preach?) is that woven into the fabric of Christian preaching should be these three emphases: (1) a steady emphasis on the glory of God as the ultimate goal of all things; (2) a steady emphasis that Jesus Christ crucified is the ground of every good that comes to God's people in every text—and that the ultimate good is Christ himself in all his glory; and (3) a steady emphasis on how to appropriate the reality of every text as a justified child of God, and to put it to use through the Spirit, by faith, for the sake of a life of love and holiness, without which no one will see the Lord.

Implications for Preaching

These three emphases are interlocking:

- God's glory shines forth in Christ's death and our holiness.

- Christ's death makes possible the heart that glorifies God and loves people.

- Our Spirit-wrought holiness has Christ crucified as its ground and the glory of God as its goal.

Those Trinitarian, interlocking emphases should be woven through all our preaching. How, and in what proportion, requires spiritual discernment, judicious biblical knowledge, insight into the hearts of your people, pedagogical gifting, and a heart overflowing with exultation in these realities. That is what we should pray for. It is a glorious gift of God to be able to take all the specific, concrete, detailed strands of each text of Scripture, see the particular wonders of each one, and weave them together with the work of Christ, the walk of the Spirit, and the glory of God in such a way that the people know it is the peculiar truth of this very text that has been seen and savored.

Aim of Part 7

The question I am asking here in part 7 is whether it is legitimate to bring these three emphases to our preaching on Old Testament texts. Will we dishonor or distort the reality that the authors aim to communicate if the fabric of our Old Testament preaching is interwoven with steady emphases on the glory of God, the cross of Christ, and the Spirit-enabled obedience of faith?

Peril of Muting or Distorting the Text

My answer is, first, "That depends." But the problem that keeps me from answering with a simple "Yes, we may dishonor the Old Testament texts," is not that we are talking about *Old Testament* texts. The problem is that *any* text can be dishonored and distorted by a misuse of overarching emphases that we apply to all of Scripture. This is why we devoted so much effort in part 5 to the rigorous attention to the very wording of the text.

I lamented that much preaching mutes the riches of biblical texts by applying a theological overlay to the text in a way that obscures detailed implications rather than making them bright and clear in the light of a wider biblical perspective. This calls for great wisdom and much analytical attention to each text. Old Testament texts can be muted and distorted, and New Testament texts can be muted and distorted.

But this distortion is not necessary in the Old or the New Testaments when we see all texts in relation to the glory of God, the cross of Christ, and the obedience of faith. Everything hangs on how that relationship is seen and how it is used to illumine the text. And that is the goal—to illumine, not obscure or suppress. The goal is that connecting the text with these larger, overarching concerns of Scripture would make the text—in its own context, and with all its specificity—*more* clear and not less clear. My assumption is that Old Testament texts, with all their peculiarity and detail, will shine more brightly *for what they really are* if the preacher links them *biblically* to the glory of God, the cross of Christ, and the obedience of faith.

What follows in this chapter and the next two is my very limited attempt to show what the word *biblically* means in this context. What is the *biblical* basis and guide for relating the glory of God, the cross of Christ, and the obedience of faith to Old Testament texts in our preaching as we give our most rigorous attention to the actual wording of the text?

Preaching the Glory of God

In chapter 13 I referred to Jonathan Edwards's astonishing book *The End for Which God Created the World*. It is one of the most thorough and compelling demonstrations of the pervasive biblical revelation that the glory of God is the ultimate goal of all things. One of his most beautiful summations of his study is worthy of quoting again:

> All that is ever spoken of in the Scripture as an ultimate end of God's works is included in that one phrase, *the glory of God.* . . . The refulgence shines upon and into the creature, and is reflected back to the luminary. The beams of glory come from God, and are something of God and are refunded back again to their original. So that the whole is of God, and in God, and to God, and God is the beginning, middle and end in this affair.[1]

How extensive and encompassing is the goal of the glory of God in the Old Testament? Or to put it more carefully, how pervasively does the Old Testament express the view that God's ultimate goal in all he does is the exaltation of his own glory? Since I hold to the essential unity of the Scriptures, I may ask, Is this view clear enough in Old Testament

---

1. Jonathan Edwards, *The Dissertation Concerning the End for Which God Created the World*, ed. Paul Ramsey, vol. 8, *The Works of Jonathan Edwards* (New Haven, CT: Yale University Press, 1989), 526, 531.

contexts to lead us to the conclusion that all Old Testament authors would affirm it? I think the answer is yes. Consider the following, by no means exhaustive, selection of passages.

God's Glory as the Goal of All Things

God's overarching statement is that he will share his glory with no other:

> I am the LORD; that is my name;
>> my glory I give to no other,
>> nor my praise to carved idols. (Isa. 42:8)

When all is said and done, God intends that his glory alone will be supremely exalted:

> The haughty looks of man shall be brought low,
>> and the lofty pride of men shall be humbled,
> and the LORD alone will be exalted in that day. (Isa. 2:11)

His aim is that the whole earth be filled with his glory and with the knowledge of his glory:

> The earth will be filled
>> with the knowledge of the glory of the LORD
>> as the waters cover the sea. (Hab. 2:14)

> Truly, as I live, and as all the earth shall be filled with the glory of the LORD, (Num. 14:21)

> Blessed be his glorious name forever;
>> may the whole earth be filled with his glory!
>> Amen and Amen! (Ps. 72:19)

Therefore, he creates the world for his glory:

> The heavens declare the glory of God,
>> and the sky above proclaims his handiwork. (Ps. 19:1)

> Bring my sons from afar
>> and my daughters from the end of the earth,
> everyone who is called by my name,
>> whom I created for my glory,
>> whom I formed and made. (Isa. 43:6–7)

God created man in his own image, in the image of God he created him; male and female he created them. (Gen. 1:27)

God's final purpose for all nations is that they glorify him:

All the nations you have made shall come
  and worship before you, O Lord,
  and shall glorify your name. (Ps. 86:9)

Who will not fear, O Lord,
  and glorify your name?
For you alone are holy.
  All nations will come
  and worship you,
for your righteous acts have been revealed. (Rev. 15:4)

Declare his glory among the nations,
  his marvelous works among all the peoples! (Ps. 96:3)

God's Glory and His Purposes for Israel

Most of the Old Testament is devoted to God's redemptive focus on Israel. Therefore, most of the statements in the Old Testament about God's pursuit of his glory relate to his purposes through Israel.

He chose Israel for himself, so he would be glorified through her:

As the loincloth clings to the waist of a man, so I made the whole house of Israel and the whole house of Judah cling to me, declares the LORD, that they might be for me a people, a name, a praise, and a glory, but they would not listen. (Jer. 13:11)

He said to me, "You are my servant,
  Israel, in whom I will be glorified." (Isa. 49:3)

As a paradigm for all divine rescues, the exodus is strewn with evidences that God was acting for his own name, that is, for his glory:

Our fathers, when they were in Egypt,
  did not consider your wondrous works;
they did not remember the abundance of your steadfast love,
  but rebelled by the sea, at the Red Sea.
Yet he saved them for his name's sake,
  that he might make known his mighty power. (Ps. 106:7–8)

> I acted for the sake of my name, that it should not be profaned in
> the sight of the nations among whom they lived, in whose sight I
> made myself known to them in bringing them out of the land of
> Egypt. (Ezek. 20:9)

Pharaoh stands out as a typical world ruler over whom God aims to
get great glory:

> I will harden Pharaoh's heart, and he will pursue them, and I will get
> glory over Pharaoh and all his host, and the Egyptians shall know
> that I am the LORD. (Ex. 14:4)

> I will harden the hearts of the Egyptians so that they shall go in
> after them, and I will get glory over Pharaoh and all his host, his
> chariots, and his horsemen. And the Egyptians shall know that I am
> the LORD, when I have gotten glory over Pharaoh, his chariots, and
> his horsemen. (Ex. 14:17–18)

> For this purpose I have raised you up, to show you my power, so
> that my name may be proclaimed in all the earth. (Ex. 9:16)

Even in the wilderness, after the exodus, God saved his rebellious people for his name's sake:

> I acted for the sake of my name, that it should not be profaned in
> the sight of the nations, in whose sight I had brought them out.
> (Ezek. 20:14)

> I withheld my hand and acted for the sake of my name, that it
> should not be profaned in the sight of the nations, in whose sight I
> had brought them out. (Ezek. 20:22)

After the exodus came the conquest of Canaan. This too God did to
make a name for himself:

> Who is like your people Israel, the one nation on earth whom God
> went to redeem to be his people, making himself a name and doing
> for them great and awesome things by driving out before your peo-
> ple, whom you redeemed for yourself from Egypt, a nation and its
> gods? (2 Sam. 7:23)

And when his people rebelled again, desiring a king to be like the nations, God, in his anger, made clear that the reason he would not forsake his people was for his own name's sake:

> Samuel said to the people, "Do not be afraid; you have done all this evil. Yet do not turn aside from following the LORD, but serve the LORD with all your heart. And do not turn aside after empty things that cannot profit or deliver, for they are empty. For the LORD will not forsake his people, for his great name's sake, because it has pleased the LORD to make you a people for himself. (1 Sam. 12:20–22)

More than once God's protection of Jerusalem was attributed to his zeal for his own name:

> I will defend this city to save it, for my own sake and for the sake of my servant David. (2 Kings 19:34; cf. 20:6)

When Israel finally was exiled from her own land, God's declarations that he would again gather her and save her were strikingly God-centered, putting all the emphasis on his own name and glory:

> Say to the house of Israel, Thus says the Lord GOD: It is not for your sake, O house of Israel, that I am about to act, but for the sake of my holy name, which you have profaned among the nations to which you came. And I will vindicate the holiness of my great name, which has been profaned among the nations, and which you have profaned among them. And the nations will know that I am the LORD, declares the Lord GOD, when through you I vindicate my holiness before their eyes. I will take you from the nations and gather you from all the countries and bring you into your own land. (Ezek. 36:22–24)

> It is not for your sake that I will act, declares the Lord GOD; let that be known to you. Be ashamed and confounded for your ways, O house of Israel. (Ezek. 36:32)

> My holy name I will make known in the midst of my people Israel, and I will not let my holy name be profaned anymore. And the nations shall know that I am the LORD, the Holy One in Israel. (Ezek. 39:7)

Isaiah's prophecy of God's mercy to Israel in exile is perhaps the most concentrated expression in all the Bible of God's purpose to act for his glory:

For my name's sake I defer my anger;
>   for the sake of my praise I restrain it for you,
>   that I may not cut you off.
> Behold, I have refined you, but not as silver;
>   I have tried you in the furnace of affliction.
> For my own sake, for my own sake, I do it,
>   for how should my name be profaned?
>   My glory I will not give to another. (Isa. 48:9–11, see also v. 20)

God's Glory in Individual Believers

Besides all these statements about God's purpose to glorify himself in the national life of Israel, there are amazing statements about God's purposes to glorify himself in the saving and helping of his individual, faithful Israelites.

God will blot out their transgressions for his own sake:

> I, I am he
>   who blots out your transgressions for my own sake,
> and I will not remember your sins. (Isa. 43:25)

> Help us, O God of our salvation,
>   for the glory of your name;
> deliver us, and atone for our sins,
>   for your name's sake! (Ps. 79:9)

> For your name's sake, O LORD,
>   pardon my guilt, for it is great. (Ps. 25:11)

> For you are my rock and my fortress;
>   and for your name's sake you lead me and guide me. (Ps. 31:3)

God will preserve life for his own name's sake:

> For your name's sake, O LORD, preserve my life!
>   In your righteousness bring my soul out of trouble! (Ps. 143:11)

> You, O GOD my Lord,
>   deal on my behalf for your name's sake;
>   because your steadfast love is good, deliver me! (Ps. 109:21)

God will lead and guide in paths of righteousness for his name's sake:

He restores my soul.
He leads me in paths of righteousness
    for his name's sake. (Ps. 23:3)

"Pervasive in All Parts of the Bible"

From this sampling of Old Testament passages, and the many others they represent, I conclude with Jonathan Edwards and Greg Beale and James Hamilton that (to use Beale's words) "God's ultimate goal in creation was to magnify his glory throughout the earth."[2] Hamilton argues that throughout the Scriptures "*the self-revelation of God* is for the glory of God."[3] This is the "ultimate end" he is referring to when he says:

> If it can be shown that the Bible's description of God's ultimate end produces, informs, organizes, and is exposited by all the other themes in the Bible, and if this can be demonstrated from the Bible's own salvation-historical narrative and in its own terms, then the conclusion will follow that the ultimate end ascribed to God in the Bible is the center of biblical theology. . . . The center of biblical theology will be the theme that is prevalent, even pervasive, in all parts of the Bible.[4]

Hamilton uses six hundred pages to show that the "if" in that quote is a reality. Not only is God's pursuit of his own glory "pervasive in all parts of the Bible," but he goes on to say toward the end of his book, "God's ultimate purpose is the main concern of the biblical authors, even when they are describing the subordinate ends on the way to the chief end."[5]

This means that we are not obscuring any text if we see reflected in its particular meaning the brightness of God's glory. To see this and bring it out in ways that honor the peculiar specifics of each text is part of the great calling of expository exultation in the Old Testament.

We turn in the next chapter to the question of what it means to preach Christ crucified from the Old Testament. I argued in chapters 15 and 16 that woven through all Christian preaching should be the steady emphasis on Christ crucified as the ground for every good that every biblical text offers God's people. Is that the case when we preach from the Old Testament?

---

2. Greg Beale, *The Temple and the Church's Mission: A Biblical Theology of the Dwelling Place of God*, New Studies in Biblical Theology (Downers Grove, IL: InterVarsity Press, 2004), 82.

3. James M. Hamilton Jr., *God's Glory in Salvation through Judgment: A Biblical Theology* (Wheaton, IL: Crossway, 2010), 53; emphasis original.

4. Ibid., 48–49.

5. Ibid., 560.

20

Expository Exultation and the Old Testament, Part 2

Preaching Christ Crucified

With regard to his ministry at Corinth, Paul said, "I decided to know nothing among you except Jesus Christ and him crucified" (1 Cor. 2:2). To the Galatian churches, he said, "Far be it from me to boast except in the cross of our Lord Jesus Christ" (Gal. 6:14). I argued in chapters 15 and 16 that this means all of Paul's preaching about any topic would be in relation to the death of Jesus, because without the death of Jesus there would not be a single good in all the world that would be a lasting benefit to any believer.

Every good that Paul could offer in any sermon or any text would be offered because it was blood bought. Apart from the blood of Jesus, we receive only God's wrath, or offers of mercy that turn into wrath through our impenitence (Rom. 2:4). But because of the cross, all who are in Christ Jesus receive "all things" (Rom. 8:32)—everything we need to do God's will, glorify his name, and come safely through the final judgment into joyful fellowship with Jesus forever.

Therefore, preaching Christ crucified does not mean simply rehearsing the events of Good Friday and Easter. It also means preaching on every text and every topic, with rigorous attention to the specific wording, and with the explicit understanding that Christ crucified is the ground of every good that comes to God's people in every moment and every text—and that the ultimate good is the all-satisfying Christ himself.

Doing It Biblically

The question now is this: May we, and should we, do this in all of our preaching from the Old Testament? Or will such a pattern of preaching distort and suppress the meaning of Old Testament texts as the author intended it? My answer is that we may, and we should, and if we do it *biblically*, Old Testament texts, with all their peculiarity and detail, will shine more brightly with the original intention of their writers—who "spoke from God as they were carried along by the Holy Spirit" (2 Pet. 1:21).

Part of what I mean by "biblically" is implied in what I just said about how to preach Christ crucified. Treating Christ crucified as the decisive ground, and Christ glorified as the final goal, of every good offered to us in the Old Testament is not an encouragement to preach speculative types and shadows from grapes and twigs. It rests on solid, clear, biblical considerations relating to all Old Testament Scripture.

How Much of the Old Testament Is Still in Force?

One issue we need to deal with briefly, though it is massive, is an issue raised by the words I just used, "every good offered to us in the Old Testament." What is offered to Christians (including Gentiles) from the Old Testament? This is not a simple question, mainly because, with the coming of the long-expected Messiah, Jesus, God's ways of dealing with his people and with the world have changed dramatically. We cannot simply go to every text in the Old Testament and assume that the way it was to be applied in Israel is the way it should be applied today.

Examples of Changes between Old and New

Following are eight examples of why we cannot merely assume Old Testament applications for today.

1. Jesus offers himself as the final sacrifice for sin. This makes the practice of sacrificing animals obsolete. That brings to an end the priestly ministry as the Old Testament developed it in great detail.

It was indeed fitting that we should have such a high priest, holy, innocent, unstained, separated from sinners, and exalted above the heavens. (Heb. 7:26)

He entered once for all into the holy places, not by means of the blood of goats and calves but by means of his own blood, thus securing an eternal redemption. (Heb. 9:12)

Christ, our Passover lamb, has been sacrificed. (1 Cor. 5:7)

2. The mystery hidden for ages, but now revealed in Christ, is this: because of the death and resurrection of Jesus, God intends for all the nations (Gentiles) to be included as fellow heirs with Israel of all the promises of God.

This mystery is that the Gentiles are fellow heirs, members of the same body, and partakers of the promise in Christ Jesus through the gospel. (Eph. 3:6)

If some of the branches [ethnic Israel] were broken off, and you, although a wild olive shoot [Gentiles], were grafted in among the others and now share in the nourishing root of the olive tree, do not be arrogant toward the branches. If you are, remember it is not you who support the root, but the root that supports you. Then you will say, "Branches were broken off so that I might be grafted in." That is true. They were broken off because of their unbelief, but you stand fast through faith. So do not become proud, but fear. (Rom. 11:17–20)

I tell you, the kingdom of God will be taken away from you [Israel] and given to a people producing its fruits [Christ's followers]. (Matt. 21:43)

I tell you, many will come from east and west [Gentiles] and recline at table with Abraham, Isaac, and Jacob in the kingdom of heaven, while the sons of the kingdom [unbelieving Israel] will be thrown into the outer darkness. In that place there will be weeping and gnashing of teeth. (Matt. 8:11–12)

3. That implies, then, that the new people of God (made of both Jews and Gentiles who believe in Jesus) are no longer an ethnically and politically defined people. The church is not a theocracy in the same way that Israel was.

4. Because the church is not a theocracy in the Old Testament sense, civil penalties prescribed for the political state of Israel do not function in the same way. When a man commits a sin at Corinth (1 Cor. 5:1), which in the Old Testament would have been punishable by death (sexual intercourse with a relative, Lev. 20:11), the New Testament process of discipline is excommunication (1 Cor. 5:3).

5. Another change introduced by the revelation of this "mystery" of the inclusion of the Gentiles is that circumcision, which once marked all the male members of the body politic of Israel, is not required in the new people of God (Gal. 2:3).

6. The food laws are no longer prescribed for the followers of Jesus. "He declared all foods clean" (Mark 7:19).

7. With the arrival of the Messiah, some compromises with man's hardness of heart, which shaped some laws in the Old Testament (such as laws pertaining to divorce), are done away with, and a new standard is expected of the disciples of Jesus.

> They said, "Moses allowed a man to write a certificate of divorce and to send her away." And Jesus said to them, "*Because of your hardness of heart* he wrote you this commandment. *But from the beginning* of creation, 'God made them male and female.' 'Therefore a man shall leave his father and mother and hold fast to his wife, and the two shall become one flesh.' So they are no longer two but one flesh. What therefore God has joined together, let not man separate." (Mark 10:4–9)

8. Finally, there is the profound change from a mainly come-see religion in the Old Testament to a mainly go-tell religion in the New Testament. God did not make the Great Commission of Matthew 28:18–20 a centerpiece of Old Testament life. But with the resurrection of Jesus, and the revelation of the mystery that Gentiles are full fellow heirs of God, the church's mission to the nations becomes central to what the church is.

This change accounts for a number of shifts. Simplicity of life, rather than the accumulation of wealth and opulent living, becomes normal. The church is not expecting the Queen of Sheba (1 Kings 10) to come admire Christian palaces. Instead the church expects to pour its resources into going to the perishing people who are ruled by all the queens and kings of the world. Besides simplicity, the crucial place of suffering, and possibly martyrdom, are now treated as normal, rather than suggesting God's displeasure.

Don't Preach What Is Not Offered and No Longer Required

The point of those eight observations is to show that when we preach from the Old Testament, we must not offer people things that God no longer intends to give. The Old Testament itself was moving toward these changes. A new covenant was promised (Jer. 31:31) that would bring profound changes. The Old Testament itself contains the promissory seeds of its transformation.[1]

What It Means to Preach Christ

So, with this caution about misapplying the Old Testament to our day, I assume that all of the Old Testament, seen in its proper place in the progress of redemptive history, is profitable for preaching (2 Tim. 3:16). And I return to my affirmation above that we may, and we should, preach Christ crucified from all Old Testament texts. This does not mean finding doubtful types and shadows. The more speculative preaching is, the more it loses its God-given authority. Rather, it means preaching on every text and every topic, with rigorous attention to the specific wording, and with the explicit understanding that (1) Christ crucified is the ground of every good that comes to God's people in every text, and (2) that the ultimate good is the all-satisfying Christ himself.

Let's take those one at a time and see why it is *biblical* to approach Old Testament passages this way. First, we will focus on my claim that Christ crucified is the ground of every good that comes to God's people through every text in the Old Testament. Second, we will focus on the claim that the ultimate good is the all-satisfying Christ himself.

1. Christ, the Ground of Every Good

First, preaching Christ crucified in the Old Testament, as I am defending it, means that our preaching is interwoven with the truth that

---

1. I won't press further into the issue of what is offered to Christians (including Gentiles) from the Old Testament. Instead I would refer you to Jason DeRouchie, *Understanding and Applying the Old Testament: 12 Steps from Exegesis to Theology* (Phillipsburg, NJ: P&R, 2017), esp. chap. 12 (pp. 396–469), where he deals with several examples of how to move from puzzling texts in the Old Testament to principled application to our day.

Christ crucified is the ground of every good that comes to God's people through every text in the Old Testament. The most important text for showing this is Romans 3:25–26:

> God put [Christ] forward as a propitiation by his blood, to be received by faith. This was to show God's righteousness, because in his divine forbearance he had passed over former sins. It was to show his righteousness at the present time, so that he might be just and the justifier of the one who has faith in Jesus.

The link with the Old Testament here is the clause "because in his divine forbearance he had passed over former sins." I take this to refer to God's forgiveness of all the sins of those in the Old Testament who appropriated the sacrificial system as God intended and received forgiveness for their sins (Lev. 4:20 and others). And I take it to refer to God's forgiveness of sins for those who, in the spirit of the sacrifices, cried out for mercy, like David after the sin with Bathsheba and Uriah (2 Sam. 12:13; Psalm 51).

Christ died for sins done before he died. What Romans 3:25 shows is that God's righteousness was *obscured* by God's passing over of these sins in the Old Testament. Indeed, his righteousness was *contradicted* in leaving so many sins without full punishment—unless something else could happen to set things right, for the blood of bulls and goats could never be sufficient payment for human sins (Heb. 10:4).

Paul says that God sent Christ to die "to show God's righteousness." Actually, he says even more. In verse 26 he says the aim of Christ's death was so that God "might be just and the justifier." It is not just that God would *seem* unrighteous without the death of Christ. He would actually *be* unrighteous. And God would be unrighteous without Christ's death because "he had passed over former sins." In other words, sin against God is of such a nature that Old Testament sacrifices could not finally cover them, but only point to the sacrifice that would (Heb. 10:4).

Here's the massive implication. The forgiveness of every sin in the Old Testament is based on the blood of Jesus. This is true, even though those who were forgiven did not yet know Jesus as we know him. They were trusting in God's promise and mercy. But God knew what he was going to do. So when he forgave sin in the Old Testament, he did so with a view to the death of Jesus as the decisive payment and covering for that sin.

Every good through every text owing to Christ. This means that apart from Christ crucified, every person in the Old Testament would receive only wrath, or gifts of mercy that turn to wrath (Rom. 2:4). Which means that every saving blessing, every lasting good, that God's people receive, including those that come through the texts of Old Testament Scripture, are owing to Christ crucified. Which means that every sermon from the Old Testament that offers any good to a Christian congregation should make that clear. A Gentile Christian in the twenty-first century possesses whatever good thing is offered in the preacher's Old Testament text, solely because it was bought by the blood of Jesus. That is exactly the same basis for its enjoyment as the basis from three thousand years ago in the Old Testament. Only now we know the glorious reality of how God did it—through Christ crucified. That is the first meaning of preaching Christ from the Old Testament.

And we should not think that Romans 3:25–26 is imposing something on the Old Testament that the Old Testament itself did not foresee. Isaiah 53 shows that a servant of God was coming someday who would bear the sins of God's people:

> Surely he has borne our griefs
>> and carried our sorrows;
> yet we esteemed him stricken,
>> smitten by God, and afflicted.
> But he was pierced for our transgressions;
>> he was crushed for our iniquities;
> upon him was the chastisement that brought us peace,
>> and with his wounds we are healed.
> All we like sheep have gone astray;
>> we have turned—every one—to his own way;
> and the LORD has laid on him
>> the iniquity of us all. (Isa. 53:4–6)

And Psalm 49 shows how the psalmist could despair of ever being ransomed by any ordinary human:

> Truly no man can ransom another,
>> or give to God the price of his life,
> for the ransom of their life is costly
>> and can never suffice. (vv. 7–8)

And yet the psalmist believed that somehow God would do this in a way the psalmist did not fully understand:

> God will ransom my soul from the power of Sheol,
>   for he will receive me. (v. 15)

Therefore, I conclude that we are being faithful both to the Old Testament and the New Testament when we preach Christ as the basis of every good that the preacher brings out of any Old Testament text for the followers of Christ. "For all the promises of God find their Yes in him" (2 Cor. 1:20).

Now we turn to the second way that we preach Christ crucified from the Old Testament.

2. Christ Himself Is the Greatest Gift He Gives

Second, preaching Christ crucified in the Old Testament, as I am defending it, means that our preaching is interwoven with the truth that the greatest good Christ died to provide was his people's enjoyment of himself. Or, to say it more fully, every gift Christ bought for his people by his blood—whether in the Old Testament era (before the price was paid) or in the Christian era (after the price was paid)—was bought with a view to pointing people through the gift to the ultimate good Christ bought, namely, everlasting, joyful worship of Jesus himself.

Christian preaching aims to bring people to see and savor the glories of all that God is for them in Jesus. It aims at worship—in all of life forever. The Old Testament foresaw a coming One who would be a glorious person with qualities they could not completely comprehend.

David calls him Lord. In Psalm 110:1, David said, "The LORD [note the all-caps Yahweh] says to my Lord [lowercase master, ruler]: / 'Sit at my right hand, until I make your enemies your footstool.'" Jesus made this verse the center of one of his conflicts with the Pharisees. His aim was to show that the Old Testament intimated that the Messiah would be much more than an ordinary man.

> [Jesus said,] "What do you think about the Christ? Whose son is he?" They said to him, "The son of David." He said to them, "How is it then that David, in the Spirit, calls him Lord, saying,

> 'The Lord said to my Lord,
> "Sit at my right hand,
>   until I put your enemies under your feet"'?
>
> If then David calls him Lord, how is he his son?" (Matt. 22:42–45)

What did Jesus mean by his rhetorical question, "If then David calls him Lord, how is he his son?" Henry Alford answers wisely:

> From the universally recognized title of the Messiah as the Son of David, which by His question He elicits from them, He takes occasion to shew them, who understood this title in a mere worldly political sense, the difficulty arising from David's own reverence for this his Son: the solution lying in the incarnate Godhead of the Christ, of which they were ignorant.[2]

This "reverence" for the Promised One that runs through the Old Testament means that Christian preaching does more than simply make explicit that every blood-bought good offered to God's people in every text of the Bible is bought by the blood of Jesus. This pervasive reverence for the coming One is also a pointer to Christ as the best gift, to which all others are pointing as supremely valuable. The assumption behind this kind of preaching is not foreign to the Old Testament. The Old Testament saints, who saw the implications of their faith most clearly, were like Simeon (Luke 2:25–34) and Anna (Luke 2:36–38), whose hearts were fixed intently to wait for the reverenced One. The glory they foresaw made this coming One the capstone of their dreams.

Capstone of all their dreams. He is going to be a Wonderful Counselor, Mighty God, Everlasting Father, Prince of Peace. He will sit on the throne of his father David. But unlike kings of old, he will reign forever:

> For to us a child is born,
>   to us a son is given;
> and the government shall be upon his shoulder,
>   and his name shall be called
> Wonderful Counselor, Mighty God,
>   Everlasting Father, Prince of Peace.

---

2. Henry Alford, *Alford's Greek Testament: An Exegetical and Critical Commentary*, vol. 1 (Grand Rapids, MI: Guardian Press, 1976), 225.

> Of the increase of his government and of peace
>> there will be no end,
> on the throne of David and over his kingdom,
>> to establish it and to uphold it
> with justice and with righteousness
>> from this time forth and forevermore.
> The zeal of the LORD of hosts will do this. (Isa. 9:6–7)

He will come as a messenger of the covenant and be the healer and delight of his people. They will rejoice over him with such abandon they will be like calves leaping from the stall:

> Behold, I send my messenger, and he will prepare the way before me. And the Lord whom you seek will suddenly come to his temple; and the messenger of the covenant in whom you delight, behold, he is coming, says the LORD of hosts. (Mal. 3:1)

> But for you who fear my name, the sun of righteousness shall rise with healing in its wings. You shall go out leaping like calves from the stall. (Mal. 4:2)

He will be crushed by God but raised from the dead. Then he will prolong his days forever, reckoning his people as righteous:

> It was the will of the LORD to crush him;
>> he has put him to grief;
> when his soul makes an offering for guilt,
>> he shall see his offspring; he shall prolong his days;
> the will of the LORD shall prosper in his hand.
> Out of the anguish of his soul he shall see and be satisfied;
> by his knowledge shall the righteous one, my servant,
>> make many to be accounted righteous,
>> and he shall bear their iniquities. (Isa. 53:10–11)

He will be the joy of the humble because he will come humbly, and riding on a donkey, but still a king:

> Rejoice greatly, O daughter of Zion!
>> Shout aloud, O daughter of Jerusalem!
> Behold, your king is coming to you;
>> righteous and having salvation is he,

> humble and mounted on a donkey,
> > on a colt, the foal of a donkey. (Zech. 9:9)

He will serve in the majesty of God, yet be a tender, caring shepherd—a perfect combination of majesty and meekness:

> He shall stand and shepherd his flock in the strength of the LORD,
> > in the majesty of the name of the LORD his God.
> And they shall dwell secure, for now he shall be great
> > to the ends of the earth. (Mic. 5:4; cf. Ezek. 34:23)

He will execute justice for God's people, and all the persecuted and wronged faithful ones will be vindicated.

> In those days and at that time I will cause a righteous Branch to spring up for David, and he shall execute justice and righteousness in the land. (Jer. 33:15)

He will bring good news to the poor, compassion to the brokenhearted, liberty to the captive:

> The Spirit of the Lord GOD is upon me,
> > because the LORD has anointed me
> to bring good news to the poor;
> > he has sent me to bind up the brokenhearted,
> to proclaim liberty to the captives,
> > and the opening of the prison to those who are bound;
> to proclaim the year of the LORD's favor,
> > and the day of vengeance of our God;
> to comfort all who mourn. (Isa. 61:1–2)

There are many more evidences in the Old Testament that the saints expected, hoped for, and rejoiced in the coming One as the capstone of their dreams. This is why they had been chosen as a people. This is why God rescued them from Egyptian bondage; why they had been given the Promised Land; why they had been disciplined in the exile; and why they had been given mercy to return. Most of all, this is why God had provided for the forgiveness of their sins. This is what Simeon was yearning for (Luke 2:29) and what Anna was fasting for (Luke 2:37). None of the Old Testament writers or saints would have considered it a distortion of their intention to trace the blood of the sacrifices to the gift of forgiveness to the bountiful blessings of God to the best gift of all, the hope of the Messiah himself.

Completion, Not Distortion

When a Christian preacher preaches Christ crucified as the decisive ground of all those gifts and Christ glorified as the final joy to which all the gifts were pointing, he is simply naming what was implicit in the hope of the Old Testament saints. This is what I mean by preaching Christ crucified from Old Testament texts *biblically*. It is preaching on every text and every topic, with rigorous attention to the specific wording, and with the explicit understanding that Christ crucified is the ground of every good that comes to God's people through every text—and that the ultimate good is the all-satisfying Christ himself. That way of preaching Christ is rooted in the Old Testament itself.

The Way to Life

There is one other assumption that has been guiding our effort to answer the question, What reality do we preach? That assumption is that there is a way to live the Christian life that leads to final salvation, and there is a way to try to live it that leads to destruction. I argued in chapters 17 and 18 that the way that leads to life is rooted in justification by faith alone, and then proceeds by that same faith to walk by the Spirit and bear the fruit of love, without which we will not see the Lord. Therefore, the task of preaching is to feed that faith with the soul-satisfying truth of God's word. That is, we are to clarify from every text how it helps us walk along the path of faith and love that leads to life. I take that to be true not only for preaching from the New Testament, but for preaching from the Old Testament as well. That is our concern in chapter 21.

21

Expository Exultation and the Old Testament, Part 3

Preaching the Obedience of Faith

In chapters 17 and 18, I showed that the aim of preaching is to help our people get on, and stay on, the path that leads to final salvation. I called it "the way of love that leads to life." There is a practical holiness without which our people will not see the Lord (Heb. 12:14). Paul calls it "the obedience of faith" (Rom. 1:5). It is urgent that our people see the necessity of how this obedience is maintained. So I tried to clarify how this "obedience of faith" relates to justification by faith alone and how persevering faith, in the power of the Holy Spirit, produces a life of sacrificial love, without which, John says, we "abide[s] in death" (1 John 3:14).

I argued that the preacher should be vigilant in all his preaching to portray God as supremely satisfying to the souls of his people. Faith is sustained not just by showing God as trustworthy, but by showing him, in all his attributes and actions, as perfectly satisfying to every dimension of human need and longing. The faithful preacher will seek to sustain such faith in the hearts of his people.

The Aim of Old Testament Preaching: Faith Working through Love

Now, the question before us is, Should the same emphasis on the obedience of faith and the way of love that leads to life be woven through all our preaching from the Old Testament? My answer is yes. Along with the glory of God as the goal of all Old Testament preaching and the cross of Christ as the ground of every good offered in Old Testament preaching, I am now going to argue that woven into the fabric of all Old Testament preaching should be the summons to be satisfied in all that God is for us in Jesus, so that, feasting on the riches of the revelation of God from Genesis to Malachi, the church today would walk in the way of love, by the power of the Holy Spirit, and thus arrive at final salvation.

In other words, Paul's aim—and ours—is no less true for Old Testament preaching than for New Testament preaching: "The aim of our charge is *love* that issues from . . . sincere *faith*" (1 Tim. 1:5). My argument will be that this aim of "faith working through love" (Gal. 5:6) is in line with the intention of the Old Testament itself, not a gospel overlay forced on a legalistic religion.

Hebrews Forges the Link with the Old Testament

My first argument is to draw our attention to the connection between Hebrews 10:32–35 and the argument of Hebrews 11—that is, the connection between the way the author portrays the Christian power to love and the Old Testament power to love, both of them "by faith." In chapter 18 I made the point that the source of radical, self-sacrificing love is the joy that comes from being satisfied with all that God promises to be for us in Jesus. The key statement was Hebrews 10:34: "You had compassion on those in prison, and you *joyfully* accepted the plundering of your property, *since you knew that you yourselves had a better possession and an abiding one.*"

In other words, the faith of these Christians felt the joy of their reward so deeply that it stilled their fears and released their love. That is, their faith was the substance and assurance of things hoped for (Heb. 11:1).[1] The all-satisfying reward of supreme and eternal pleasure with God in the resurrection was tasted—embraced, experienced, felt—as real in the present with such joy that they risked everything to love their imprisoned brothers and sisters. And, in view of the rest of Hebrews, they knew that this reward and this joy were secured by the death of Jesus (Heb. 7:27; 9:12; 10:10).

---

1. See chap. 18 for an explanation of how faith is both the *assurance* and the *substance* of things hoped for (Heb. 11:1).

That is how the gospel of Christ—the good news of blood-bought forgiveness and the hope of everlasting joy—gives rise to faith and love in the New Testament. That was the argument of chapters 17 and 18. Now notice from Hebrews 11 that, in the mind of this inspired writer, *faith and obedience work the same way in the Old Testament.*

The phrase "by faith" occurs eighteen times in Hebrews 11 and is described as the way the Old Testament believers received their blessings and walked in the path of obedience. "By faith Abel offered to God a more acceptable sacrifice" (v. 4). "By faith Enoch . . . pleased God" (v. 5). "By faith Noah . . . constructed an ark" (v. 7). "By faith Abraham obeyed" (v. 8). "By faith Sarah . . . received power to conceive" (v. 11).

Christian Love and Old Testament Love Have the Same Root: Faith

We saw in chapter 18 that the author of Hebrews, in fact, intentionally describes the dynamics of Moses's act of love in Hebrews 11:24–26 as virtually identical with the New Testament dynamics of love in Hebrews 10:32–35. The Christians rejoiced in the hope of a better possession and an abiding one (10:34). Moses looked to the reward (11:26). The Christians chose to be plundered in the service of their suffering friends (10:34). Moses chose "to be mistreated with the people of God" (11:25).

The point is that God's way of creating radical love that leads to life is the same in the Old and New Testaments. It is by faith. And that faith means being satisfied in all that God promises to be for us in Christ. The difference between the Old and New Testaments in regard to this path of obedience is that in the New Testament we have a fuller knowledge of Christ and how he came to purchase every good that believers enjoy—then and now, in every age.

The Good News of Faith Preached to Israel

Lest we miss his point about the life of faith in the Old Testament, the writer of Hebrews has an astonishing statement in Hebrews 4:2. Here's the context:

> To whom did [God] swear that they would not enter his rest [the Promised Land pointing to a deeper "rest"], but to those who were disobedient? So we see that they were unable to enter *because*

> *of unbelief.* Therefore, while the promise of entering his rest still stands, let us fear lest any of you should seem to have failed to reach it. For *good news came to us just as to them*, but the message they heard did not benefit them, because *they were not united by faith* with those who listened. (Heb. 3:18–4:2).

What is astonishing here is not so much that the key fault of the people of Israel is called "unbelief" (3:19), but rather that the message they received is called "gospel" or "good news": "Good news came to *us just as to them* [*esmen euēngelismenoi kathaper kakeinoi*]" (4:2). In other words, even though they didn't have access to all the knowledge we do, because the Messiah had not yet come and died and risen, nevertheless, the revelation of God's nature and his ways and his promises was such that the path of blessing and salvation and hope and final joy was manifestly the path of *faith*—the good news of being satisfied with all that God promised to be for them, even though they did not yet know what we know about the Messiah.

So my first argument that all preaching from the Old Testament should aim to awaken faith leading to love and final salvation is that the book of Hebrews points us in that direction. When Hebrews 6:12 tells us not to "be sluggish, but imitators of those who *through faith* and patience inherit the promises," the author has in mind most immediately Abraham as our chief model: "Abraham, having patiently waited, obtained the promise" (Heb. 6:15). In this, Hebrews is in step with the apostle Paul's understanding of the Old Testament's emphasis on faith. So we turn for our second argument to Paul's writings.

Paul's Example of Abraham

Paul joins Hebrews in encouraging us that all our preaching from the Old Testament should aim to awaken faith leading to love and final salvation. His most prominent way of doing this is by making Abraham the paradigm and father of all *Christian* believers, while showing how the Mosaic law does not contradict the life of faith. The entire fourth chapter of Romans unfolds the faith of Abraham as the pattern and root of Christian faith. "What does the Scripture say? 'Abraham *believed* God, and it was counted to him as righteousness'" (v. 3). Then Paul points out that God justified Abraham by faith *before* he was circumcised (v. 11). Then he draws this conclusion: "The purpose was to make him the father of *all who believe* without being circumcised, so that righteousness would be counted to them as well" (v. 11). That would be all Gentile believers who trust Christ for righteousness, not circumcision. This faith we share with Abraham is not only counted as our justification, but it also leads to an obedient life. Thus Abraham was "the father of [those who] . . . *walk in the footsteps of [Abraham's] faith*" (v. 12).

We have several reasons for seeing Paul's description of Abraham's life of faith as normative for all of God's people in the Old Testament. Abraham was not an exception among Old Testament saints as though his way of being justified and sanctified was unique. Paul portrays him as the paradigm for all true covenant members—then and now. For example, even here in Romans 4 Paul includes the testimony of David, not just Abraham, to make the point that justification comes *by faith*, not works: "Just as David also speaks of the blessing of the one to whom God counts righteousness apart from works: 'Blessed are those whose lawless deeds are forgiven, and whose sins are covered; blessed is the man against whom the Lord will not count his sin'" (Rom. 4:6–8).

Unbelief Is the Root of All Israel's Failures

Just as important as particular examples of Old Testament faith, such as Abraham and David, are Paul's general statements that the failure of faith was the reason Israel failed in the path of obedience to God. For example, in Romans 11 Paul describes the true Israel as a natural olive tree, while the individual branches are individual Israelites. His explanation why some of these branches were broken off from true Israel is their *unbelief*. And his explanation for how Gentiles—"wild olive shoots"—can be grafted in to true Israel is *faith*:

> If some of the branches were broken off, and you, although a wild olive shoot, were grafted in among the others and now share in the nourishing root of the olive tree, do not be arrogant toward the branches. If you are, remember it is not you who support the root, but the root that supports you. Then you will say, "Branches were broken off so that I might be grafted in." That is true. They were broken off *because of their unbelief*, but *you stand fast through faith*. So do not become proud, but fear. (Rom. 11:17–20)

That is a sweeping statement about what the Old Testament required of all Israel, all the time. It required faith. This is not a narrow statement about *some* Jews in some parts of the Old Testament. This is an all-inclusive assessment of why Israel failed, wherever she failed: "because of their unbelief."

They Did Not Reach the Law Because of Unbelief

Another example of Paul's overarching assessment of what the Old Testament requires is found in Romans 9:30–32:

> What shall we say, then? That Gentiles who did not pursue righteousness have attained it, that is, a righteousness that is by faith; but that Israel who pursued a law that would lead to righteousness *did not succeed in reaching that law*. Why? Because *they did not pursue it by faith*, but as if it were based on works. They have stumbled over the stumbling stone.

The failure to "reach the law" was owing to the failure to see how the law pointed to a life of faith. We will see later how the Mosaic law actually brought about death and condemnation, but in the larger context of the Old Testament it was intended to lead Israel to faith and to a gracious Redeemer. But Israel's failure referred to here is the attempt to use the law to establish her own righteousness (Rom. 10:3).

They failed to see that law keeping itself was not the ground of justification. The reason it wasn't is that once you step onto the path of law keeping as the ground of justification, you are bound to keep the whole law, and no one could. That's essentially what Paul said in Galatians 5:2–3: "Look: I, Paul, say to you that if you accept circumcision, Christ will be of no advantage to you. I testify again *to every man who accepts circumcision that he is obligated to keep the whole law*."

In other words, if you choose the path of law keeping as the basis of your justification with God, you embrace an obligation to keep the *whole* law. Or, as James says, "whoever keeps the whole law but fails in one point has become guilty of all of it" (James 2:10). Law keeping is a hopeless ground for acceptance with God. "By works of the law no one will be justified" (Gal. 2:16). "All who rely on works of the law are under a curse" (Gal. 3:10). "By works of the law no human being will be justified in his sight" (Rom. 3:20).

But Paul's point in Romans 9:32 ("they did not pursue it by faith") is that if Israel had rightly understood the law's design, they would not have made this mistake (of seeking justification by law keeping) but would have been led to faith in God's gracious promises of a Redeemer, "for the goal of the law is Christ for righteousness to everyone who believes" (Rom. 10:4, my translation).

Old and New Testaments Teach One Way That Leads to Life: Faith

We have seen from Hebrews and from Paul that the way of life required of God's people in the Old Testament is the life of faith. Obedience to the commands of God, summed up in love (Lev. 19:18; Rom. 13:9), is the obedience that comes from faith (Rom. 4:12; Hebrews 11), just as it is in the New Testament (Rom. 1:5; 1 Tim. 1:5).

To establish this claim more fully, we may ask whether the Old Testament itself teaches this. We've seen that Hebrews and Paul do. What about the Old Testament? We start with the Pentateuch—the first five books of the Bible, often called the Law. Does the Pentateuch summon the people of God to a way of life that is rooted in faith in God's gracious promises, or is it founded on law keeping as the ground of justification? Crucial to answering this question is to distinguish the Pentateuch as a whole from the Mosaic law in particular. We will see in a moment how the Pentateuch itself makes this point, but notice that Paul saw it this way as well:

> The promises were made to Abraham and to his offspring [as narrated in the Pentateuch!]. . . . The law, which came 430 years afterward, does not annul a covenant previously ratified by God, so as to make the promise void. For if the inheritance comes by the law, it no longer comes by promise; but God gave it to Abraham by a promise. (Gal. 3:16–18)

You can see how Paul distinguishes "the law" from other parts of the Pentateuch—in this case, the parts of Genesis that tell the story of Abraham. This means that when Paul refers negatively to the "old covenant" (2 Cor. 3:14) as a "ministry of death" (2 Cor. 3:7) and a "ministry of condemnation" (2 Cor. 3:9), he is not talking about the entire Pentateuch, let alone the whole Old Testament. He is talking about the Sinai covenant. This is what he had in view when he said, "The law came in to increase the trespass" (Rom. 5:20), and "the law brings wrath" (Rom. 4:15), and "through the law comes knowledge of sin" (Rom. 3:20), and "the law is not of faith" (Gal. 3:12).

But in saying that the law is not of faith (Gal. 3:12), he is not saying that the point of the law, in its Old Testament context, is to commend a way of life that contradicts faith. "Is the law then contrary to the promises of God? Certainly not!" (Gal. 3:21). Rather, he is saying that the negative effects of the law, through its use as a basis of justification (Lev. 18:5; Gal. 3:12; Rom. 10:5), were in fact providentially ordained by God to show Israel that they need Christ and they need faith.

Paul says this negatively in Romans 3:19–20:

> Whatever the law says it speaks to those who are under the law, so that every mouth may be stopped, and the whole world may be held accountable to God. For by works of the law no human being will be justified in his sight, since through the law comes knowledge of sin.

And he says it positively in Galatians 3:22–26:

> The Scripture imprisoned everything under sin, so that the promise by faith in Jesus Christ might be given to those who believe. Now before faith came, we were held captive under the law, imprisoned until the coming faith would be revealed. So then, the law was our guardian until Christ came, in order that we might be justified by faith. But now that faith has come, we are no longer under a guardian, for in Christ Jesus you are all sons of God, through faith.

When Paul says, "Before faith came . . ." (v. 23), he does not mean that there was no saving faith in the Old Testament (which would contradict what he had just said in Galatians 3:6, "Abraham *believed* God, and it was counted to him as righteousness"). Rather, he was saying, "before *this* faith came . . ." namely, the faith just referred to in the previous verse (v. 22), "faith in Jesus Christ." The law kept reminding Israel that justification would have to be by faith in a Redeemer (Gal. 3:24), not by law keeping.

The Pentateuch's Negative View of the Law

The Pentateuch as a whole was already making the point that Paul drew out. There is a tension between the life of faith foregrounded by the story of Abraham and the failures of Israel under the Mosaic law. This tension is meant to warn against law keeping as a way of justification and to direct attention to the life of faith. One way this tension is seen is that *until* the giving of the law in the Pentateuch, every mention of faith is positive—people believed.

> [Abraham] *believed* the LORD, and he counted it to him as righteousness. (Gen. 15:6)

> The LORD said to Moses, "Put out your hand and catch it by the tail"—so he put out his hand and caught it, and it became a staff in his hand—"that they may *believe* that the LORD, the God of their fathers, the God of Abraham, the God of Isaac, and the God of Jacob, has appeared to you." (Ex. 4:4–5)

> The people *believed*; and when they heard that the LORD had visited the people of Israel and that he had seen their affliction, they bowed their heads and worshiped. (Ex. 4:31)

> Israel saw the great power that the LORD used against the Egyptians, so the people feared the LORD, and they *believed* in the LORD and in his servant Moses. (Ex. 14:31)

> The waters covered their adversaries;
>   not one of them was left.
> Then they *believed* his words;
>   they sang his praise. (Ps. 106:11–12)

> The LORD said to Moses, "Behold, I am coming to you in a thick cloud, that the people may hear when I speak with you, and may also *believe* you forever." (Ex. 19:9)

But every mention of faith *after* the giving of the law in the Pentateuch is a reference to failure. Which fits with Paul's lament about the negative effects of the law.

> The LORD said to Moses, "How long will this people despise me? And how long will they *not believe* in me, in spite of all the signs that I have done among them?" (Num. 14:11)

> The LORD said to Moses and Aaron, "Because you did *not believe* in me, to uphold me as holy in the eyes of the people of Israel,

therefore you shall not bring this assembly into the land that I have given them." (Num. 20:12)

In spite of this word [how God carried them in the wilderness] you did *not believe* the LORD your God. (Deut. 1:32)

When the LORD sent you from Kadesh-barnea, saying, "Go up and take possession of the land that I have given you," then you rebelled against the commandment of the LORD your God and did *not believe* him or obey his voice. (Deut. 9:23)

> [God's] anger rose against Israel [when they murmured at
>   having no meat],
> because they did *not believe* in God
>   and did not trust his saving power. (Ps. 78:21–22, cf. 32)

They despised the pleasant land,
    having *no faith* in his promise. (Ps. 106:24)

One way to draw out the implications of the way the Pentateuch was put together is to say that the Pentateuch is to the Old Testament what Galatians is to the New Testament. The Pentateuch shows how the failures of the Mosaic law (that is, the Sinai covenant) fit into the larger point of the Pentateuch, which is that "the Pentateuch is intended to teach 'faith' in God."[2]

Psalms: Window on the Heart That God Wills

I am trying to show that Paul and Hebrews represent the Old Testament's own view when they teach that the way of life taught throughout the Old Testament is the obedience of faith (Rom. 9:32; 11:20; Hebrews 11). I offer one last line of evidence. The book of Psalms represents the prayer book of Israel. It gives us a glimpse into the heart religion behind the formal rituals. Therefore, the book of Psalms shows us more directly than other books how the heart of the Old Testament saints laid hold on God and lived out their faith.

The psalms abound with references to *trusting* God, and *taking refuge* in God, and *waiting* for God, and *hoping* in God, and *being*

---

2. John Sailhamer, *The Pentateuch as Narrative: A Biblical Theological Commentary* (Grand Rapids, MI: Zondervan, 1992), 61.

satisfied in God. I will mention only a few places that bring us toward our conclusion about preaching from the Old Testament, namely, that we should preach to satisfy the hearts of our people with all that God is for them in Jesus, and thus empower the way of love that leads to life.

Faith in the Psalms Is More Than Trusting God for Help

Trusting the Lord, delighting in him, and doing his will come together in Psalm 37:3–5:

> *Trust in the* LORD, *and do good*;
>   dwell in the land and befriend faithfulness.
> *Delight yourself in the* LORD,
>   and he will give you the desires of your heart.
> *Commit your way to the* LORD;
>   *trust in him*, and he will act.

I think this cluster of realities (trust, doing good, befriending faithfulness, delighting in God, and committing our way to God) is representative of how the psalms expect us to live. Doing good—loving our neighbor as we love ourselves (Lev. 19:18)—flows from trusting God. And trusting is always more than simply counting on God to help us. Faith is always, at its best, receiving God as our reward, not just our rescuer; our delight, not just our deliverer.

> Our heart is *glad* in him,
>   because we *trust* in his holy name. (Ps. 33:21)

> I will go to the altar of God,
>   to God *my exceeding joy*. (Ps. 43:4)

> I have *trusted* in your steadfast love;
>   my heart shall *rejoice* in your salvation. (Ps. 13:5)

> You give them drink from the river of your *delights*.
>   For with you is the fountain of life. (Ps. 36:8–9)

> My soul *thirsts* for you;
> my flesh *faints* for you,
>   as in a dry and weary land where there is no water.
> So I have looked upon you in the sanctuary,
>   beholding your power and glory.

> Because your steadfast love is *better than life*,
> > my lips will praise you. (Ps. 63:1–3)

> May all who seek you
> > *rejoice* and *be glad* in you. (Ps. 40:16)

> Whom have I in heaven but you?
> > And there is nothing on earth that I *desire* besides you.
> My flesh and my heart may fail,
> > but God is the strength of my heart and *my portion* forever.
> > > (Ps. 73:25–26)

Implications for Preaching from the Old Testament

Based on these observations from the book of Hebrews and from Paul and the Pentateuch and the Psalms, my conclusion is that the Christian preacher is warranted to come to any Old Testament text, give rigorous attention to its wording in order to see what is really there—the riches it contains about God and man and life—and then show how these riches serve to sustain faith. Or to say it another way, the preacher should endeavor with every text to show that God is supremely satisfying for the human soul, and that this overflowing satisfaction bears fruit in a life of love that leads to final salvation. And, of course, as we saw in chapters 19 and 20, this new life and this final salvation have been secured for the believer by the blood of Christ and are destined ultimately to magnify the greatness of God.

The New Covenant and the Spirit

One last thing begs to be observed. The Old Testament makes the promise that a new covenant is coming:

> Behold, the days are coming, declares the LORD, when I will make a new covenant with the house of Israel and the house of Judah, not like the covenant that I made with their fathers on the day when I took them by the hand to bring them out of the land of Egypt, my covenant that they broke, though I was their husband, declares the LORD. (Jer. 31:31–32)

This new covenant will bring to God's people a new heart and new spirit:

> I will give them one heart, and a new spirit I will put within them. I will remove the heart of stone from their flesh and give them a heart

of flesh, that they may walk in my statutes and keep my rules and obey them. And they shall be my people, and I will be their God. (Ezek. 11:19–20)

That will happen by the work of God's own Spirit: "I will put my Spirit within you, and cause you to walk in my statutes" (Ezek. 36:27). It will be based on the forgiveness of sins: "I will forgive their iniquity, and I will remember their sin no more" (Jer. 31:34). And it will result in a glorious ability to love God as our supreme treasure: "The LORD your God will circumcise your heart and the heart of your offspring, so that you will love the LORD your God with all your heart and with all your soul, that you may live" (Deut. 30:6).

The New Covenant Purchased by the Blood of Jesus

This new covenant was purchased and secured by the blood of Jesus. In Luke 22:20 Jesus said, "This cup that is poured out for you is the new covenant in my blood." This means, first, that the foretastes of the new covenant that Old Testament saints certainly enjoyed were a preliminary blessing of the death of Jesus in advance of his coming (as we saw in chapter 20).

But the purchase of the new covenant by Jesus also means that it would be contrary to the intention of the Old Testament itself if we preached the Old Testament as if the new covenant had not been already inaugurated by the blood of Christ. Everything in the Old Testament was in anticipation of this. To preach from the Old Testament as though we were still in a moment of anticipation for what has come would certainly dismay the Old Testament writers, if they were allowed to look down from heaven.

Therefore, the Christian preacher listens long and hard to all that the Old Testament text has to say in its original context. He digs deep into the actual wording for all that this gold mine has to give. Then, with the gold in hand, he traces its price down into the work of Christ, who bought it for the saints; and he traces its luster up to the glory of God, as its origin and goal; and he offers it to all who will believe as the all-satisfying treasure of the universe; and finally, he points to the path of love that leads to life.

Concluding Thoughts

A Dangerous and Glorious Calling

Expository exultation is a unique kind of communication. It is something not brought from the world into the service of the church. Nor can the world take it from the church and use it for its own purposes. It is different, radically different, from anything in the world.

In a Class by Itself

First, there is God. Then there is his work and his way in the world—his creation and redemption and providence. Then there is his book, his infallible book, the Bible, written by mere men, carried along by the Holy Spirit. Then there is a divine calling, a mystery of providence, family, church, desire, delight, duty. A preacher comes into being.

Then there is the sweat and prayer of preparation—the pounding on the closed door of the text, until it cracks, and beams of light shine out. Then there is the seeing of truth and wisdom and power. And then there is the laughter of joy and the tears of repentance, and in both, the savoring, O the savoring, of the glory. Then all day, and if necessary all night, the work of reason and imagination, praying, toiling, weaving dark and bright strands of truth into a fathomable fabric, a message to enfold the people.

Then while praying (again and again), there is the opening of the mouth, the heralding of the horrors and the glories. There is the explaining, the clarifying, the showing, the amazement, the rejoicing, the exultation, the offering, the pleading, the looking in the eyes. And all the while, there is the utter self-engagement, and, please God, the utter self-forgetting in the brightness of the truth. And then, God knows, the everlasting fruit, and weariness and thankfulness. And it all begins again.

There is nothing comparable to this. Expository exultation is unique.

Beautifully Made for Worship

For all its essential value in the service of evangelism, expository exultation is God's design and gift for his people gathered in worship. No other form of speech is as beautifully fitting in this God-exalting wonder called "worship."

God exists as one who knows himself perfectly in the eternal image of his Son. And he exists as one who is infinitely pleased by the one he thus knows. And we, the creatures of this glory-knowing, glory-loving God, are made in his image. We too exist to know God and to be pleased with God—to see and savor and show his glory. This is the essence of what it means to be human.

The gathering of God-seeing, God-savoring, God-showing human beings in one place to join their hearts and minds and voices in making much of this God is a miracle, and a miracle in the making. About to come into being is the miracle of corporate worship. And one indispensable flame that the Spirit uses to ignite that miracle, and make it burn, is the preaching of the word of God. By grace, the light and heat of worship spread. The preacher has come burning and shining. In his preaching, he is worshiping and awakening worship. He has come seeing and savoring and showing the beauty and worth of God. He is overflowing with the truth of exposition and the warmth of exultation.

Savoring God Is an End in Itself

The preacher is aware, and his people are aware, that the miracle of Bible-saturated, Christ-exalting, God-treasuring worship is a God-pleasing end in itself. God is being enjoyed here not as a means of making the budget. We are trembling in his presence not as means of political impact. We are exulting in God's power not to impress visitors. God is an end in himself. And our delight *in him* is our end, or it is not in *him*.

Savoring God Has a Thousand Good Effects

And yet the preacher knows, and the people know, that the ripple effect of this hour—this authentic, miracle hour of meeting God in worship—is unfathomable in its depth and extent. Because of this encounter with God, and this Spirit-anointed expository exultation, a thousand problems that had not yet come into being are solved in people's lives. A thousand decisions are shaped for good without any conscious forethought. A thousand relational corruptions are averted. And hundreds of hearts are softened in the presence of God so that impossible obedience suddenly seems possible—like saying, "I'm sorry; I was wrong." And yet we do not gather for this. We gather to see and savor God. He is the end. And where we try to make him a means, worship begins to die.

Everything Affected

The preacher knows, and the people know, that preaching and worship services are not the totality of the life of the church. There are a hundred worthy ministries for the children and the young adults, the men and the women, the singles and the married, the grieving and the aged. There are untold possibilities of reaching out to the unbelieving world. There are countless good deeds to show the glory of our Father in heaven. There are more ways to meet in small groups than we can imagine, to encourage each other and pray for each other and care for each. The preacher knows this, and makes no pretense that preaching is all people need.

But the preacher also knows this: if he fails in his expository exultation, if corporate worship languishes in lifelessness because the word of God does not come with clarity and faithfulness and soul-satisfying power, all the ministries suffer. Preaching is not everything, but it affects everything. It is the trumpet of truth in the church. And it echoes in every ministry and every household, for joy and strength and love and perseverance—or not. If every part of the engine is in working order but the spark plug fails to fire in its appointed rhythm, the whole car lurches or stops.

All Replacements Will Fail

Nothing can replace preaching. Books are wonderful. Who has not been deeply affected by a great book? Lectures and discussions and drama and poetry and film and paintings are powerful. But any effort to replace preaching with anything else will—sooner or later—fail.

People have tried experiments that replace preaching. Marginal, disillusioned people flock to the experiment. It lasts a few years. And it dies. Meanwhile preaching goes on from decade to decade and century to century. Why? Because God has created and appointed this unique, anointed embodiment of his word for the explanation and celebration of his glory and his worth.

The Lord Will Stand by You

If God has called you to preach, the task, of course, is humanly impossible. Preaching is worship. And preaching aims to awaken worship. Both worshiping and awakening worship are miracles. They are not mere choices. You cannot worship at will any more than you can be thrilled at will. It is a work of God, opening our eyes to the ultimately thrilling. But he who called you is faithful. He will do it. I testify from forty years in the ministry of the word, through the best and the worst of times, God loves to help the preacher who is desperate to make the word plain for the holy happiness of his people, by the blood of Jesus, for the glory of God. He will help you.

"The friendship of the LORD is for those who fear him, / and he makes known to them his covenant" (Ps. 25:14). If you accept this calling, and fear him and trust him, you will know an intimacy like no other. He will take you into his counsel and show you things you could not have seen any other way. He will work wonders for you. After a full day's "fruitless" labor over his word, distressed at the lateness of the hour, on your knees, through tears, in one five-second flash you will see the reality of the text. You will apprehend in an instant how the text works. It is a gift. He will make sure you know this. Again and again. Your labor for his glory, in the name of Jesus, for the good of his people, will never be in vain.

How many times have I trembled that I was not sufficient for this moment, or this great crowd, or this tiny gathering, or this painful topic, or this inscrutable text? And, as I have ventured on, trusting that his word never comes back empty, he has stood by me. He is faithful. "The Lord stood by me and strengthened me, so that through me the message might be fully proclaimed" (2 Tim. 4:17). He will do this for you, if you trust him and give yourself utterly to his word, confident in the cross, loving your people, and glorying in the worth and beauty of God.

Immortal till Your Work Is Done, and After

Every calling of God is good. To be sure, faithfulness in every calling—even in the smallest task—is greatness in heaven. "If anyone would be first, he must be last of all and servant of all" (Mark 9:35). But some callings, because of their potential for helping and hurting so many, are dangerous and glorious in a special way. "Not many of you should become teachers [or preachers], my brothers, for you know that we who teach [and preach] will be judged with greater strictness" (James 3:1).

If you hear this call and accept, you will embark on a great and dangerous work. Ambassadors of the king are not safe in enemy territory—unless they are protected and empowered by the king himself. But safety is not our goal. Our king will keep us, and use us, as long as he pleases. That will be a perfect term of service. We are, as Henry Martyn, the missionary to Persia, said, immortal till our work is done. And, of course, he would agree, we are immortal *after* our work is done and we are gone.

As I look back over four decades of preaching, I bear witness that it has been worth every effort and every cost. I hope and pray that this book will go with you, and prove, again and again, to be the kindling of the Spirit's flame in your expository exultation.

General Index

Scripture Index

✳ desiringGod

Everyone wants to be happy. Our website was born and built for happiness. We want people everywhere to understand and embrace the truth that *God is most glorified in us when we are most satisfied in him.* We've collected more than thirty years of John Piper's speaking and writing, including translations into more than forty languages. We also provide a daily stream of new written, audio, and video resources to help you find truth, purpose, and satisfaction that never end. And it's all available free of charge, thanks to the generosity of people who've been blessed by the ministry.

If you want more resources for true happiness, or if you want to learn more about our work at Desiring God, we invite you to visit us at www.desiringGod.org.

www.desiringGod.org

Experience the Transforming Power of God's Word

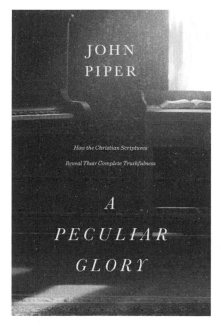

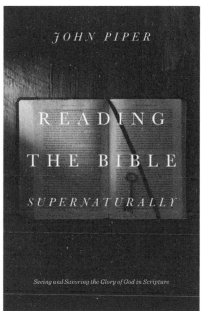

For more information, visit crossway.org.